Googling Security

Googling Security

HOW MUCH DOES GOOGLE KNOW ABOUT YOU?

Greg Conti

♣♦ Addison-Wesley

Upper Saddle River, NJ · Boston · Indianapolis · San Francisco
New York · Toronto · Montreal · London · Munich · Paris · Madrid
Cape Town · Sydney · Tokyo · Singapore · Mexico City

Library of Congress Cataloging-in-Publication Data available on request.

ISBN-13: 978-0-321-51866-8
ISBN-10: 0-321-51866-7
Text printed in the United States on recycled paper at RR Donnelley in Crawfordsville, Indiana.
First printing October 2008

Editor in Chief
Karen Gettman

Acquisitions Editor
Jessica Goldstein

Development Editor
Sheri Cain

Managing Editor
Kristy Hart

Project Editor
Jovana San Nicolas-Shirley

Copy Editor
Krista Hansing Editorial Services, Inc.

Indexer
Erika Millen

Proofreader
Kathy Ruiz

Publishing Coordinator
Romny French

Cover Designer
Gary Adair

Compositor
Bronkella Publishing

For Nicholas

Contents

Preface

The rise of the information economy dramatically shifted how we conduct business and live our lives. In the competitive world of business, the organization that has the best access to information can make more timely and effective decisions than its rivals, creating a distinct advantage. In our day-to-day lives, easier access to information and improved methods of communication enrich virtually every facet of our existence. At the heart of this revolution is the Internet, particularly the World Wide Web.

Shortly after the formation of the web in the early 1990s, its commercialization began in earnest. Online companies struggled to find business models that worked in this brave new world, where many of the traditional rules of business no longer applied. The combination of free, easy-to-use tools, along with targeted advertising, emerged as one of the most viable approaches. Customized advertising, by definition, requires insight into the needs of the individual user, which, in turn, requires logging and data mining to be most effective. As a result, online companies have logged virtually every conceivable type of data associated with our use of web-based tools. The existence of this data enables online companies to constantly improve our user experience and support their goal of selling customized advertising.

The value of this data is unprecedented in the history of mankind. If you consider the sum of your online searching, mapping, communicating, blogging, news reading, shopping, and browsing, you should realize that you've revealed a very complete picture of yourself and placed it on the servers of a select few online companies. The thin veneer of anonymity on the web is insufficient to protect you from revealing your identity. If you aren't even a little concerned, you should be. The value of this information is staggering and ripe for misuse. The threat is even worse when you consider the sum of the disclosures of your company. Everything from the dark little secrets of the corporate executives to the strategic plans of the company exists on someone else's servers. Like water rising behind a dam, this is an issue we need to address sooner or later. Today there are *only* one billion Internet users; however, this value represents just 18% of the world population. Web-based information disclosure will certainly grow as billions more users join us online. Although there is no miracle cure on the horizon, this book is a first step toward a solution. This book clearly illustrates and analyzes the problem of web-based information disclosure and provides you with countermeasures that you can employ now to minimize the threat.

WHO SHOULD READ THIS BOOK

Stated simply, if you use the web, you should read this book—unless, of course, you have nothing to hide. Not everyone is a pedophile or a terrorist, right? However, I argue that you wouldn't want everything from your health to your politics to your social network stored on someone's server, even if that someone is Google or one of its competitors. Perhaps today this won't be a problem, but history has shown that information leaks, privacy policies change, companies merge, data spills, and attacks occur. The mere existence of this information, and the power it proffers, ensures that it will be coveted by many, including business competitors, insurance companies, law enforcement officials, and governments.

As with any book, there are limits on what can fit between two covers. I've chosen to address a broad range of topics, to make the contents as accessible as possible (and increase the positive impact of the book), but at the same time give enough technical detail to provide insight into the technical challenges that exist behind the scenes. My intent is to raise awareness of the privacy implications of using the tools of Google and other online tools. The threat of web-based information disclosure is an open problem; I've attempted to outline the problem in detail, but complete solutions do not exist. For many, this book will be eye opening. However, I believe some IT and security professionals will have considered some of the points the book brings up. That being said, there will be insights and ah-ha moments for even the most security-savvy readers.

WHY GOOGLE?

This book studies the security implications of using Google's products and services. Why am I picking on Google when other companies offer similar products and services? Frankly, Google's success and marked innovation makes it the subject of this book. True, many other online companies offer similar products and services, but none comes close to the innovative and comprehensive offerings of Google. Much imitated but rarely surpassed, Google is truly the market leader and *the* company to beat when it comes to online services. Because of its success, Google has been the first to encounter many unanticipated challenges. What do you do when the U.S. Department of Justice subpoenas your search query logs? What do you do when China refuses you access to its two billion potential customers unless you place your servers inside China and comply with the government's requests to censor search results? How does Google find the ethical, and profitable, path when even a simple change in its search-ranking algorithm could make one person a millionaire or destroy a thriving business? Because of Google's sheer size, the tiniest changes have tremendous impact. Even a simple change in Google's default background color from white to an energy-conserving black could save 750 Megawatt hours per year.[1] You can easily see that ethical challenges abound for Google. By its very oft-quoted motto "Don't be evil," Google has set a very high ethical bar for itself. Any perceived deviation draws intense criticism.

Google's mission to "organize the world's information and make it universally accessible and useful" is very admirable and has already made many aspects of our lives easier. Google pursues this mission by offering high-quality tools, often for free. However, by using the tools offered by Google and its competitors, we are actually paying for their use with micropayments of personal information. By studying our interactions with Google, we are studying virtually the entire range of available offerings from *any* competing company. Throughout this book, I analyze the implications of using Google's tools and services, but when appropriate, I include other similar offerings from different vendors. I also include detailed discussion of the threat posed by Internet service providers (ISPs). ISPs have similar visibility on your online activities, although from a different network vantage point. Online companies see information streams from across the planet from hundreds of millions of users. ISPs see all activities from their customers but lack the global reach of Google.

Personally, I am a big fan of Google and use many of its services on a daily basis. By no means do I want Google to fail. However, we have to recognize and address the problem of web-based information disclosure before we reach a point of crisis—a point that I believe is rapidly approaching. We felt a tremor of this problem when AOL inadvertently released the search activity of 658,000 users in 2006.[2] My goal with this book is to outline the problem so we can all start making more informed decisions regarding our use of "free" web tools, as well as jointly seek solutions that will allow companies such as Google to innovate and thrive, while still meeting the privacy requirements of individuals and organizations. In short, by having such a high-grade product, Google makes itself a high-profile target, and that's a problem. It is certainly fair game to consider what we provide to Google and how Google protects that product.

It is important to note that this book is based entirely on publicly available information. I did not seek out any proprietary or internal-use information. As you will see, publicly available information is more than enough to understand the problem.

A MAP OF THE BOOK

The book covers many facets of the problem of web-based information disclosure as seen through the lens of Google's tools and services. The first chapter, "Googling," is an analysis of Google, its capabilities, its motivations, and its reach; it provides an overview of the types of information individuals and organizations reveal when using the wide variety of tools Google makes available. Chapter 2, "Information Flows and Leakage," places these disclosures into big-picture context by studying the same information flows, seen from the vantage point of network service providers and individual workstations.

Chapter 3, "Footprints, Fingerprints, and Connections," studies the information we leave behind as we use the web and how this information can be used to profile our behaviors, be tied to our real-world identities, and be connected with other users, businesses, and groups. Chapters 4–6 deeply examine the risks associated with major classes of online tools, including search, communication, and mapping. Chapter 7, "Advertising and Embedded Content," illustrates the increasing number of ways users can be tracked as they browse hundreds of thousands of (non-Google) web sites, thanks to embedded advertising, YouTube videos, and similar content.

Chapter 8, "Googlebot," describes how Google and other large online companies collect and process information around the clock using an army of automated web crawlers. Chapter 9, "Countermeasures," presents techniques for reducing the impact of web-based information disclosure. Finally, Chapter 10, "Conclusions and a Look to the Future," analyzes current trends and illustrates what future risks could lie ahead.

The web is an ever-growing and continuously evolving space. Although I have carefully chosen the most relevant topics to include here, a single book is not sufficient to document and analyze the full range of current and future possibilities. With this in mind, I encourage you to visit this book's companion web site at www.informit.com/title/9780321518668 for additional information.

ENDNOTES

1. "Change Google's Background Color Background Color to Save Energy?" Slashdot.org, 27 July 2007. http://hardware.slashdot.org/hardware/07/07/27/054249.shtml, last accessed 25 September 2007.

2. Ryan Singel, "FAQ: AOL's Search Gaffe and You," Wired.com, 11 August 2006. www.wired.com/politics/security/news/2006/08/71579, last accessed 25 May 2008.

Acknowledgments

With any large undertaking, many people have contributed to making this book a success. However, rather than inevitably leave someone out, I simply thank the following communities: Annual Computer Security Applications Conference, Black Hat, Communications of the ACM, DEFCON, Digg, Electronic Frontier Foundation, *IEEE Security & Privacy Magazine,* International World Wide Web Conference, Interz0ne, New Security Paradigms Workshop, Slashdot, Symposium on Usable Privacy and Security, West Point, Wikipedia, and Workshop on Privacy in the Electronic Society.

However, there are still a few people I need to single out. First, I'd like to thank John Battelle for his seminal work on web-based information disclosure in his "database of intentions" writings and in his book *The Search: How Google and Its Rivals Rewrote the Rules of Business and Transformed Our Culture* (Portfolio Trade, 2006). I'd also like to recognize Johnny Long for his excellent work in Google hacking and his well-written book *Google Hacking for Penetration Testers* (Syngress, 2007). He clearly laid out the wealth of security information that can be found in Google's database. I hope to complement his work in my book by examining the inverse, what information we provide to Google and other online companies. At Addison-Wesley, I would like to thank Jessica Goldstein, Romny French, Sheri Cain, and Jovana San Nicolas-Shirley. I'd also like to thank my technical reviewers 3efd09cddc148ee790d17e35ae323852,[1] David Blake (aka StankDawg), Sergey Bratus, Anna Shubina, and Lenny Zeltzer. Of course, any mistakes you find in the text are purely my own. Finally, I'd like to thank Google for making such an awesome suite of tools that people would need to write books about them.

---

[1]   This is an MD5 hash of the reviewer's name. Cryptographic hash functions are designed to take an input and generate a fixed-size string; reversing the operation is extremely difficult. This way, it is possible for the reviewer to prove that (s)he helped with the book (which (s)he did significantly), but will make it (nearly) impossible to work backward from the hash to the name.

About the Author

Greg Conti is an assistant professor of computer science at the U.S. Military Academy in West Point, New York. His research includes security data visualization, usable security, information warfare, and web-based information disclosure. He is the author of *Security Data Visualization* (No Starch Press, 2007) and has been featured in *IEEE Security & Privacy* magazine, *Communications of the ACM,* and *IEEE Computer Graphics and Applications* magazine. He has spoken at a wide range of academic and hacker conferences, including Black Hat, DEFCON, and the Workshop on Visualization for Computer Security (VizSEC). Conti runs the open source security visualization project RUMINT. His work can be found at www.gregconti.com/ and www.rumint.org/.

Googling

googling (gü-gəling): To use the Google search engine to obtain information on the World Wide Web[1]
—*Merriam-Webster Online Dictionary*

Have you ever searched for something you wouldn't want your grandmother to know about? This question got me thinking about what is locked in the archives of Google's databases and led me to several years of research into its products and services. What I found was a deep and wide range of free tools used without concern by millions of people, a complacency I patently disagree with. Contributing to Google's success is the widely regarded notion that Google is adhering to its informal motto of "Don't be evil." Google stock has enjoyed a meteoric rise, despite the specter of the technology bubble. Public perception of Google is at an all-time high, and why shouldn't it be? Google largely gives away its services for free. From the individual's perspective, this is a business model that he or she can live with. But therein lies the risk. The services aren't actually free; they come at the cost of your personal information.

In a famous study, people interviewed on the streets of London gave away their passwords in return for a candy bar.[2] In Google's case, we don't trade information for candy bars, but free services such as search, e-mail, and satellite mapping. The information we provide is also key to Google's business model. By carefully taking advantage of the information we disclose, Google has found effective ways to make money. Given that Google makes money by better targeting their advertisements, it is unlikely that they will truly discard information they've carefully mined one e-mail and web search at a time.[3]

We face a spectrum of risk. Google might truly be altruistic and might act entirely in your best interest. Then again, Google might be evil, might use your personal information, and might regularly exploit your trust in all sorts of nefarious activities. As a publicly held business, Google is legally bound to operate in the best interest of its shareholders, not necessarily yours. Inevitable conflicts will arise over pleasing the shareholders, and Google will weigh the potential of making a greater profit against exploiting its capabilities, including its stockpile of personal information, to the fullest extent of the law. In conducting research for this book, I examined Google's privacy policies, and they share a common theme: Google will collect personal information from you "to provide you with a better experience."[4] Unfortunately, just possessing such knowledge on so many people and organizations is tremendously dangerous.

Even assuming that Google has the best of intentions for the foreseeable future, you still face a great risk. Google's privacy policy alone will not protect you. Network connections from your personal computer to Google's servers make many of your activities visible to an eavesdropper. Your search activity is unencrypted and is typically easily visible on the network. Even if the connection is secured using SSL encryption[5] from your browser, the information will still be decrypted at Google's servers.[6] So even if we assume that no one can eavesdrop on your activity, encryption eliminates only a part of the problem because Google is a trusted partner in the communication. Subpoenas have forced online services to reveal archived information. A rogue employee or malicious individual attacking across a network cares little about the law or Google's privacy policy. Mishaps occur. Consider the loss of the account information of 1.2 million U.S. government credit card users due to a lost Express Mail package containing backup tapes.[7] Google distributes a number of free software utilities that run on your personal computer, and if one of these applications has a vulnerability, your entire personal computer is at risk. This problem has already manifested itself. The Google Desktop application recently proved vulnerable to an attack by malicious web site operators, exposing the contents of the user's hard drive.[8]

Despite Google's best efforts to secure its facilities, even physical attack is possible. But if you further assume strong market forces or even malicious intent, the picture darkens significantly. It is technically feasible for Google to create comprehensive dossiers on its users, as well as determine the personal and professional interconnections between them. You might disagree and think that Google will be unable to connect the pieces of apparently innocuous bits of information, but I feel certain that its top-tier talent in data mining,[9] algorithms, information retrieval, artificial intelligence, and machine learning would have no problems doing so. In fact, they are likely doing it now to "improve your experience."

Google is a global organization with at least 159 international domains and is available in more than 112 languages. Chances are, you are a frequent user. Even if you have never used Google, people have searched for you, your associates, and your company. Google's automated Internet browsing script, known as Googlebot, relentlessly trolls the web, gathering information around the clock, feeding Google's databases. Google's corporate mission is to "organize the world's information and make it universally accessible and useful." With that wealth of information gathered in the pursuit of that goal comes great power, the need for careful stewardship, and the potential for corruption.

Regardless of where you stand in your beliefs of Google's benevolence, this book is relevant to you. We take a close look at Google's services and examine the threats associated with each. We also provide you with countermeasures to help you protect yourself and your organization. At the end, you should have a far clearer understanding of the problem and be much better prepared to reduce the risk.

THE DIGITAL BIG BANG

Google's success is a product of the growth of the World Wide Web and the Internet. The web was created in 1989 and has enjoyed unprecedented growth.[10] In 1993 there were approximately 130 web sites, and in 1997 there were 650,000.[11] Although exact statistics are difficult to determine, there are at least 100 million web sites[12] and 15 billion to 30 billion web pages[13] today. The Internet, which includes the World Wide Web but also other services such as e-mail and instant messaging, has more than one billion users. The amount of data contained on the Internet is even more difficult to determine, but in 2003, University of California Berkeley researchers Peter Lyman and Hal Varian estimated that the surface web[14] contained 167 terabytes (TB), instant messaging contained 274TB, the deep web contained 91.8 petabytes (PB), and original e-mails contained 440.6PB.[15] A more recent study by research firm IDC stated that humans produced 161 exabytes (EB) of digital information in 2006 and will increase sixfold to 988EB by 2010.[16]

These numbers might seem large, but plenty of room for growth in both web and Internet usage still exists, when you consider that only 18% of the world's population currently has Internet access. Growth continues to be dramatic, with Africa, Asia, the Middle East, and Latin America seeing the most significant gains.[17] With only 18% of the population having Internet access and Google already enjoying more than 4.1 billion search queries and more than 117 million unique users (across all their applications and subsidiary companies)[18] per month in the United States alone,[19] we have seen only the tip of the iceberg when it comes to our information disclosure via the web.

> **NOTE**
>
> Google was crowned the world's most visited web site, with more than 500 million unique visitors.[20] This is roughly half of the global Internet population.

GOOGLE: THE NATION-STATE

Prudent security professionals analyze a potential adversary based not only on the adversary's stated intent and visible actions, but also on its capabilities. In other words, what could the entity do, if it were so inclined? By using this approach, analysts better understand the risks involved. If you consider the resources that Google has at its disposal and the power it possesses, I place it on the level of a *nation-state*, a sovereign entity equivalent to a nation. I view Google as the equivalent of a nation-state because of its top-tier intellectual talent, financial resources in the billions of dollars, and world-class information-processing resources combined with ten years of interaction data. For example, as of this writing, Google's revenue was $13.4 billion[21] which places it in the top 100 countries[22] on the planet, if you assume that the Gross Domestic Product (GDP) is roughly equivalent to revenue. However, raw figures do not tell the entire story. The buzz surrounding Google is tremendous. As the dotcom bubble burst, Google was able to cherry-pick some 10,000 of the world's best and brightest.[23] Google's stable of talent, which includes more than 600 Ph.D.s, again gives it the intellectual resources of a nation-state. In addition, consider what this level of expertise and financial resources could do with archives of billions of user queries and other interaction data, as well as more than 450,000 servers located in about 25 locations.[24] If you assume that each of these servers is based on a reasonably fast commodity PC,[25] you have a supercomputer capable of 5,850 petaflops, or about 20 times faster than IBM's BlueGene/L system, which ranked number one on the top-500 supercomputers listing.[26] My back-of-the-envelope calculation is supported by Google's CEO Eric Schmidt, who described Google as building the world's largest supercomputer.[27] Some experts even speculate that Google is capable of keeping the entire web in RAM.[28] To give you a feel for the type of experts in Google's employ, see Table 1-1, taken from a Google Labs solicitation.[29] Note the presence of skills such as data mining, profiling, information retrieval, machine learning, and artificial intelligence, which foreshadow possible advances in the exploitation of Google's information stockpile.

Table 1-1   List of Desired Skill Sets from a Google Labs Employment Advertisement

Algorithms	Artificial intelligence
Compiler optimization	Computer architecture
Computer graphics	Data compression
Data mining	File system design
Genetic algorithms	Information retrieval
Machine learning	Natural language processing
Operating systems	Profiling
Robotics	Text processing
User interface design	Web information retrieval

Google also possesses a ubiquitous global and multicultural presence, perhaps without peer. Its search interface is available in an astonishing 112 languages[30] (see Table 1-2), and it offers 159 country-specific portals[31] (see Figure 1-1). This achievement is even more astonishing when you consider that the United Nations membership, which includes virtually every national government on the planet, has only 192 members.[32] By offering a ubiquitous and tailored front end to essentially every Internet-capable person on Earth, Google has become the gold standard in international accessibility. However, this global reach also magnifies the threat of web-based information disclosure. Because Google is so readily available and easy to use, more people across the planet will divulge their personal information.[33] You might wonder why I call information such as search queries "personal information"; the next section, "Just Google It," explains in great detail.

Table 1-2   Google's Interface Is Available in 112 Languages. Web-Based Information Disclosure Is Not Just a U.S. Phenomenon.[34]

Afrikaans	Albanian	Amharic	Arabic
Armenian	Azerbaijani	Basque	Belarusian
Bengali	Bihari	Bosnian	Breton
Bulgarian	Cambodian	Catalan	Chinese (Simplified)
Chinese (Traditional)	Corsican	Croatian	Czech
Danish	Dutch	English	Esperanto

continues

Table 1-2   Continued

Estonian	Faroese	Filipino	Finnish
French	Frisian	Galician	Georgian
German	Greek	Guarani	Gujarati
Hebrew	Hindi	Hungarian	Icelandic
Indonesian	Interlingua	Irish	Italian
Japanese	Javanese	Kannada	Kazakh
Korean	Kurdish	Kyrgyz	Laothian
Latin	Latvian	Lingala	Lithuanian
Macedonian	Malay	Malayalam	Maltese
Marathi	Moldavian	Mongolian	Nepali
Norwegian	Norwegian (Nynorsk)	Occitan	Oriya
Pashto	Persian	Polish	Portuguese (Brazil)
Portuguese (Portugal)	Punjabi	Quechua	Romanian
Romansh	Russian	Scots Gaelic	Serbian
Serbo-Croatian	Sesotho	Shona	Sindhi
Sinhalese	Slovak	Slovenian	Somali
Spanish	Sundanese	Swahili	Swedish
Tajik	Tamil	Tatar	Telugu
Thai	Tigrinya	Tonga	Turkish
Turkmen	Twi	Uighur	Ukrainian
Urdu	Uzbek	Vietnamese	Welsh
Xhosa	Yiddish	Yoruba	Zulu

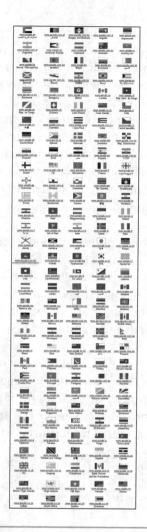

Figure 1-1 Google offers 159 country-specific portals, facilitating global ease of use and data collection.

JUST GOOGLE IT

Somewhere in the eight years between the formation of Google (the company) in 1998 and the inclusion of *google* (the verb) in the Oxford English dictionary in 2006, *Google* became a household word, joining the ranks of Coke, FedEx, Frisbee, Rollerblade, Spam, and Xerox. Beating out its many rivals, Google has become *the* destination of choice for some 500 million unique visitors each year. Each of these visitors, *including you and me,* shares tremendous amounts of personal and corporate information via Google's easy-to-use web tools. This is a tremendous amount of information to share with one company, and it requires a great deal of trust, even with a company whose informal motto is "Don't be evil."[35] For the past ten years, we've have been pouring all facets of our lives into the servers of Google and similar companies. Whether the information is accidentally spilled, stolen, subpoenaed[36], or just data-mined for all its worth by companies similar to Google, you should be concerned that so much information about you is stored on someone else's servers. The AOL data spill of 2006[37] taught us that this concern is warranted and that the information we share is extremely sensitive and often personally identifiable.[38] Let's take a closer look at what you and 500 million other Google users are revealing.

When thinking about the problem of information disclosure, one useful way is to apply the Sobiesk Information Disclosure Metric (SIDM).[39] The Sobiesk Information Disclosure Metric is the percentage of information that you would share with an online company that you would not want shared publicly. Expressed as a percentage, SIDMs of 10% to 35% are most common, but they vary according to the user's trust of each online company. This is a telling statement and should highlight the sensitivity of what people are sharing with Google.

Google gathers information through several primary vectors: information you provide directly through your use of their tool suite, information harvested by the Googlebot web crawler, web surfing demographics from the Google AdSense and Google Analytics services, information provided to Google by other users through their use of Google's tools, and information acquired from third-party databases and business partners (see Figure 1-2).

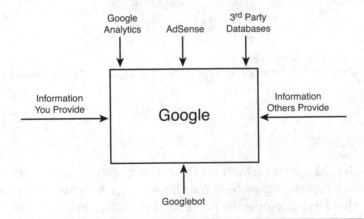

Figure I-2 Google gathers information through a wide variety of vectors.

INFORMATION DISCLOSURE: A CLOSER LOOK

Online companies offer hundreds of free tools and services. Over time, use of these tools divulges significant information regarding each user's personal and professional life, as well as that of their friends, family, and employer. The tools include a wide range of applications, including search, language translation, data storage, e-mail, mapping, and finance, as well as online office applications such as word processing, calendaring, and spreadsheets. Innovation is widespread, and new applications are added every day. The amount of information you disclose depends on the type of tool that you use. Figure 1-3 shows one possible scenario. Your usage will certainly differ, but envision plotting the services you do use on a similar chart. Note that, over time, as your usage continues, the sum of your disclosures will increase. Thus, positions on the line will slide to the right. It is important to note that comprehensive tools to measure web-based information disclosure do not yet exist, so the approach I'm taking here is theoretical. Measuring "the sum of your disclosures" is a hard problem that merits future research. For example, it is possible to measure the amount of raw data that users disclose, but this data could be repetitive, as in the case of many similar search queries, or could otherwise contain little to no information content.

Figure 1-3 Information disclosure by service, from less (left) to more (right) for a notional user. Information disclosure occurs when you use virtually any online tool but is significantly more risky when a single company offers many services.

Although these tools are quite powerful and easy to use, they also entice you to disclose sensitive information at an alarming rate. Each individual interaction, such as a web search, might seem insignificant in isolation, but the sum total (perhaps accumulated over years of using a wide range of tools) paints an alarmingly clear picture of your life. Counterintuitively, the more easy-to-use these tools are, the more information you are enticed to disclose, and hence the greater the information disclosure risk. See Table 1-3 for examples of services and the types of information you disclose when using them.

Table 1-3 Listing of Google's Tools and Services and Associated Information Disclosure Examples

Service	Information Disclosure Examples
Alerts	Topics and news stories that you are interested in.
Blog Search	Topics you are interested in.
Blogger	Blogs you read and contents of your posts.
Book Search	Topics of interest and books you read.
Calendar	Your day-to-day personal and professional schedule.
Catalogs	Items you wish to purchase.
Code	Your computer programming skill set and the kind of problems you are working on.
Co-op	Your web site.
Checkout	Items you purchased.
Desktop	A unique application number is sent to Google when Google Desktop checks for updates. Potential vulnerabilities could disclose the contents of your computer.
Directory	Topics you are interested in.
Docs & Spreadsheets	Your writings and financial information.
Earth	Locations of interest.
Finance	Your investments.
Gmail	Your communications and responses from contacts.
Groups	Groups you are affiliated with and subjects that interest you.
iGoogle	Information sources of interest.
Images	Topics of interest.
Labs	Your computer use expertise level.
Maps	Locations of interest, travel plans, and routes.
Maps for Mobile	Your location.
Mobile	Your location and phone number.

Service	Information Disclosure Examples
News	News stories of interest.
Notebook	Web pages you've surfed and your comments on each.
Orkut	Family, friends, and colleagues.
Pack	A unique application number is sent to Google when Google Pack checks for updates. Potential vulnerabilities could disclose the contents of your computer.
Patent Search	Patent ideas and strategic plans.
Picasa	(Potentially) Your image and those of your acquaintances.
Product Search	Items you plan to purchase.
Scholar	Your academic background and expertise.
SMS	Contents of text messages and your phone number.
Specialized Searches	Spelling and mathematical ability.
Talk	Contents of your communications.[40]
Toolbar	(Potentially) Your web search activity.
Translate	Your native language.
Video	Topics of interest.
Web Accelerator	The speed of your Internet connection. Web pages you are reading through this service.
Web Search	Topics of interest.
Web Search Features	Your computer use skill level.
YouTube	Topics of interest.

By reviewing the table, you should see the dizzying array of services Google provides. I cover many of them in detail later in the book. But for now, the key idea is to understand that each service discloses something important to the online company. The more offerings a given company provides, the greater amount of information on you they possess and, thus, the greater power you provide them. Figure 1-4 shows one possible scenario of online tools you might use. In the figure, I've grouped activities by the online company whose tool you used. The size of each sphere indicates the total amount of information you've provided. Overlapping spheres represent cooperative agreements, such as eBay's hosting of Google advertising.[41] Also, in an earlier version of this image, I included DoubleClick as a separate entity, but with Google's recent acquisition of the company, I've included DoubleClick inside of Google and increased the size of Google's sphere accordingly.

Figure 1-4   Aggregated information disclosure by company for a notional user

RISKS

So far, we've seen that Google possesses tremendous capabilities and has a global reach, and that we feed it information at a tremendous rate. As we examine the security impact of Google and other online companies, we must ask ourselves what risks are associated with our use of their tools and services. At the heart of this debate is the value of the information we provide. In the security community, a traditional risk assessment involves a comparison between the cost of security and the value of what is protected. In the case of web-based information disclosure, this question is one of the value of the tool vs. the value of the information we provide. I argue that many people take the short-sighted view that each individual disclosure is unimportant, but they fail to consider the sum of all their activities. In addition, most people are unaware of the full spectrum of their disclosures across all the services they use and the fact that the disclosures can be aggregated, data-mined, and tied together across many sites and social groups. They are also unaware that their real-world identity can, in many cases, be determined with a relatively small amount of online activity. As you consider these points, ask yourself the following questions:

- How frequently do you use the free tools offered by Google and other companies?
- Do you have a registered user account with these companies?
- Have you ever disclosed information you wouldn't share with your family, friends, employer, or government?
- If this information fell into the wrong hands, what are the implications?
- How frequently do you delete cookies from your computer?
- How many of your employees or coworkers frequent these same tools?
- What is the value of the aggregated information they've disclosed to your competitors via their free online tools?
- How likely is it that the information will be misused?
- Across the global population of one billion Internet users, how much power are we placing into the hands of a few online companies?
- How will future advances in data mining, as well as changes in the law and corporate leadership, impact your answers?

These questions should help you start thinking about the real-world impact of the problem. Let's look at some possible scenarios.

INFORMATION DISCLOSURE SCENARIOS

Despite our best intentions, insight can be garnered from the most unlikely pieces of information. Take, for example, the simple act of ordering a pizza. This may seem innocuous, but in Washington, D.C., a sudden surge in pizza orders at the White House or Pentagon can signal a major crisis, as occurred during the Gulf War and the Monica Lewinsky scandal.[42] Far more than ordering a pizza, we disclose sensitive information about ourselves, our friends, and our employer on a daily basis for a period of years. Similarly, the web contains an additional trove of information that can be captured using Googlebot or other webcrawlers, scripts that index web pages, and added to the equation. From these sources, online companies know a great deal about our lives, from the least significant aspects to our most important personal crises. Consider the following examples.

- Your company's research department discovers a new technology. They use Google's patent database to search for any related patents. (They didn't choose the United States Patent and Trademark Office's site because they preferred Google's ease of use.) Their searches (including successful and unsuccessful outcomes) reveal the core ideas behind the new technology.

- An AIDS support group chooses a new meeting location. The organizer sends out an e-mail, with a link to directions in Google Maps, to all the group's members using his Gmail account. He has disclosed the entire membership of the group (via e-mail addresses), the topic of the meeting (in the body of his e-mail), and the IP addresses of all the members who click on the link. In addition, identifying cookies were likely placed on each member's computer when they visited the site. Later searches for the same location might indicate new group members.

- A company is experiencing hard times. Employees secretly start using their computers to search for job openings and news about their employer.

- A company plans to launch a new strategic initiative. For three months, the company researches manufacturers in a small province in China using Google.

- A man searches for the cover name of a sensitive project. Not discovering the name in the search results, he continues to search for related topics.

- A women becomes pregnant. She searches on obstetricians and baby names. Later she searches for abortion clinics. Two weeks later, she searches for counseling centers.

- A law enforcement agency uses an online search engine to check the background of potential leads and anonymous sources for most of their active cases.

- A hacker prides himself in the anonymity of his handle. His photo and his real name aren't available online. A fan of his work overhears his name at a conference and that night searches for the hacker's web site using a query that includes both the hacker's real name and his handle.

- Malware researchers in a security service company pride themselves on having collected the greatest amount of undisclosed vulnerabilities. They frequently use Google to research each new vulnerability and confirm that it hasn't been discovered.

- A company with a mobile workforce chooses to place its financial books in Google Spreadsheet so sales representatives can access the information from around the globe.

- A man develops possible symptoms of lung cancer. He conducts searches on the disease. He later searches on cancer treatment centers in the area. Six months later, his wife searches for funeral homes.

This list could go on forever. Whether you are trying to protect corporate intellectual property or just the privacy of your personal life, the key idea is that you shouldn't underestimate the importance of your disclosures, particularly over time. The better you understand this value, the better you can evaluate the acceptable risk when using different types of online tools. It is important to note that this list includes innocent uses of online tools. I could have just as easily included controversial or criminal uses such as pedophiles seeking vulnerable children, terrorists sharing bomb-making instructions, serial killers researching how to hide their tracks, or drug dealers communicating with suppliers. These rare scenarios are often used as public relations levers by governments and others, to jeopardize the privacy of law-abiding Internet users such as those in the previous list.[43]

TREND AWAY FROM THE DESKTOP

The problem of web-based information disclosure is compounded by the general trend away from the desktop to web-based applications. During the first decades of the personal computer revolution, individual computers become increasingly more powerful, in terms of both raw processing power and hard disk storage. Network access, on the other hand, was slow or nonexistent. As a result, desktop applications reigned supreme. Perhaps the best example is that of Microsoft Office running on Microsoft Windows. The rise of the World Wide Web, combined with easy access to always-on high-speed Internet, has changed the landscape. No longer are users tied to large desktop applications and monolithic operating systems. Well-designed web applications are now starting to replace their PC-bound counterparts. We are seeing the early rumblings of this trend now. Google has developed or acquired web-based replacements for word processing, e-mail, calendaring, spreadsheet, and presentation software. As an added bonus, such users can access their data from anywhere on the planet.[44] They need only a browser and an Internet connection to do their work. Browsers exist for all major operating systems, so being locked into a given operating system is becoming increasingly irrelevant. Although with desktop applications we typically see upgrades occurring infrequently, centralized web applications can be updated on a continuous basis. One of the largest obstacles to the adoption of web-based applications is the necessity for extremely reliable network connectivity, which has yet to be achieved but is becoming more of a reality every day. Another major concern is security.

By placing applications, and their data files, on centralized servers, we lose control of our data. Critical information that was once safely stored on our personal computers now resides on the servers of online companies. In the past, we possessed the entire application on our machines and could use it as long as we wanted. With web-based applications, we could find both access to the application and our data at risk by placing both in the hands of a third party.

DATA RETENTION AND PERMANENCE

A major issue regarding web-based information disclosure is the question of data retention. The key idea is that our online activities are scrupulously logged and retained, as is the data we provide using web-based office applications, in most cases for an indeterminately long time. Although a handful of online companies, including Google, have made gestures toward anonymizing logs after a period of time, for security purposes, it is prudent to assume that everything you are doing online is retained forever. Don't get me wrong—in some cases, it might be reasonable for companies to retain some data. Data retention is required to provide and improve services, conduct research, and sell advertising. That being said, acquiring the minimal amount of data, ensuring that it will be carefully protected, and eliminating or reducing the opportunity for abuse are all key to finding a legitimate balance between privacy and innovation. Ultimately, the key is to provide transparency, letting the user know exactly what is being retained and for how long. Let us be informed partners in the management of our data.

To its credit, Google provides reasonably readable privacy policies. That being said, these policies are vague in some instances and overly broad in others. I discuss these instances throughout the book when covering Google's key services. Privacy policies do matter to some end users. Researchers from Carnegie Mellon University found that some end users would pay more for items purchased online if they believed the business they purchased from would protect their privacy.[45] Online companies are similarly testing whether privacy policies can provide a competitive advantage. For example, major search engines are taking different approaches to anonymization and data retention. Ask.com, AOL, and Microsoft all delete search data after a given period of time ("within hours," 13 months, and 18 months, respectively). Google and Yahoo! partially anonymize their search data, by removing portions of identifying information from their logs, after 18 months and 13 months, respectively. In addition to competitive advantage, online companies are beginning to feel regulatory pressure both in the United States and in Europe.[46] Government oversight, often in the form of government regulation, occurs when individual companies and industries prove unable to regulate themselves.

Note that a significant legal difference exists between data that is stored on one's computer and data that is stored on Google's servers. When someone stores documents or e-mail on a home computer's hard drive, the data receives strong Fourth Amendment protections. When the data is stored on the servers of Google or another online company, it might be protected only by Congressional statutes such as the Electronic

Communications Privacy Act.[47] The U.S. legal system infers that if you are comfortable storing data on Google's servers, where its employees may have access to it, the data isn't truly private. A full discussion of this subject is beyond the scope of this book, but it is important to note that an important legal distinction exists between information on one's home computer and information that users store on Google's servers.

TRUST

In many ways, web-based information disclosure comes down to trust. Do you trust that the information you provide will be kept private and used only in ways that you would approve of? Of course, whenever you use your computer, you actually trust a great many people and companies. Your computer depends on hardware (chips, motherboards, peripherals), software (BIOS, operating system, myriad applications), protocols (Domain Name System, IP, TCP, UDP), algorithms (SSL, MD5), and networks (network device manufacturers, ISPs, Internet backbone providers). The truth is, you must trust the computers and personnel at online companies you interact with. Any break in this chain of trust, however, could defeat your best efforts at security.

INFORMATION IS A SLIPPERY THING

At this point, I hope I've convinced you that the information we provide is important and conveys tremendous power. I believe that Google and other online companies are doing their best to protect this information. It is one of their most valuable assets, so protecting it is clearly in their best interest to do so. Data-mining this information is essential to the business model of targeted advertising, and eroding the trust of consumers would be counterproductive, if not deadly. However, data is a slippery thing. History has taught us that it is almost impossible to control the flow of information, despite even the best safeguards. As a simple example, we've all seen e-mails that were inadvertently sent to the wrong recipients. Just a simple slip, such as clicking Reply To All or failing to send an e-mail using blind carbon copy (BCC), allows sensitive information to fall into the wrong hands. The latter happened in October 2007 with a U.S. House of Representatives e-mail to whistle blowers. Intended to be sent anonymously using BCC, it was instead sent to more than 150 people who had contacted the committee, with every e-mail address visible. For good measure, the Vice President of the United States was CC'd on the e-mail![48] Oops. Similarly, large databases containing sensitive information are exposed with disturbing regularity. The Privacy Rights Clearinghouse estimates that 167.7 million records containing sensitive information have been involved with data breaches from 2005 to 2007.[49] The security community has a saying that services can be "cheap, fast, or secure (choose two)." Online companies are trying to do all three to maximize profit. Problems are sure to arise. Let's look at some ways in the following sections.

DELIBERATE SHARING WITH THIRD PARTIES

Companies form strategic alliances and partnerships, which include sharing of your information. If you read the privacy policies of online companies, you will likely discover wording that allows this to take place. Google's privacy policy[50] states that it "may share aggregated non-personal information with third parties outside of Google." However, if you are a registered user of a Google service, or otherwise voluntary provide personal information, the sharing is even less restrictive. Privacy policies can change when companies merge. You must consider that your information might be shared at some point when you deal with an online company.

ACCIDENT

Data spills and accidents happen. You only have to read the headlines to hear about large companies accidentally losing control of sensitive personal information. I've already discussed the AOL incident. However, other large corporations have also done so. Citigroup lost control of back-up tapes containing names, account history, and Social Security numbers of more than 3.9 million customers while shipping the tapes via UPS. Citigroup Executive Vice President Kevin Kessinger stated, regarding the loss, "We deeply regret this incident, which occurred in spite of the enhanced security procedures we require of our couriers." Similarly, Bank of America lost 1.2 million records of its charge card customers, Time Warner lost personal information on 600,000 current and former employees, a hard drive containing records on 500,00 military health beneficiaries was stolen from the offices of Department of Defense contractor TriWest,[51] and a Veteran's Administration laptop was stolen containing 26.5 million veterans' Social Security numbers.[52] This last incident was the largest Social Security number breach in history and was believed to contain the Social Security number of virtually every living U.S. veteran.[53] Again, the list could go on and on, and again each of these organizations went to great lengths to protect sensitive information—but the losses occurred anyway. Large online companies are not immune to such incidents.

MALWARE AND SOFTWARE VULNERABILITIES

Malicious software presents a significant concern from two main perspectives: the end user and the online company. A rampant threat, malicious software can attack and reside on your personal computer, those of your employer, and machines of online companies. Malicious software can come in many forms, such as software that captures your key strokes, a rootkit that hides itself and provides concealed functionality to an attacker, or a trojan that allows remote control of your computer. Today's best attempts to protect against malicious software are only partially effective. Firewalls attempt to block unauthorized network connections but must allow at least some traffic through to allow basic network access such as web browsing and e-mail. Intrusion-detection systems monitor network communications and attempt to identify suspicious activity. Antivirus and antispyware software monitors individual systems and also attempts to identify suspicious activity. However, intrusion-detection systems, antivirus software, and antispyware software are best at detecting known attacks that match an existing signature. New attacks typically do not match any existing signatures, leaving computers vulnerable. When companies rely on homogenous hardware and software to create economies of scale, the risk is even more severe. One common vulnerability could cause catastrophic destruction. Even if computers have been successfully secured against traditional network attacks, attackers are increasingly attacking applications, particularly browser software and e-mail applications. By creating specially crafted web pages and e-mails, attackers can successfully compromise many systems. Although they are hardened against attack, web browsers and e-mail applications are still vulnerable. New attacks occur with disturbing regularity.

The end result of these vulnerabilities is that it is almost impossible for you, your employer, and online companies to provide impervious protection against attack; therefore, your data is at risk. No one is immune, even Google. If anything, Google is an even *bigger* target because of the amount of data it has. For example, researchers found a vulnerability in Google Desktop and Internet Explorer that exposed web surfers' hard-drive data to malicious web sites.[54] Another good example is the vulnerability that existed in Google's Gmail that granted attackers access to the victim's e-mail account.[55]

TARGETED ATTACK

The information that online companies collect is of tremendous value, which guarantees that many will covet it. In this section, we look at some of the many ways attackers can acquire the data by penetrating the security defenses of online companies. Booz Allen,

Unisys, Hewlett-Packard, and Hughes Network Systems have all been subject to sophisticated targeted attacks.[56] I'll bet that every large company has been targeted as well; the incidents just haven't been reported or detected.[57]

I've already discussed malicious software in general; however, there is an increasing trend of specificity in attacks. Attackers are creating custom attacks against individual companies or even small groups of employees. A recent trend for such attack has been the use of a malicious PDF. As an example, an attacker emailed a specially crafted PDF file to specific employees of a large company, appearing to be a legitimate internal report. The PDF file, however, was modified to exploit a vulnerability in the PDF viewer software and quietly compromised internal systems. This is just one example; researchers are discovering similar new vulnerabilities and techniques every day.[58]

The chance of an *insider threat*, an attack by a trusted employee, is another important consideration. To make use of the data they collect online, companies must give at least some of their employees access to it. This fact opens the door for employees to abuse this trust for fun or profit. At large online companies, presumably, strong safeguards are in place to vet individuals and control access to the data, but history has shown that such measures are insufficient. Take, for example, the highly trusted FBI agent Robert Hanssen and veteran CIA officer Aldrich Ames. Both went through extensive screening procedures and both gave highly sensitive classified information to the KGB in return for cash and other valuables.[59, 60] It is hard to imagine more rigorous screening procedures than those employed by the CIA and FBI; surely the same risks exist within online companies.

Companies can be attacked in many other ways. Social engineering is the art of manipulating people into disclosing sensitive information such as passwords or network addresses. Classic examples include calls by seemingly senior corporate officers to tech support requesting help in accessing their computers and pretty women chatting up male employees in bars. More intense corporate espionage is also probable. Although it is unlikely that a paramilitary team will storm into the data centers of Google or Yahoo!, it does remain a possibility. In a more personal approach, it someone puts a gun to an employee's head, that person will happily provide passwords, cryptographic keys, and PIN numbers, a process called "rubber house cryptanalysis."

The more valuable the asset, the more likely others will attempt to acquire it. Although it is hard to put a price on the information troves of Google and other online companies, it is safe to assume that they are extremely valuable, motivating disgruntled employees, competitors, and even governments to apply a great deal of effort to acquire this information.

LEGAL COMPULSION

Online companies are not immune to legal requests for information and other related pressure. To compound the problem, online companies must comply with myriad national and international laws to operate globally. If these companies want to operate in a given country, compliance is a cost of doing business. Perhaps the most controversial of these countries is China. To have access to China's 1.3 billion potential consumers, companies such as Cisco, Google, Yahoo!, and Microsoft must rigorously comply with China's laws and regulatory requirements. As an example, in 2007, China announced that foreign media companies must seek prior approval before distributing pictures, graphics, and news.[61] These companies have no real choice but to comply. Conflicts between user privacy and law are sure to occur. In 2005, Yahoo! was accused of providing information to Chinese officials that led to the jailing of a Chinese writer for divulging state secrets.[62] In 2006, the U.S. Department of Justice issued a far-reaching subpoena[63] demanding disclosure of two full months' worth of search queries and all the URLs in Google's index.[64, 65] To its credit, Google successfully fought off this attack, while other companies, including Yahoo!, complied.[66] This action by the Department of Justice is significant because it sets an important precedent to gaining legal access to user data retained by online companies. However, in many other cases, Google did release information. As an example, in 2008, Indian police sought help in identifying a man posting vulgar comments about Sonia Gandhi, the President of the Indian National Congress. In this case, Google supplied information, which was used to track down the man. He now faces imprisonment for up to five years.[67]

IT'S JUST BUSINESS

At the end of the day, I believe data retention and data mining are about running a profitable business. The more information we provide and the better the ways of analyzing it, the more valuable advertising based on it will become. Make no mistake, online advertising is a billion-dollar industry and the core business model of companies such as Google. However, the tension between the needs of the shareholders and the privacy concerns of individuals makes me certain that user privacy will not always come out on the best end of the bargain. By law, companies must operate in the best interests of their shareholders, not necessarily their users. Although the law provides protection for shareholders, online companies have great flexibility in setting their own rules in the form of privacy policies and terms of service agreements. Many naive web users implicitly assume their privacy will be protected and fail to consider data retention, mining, and sharing. Indeed, data retention and analysis is usually couched in terms of "improving your user experience," but these policies are designed to maximize profit, by allowing data mining as well as sharing data with third parties. Also, don't forget these policies are malleable—that is, they can be rewritten at any time, a common practice. What today is an ethical company may tomorrow be a serious threat, putting sensitive information into the hands of third parties or relying on them for critical business needs. Competition in the business world creates pressure to do the wrong thing. Imagine if a company had the power to legally double its profits at the expense of some reduction in user privacy. Which direction do you think it would choose? This becomes a problem only if the choice becomes public. Declining profitability, mergers, and changes in leadership all have a way of changing corporate morals.

Google Addiction and Dependence

Can a company be too successful? The tools that Google provides are wonderfully efficient and effective. Hundreds of millions of users rely on them for information and communication on many aspects of their daily lives. Google's tools provide some of the best that the web has to offer. This strength is also a weakness. How many people and businesses are dependent on these services? I know I am. I've tried to use other search services, and, frankly, they are generally mediocre. Whether the loss of these services is due to external forces, such as a distributed denial of service attack, accident,[68] or corporate decision making, the risk is severe. I don't regularly use Gmail, but for those who do, imagine if the service was discontinued. How much time and effort would it take for you to create and distribute a new e-mail address to all your friends? What about the data you've stored on Gmail, including the archives of your e-mails and files? Google threatened to do this in Germany, ironically, in response to proposed legislation that mandated data retention.[69, 70] How about you and your employer? Try going for a day without using any of Google's services.[71] Companies and individuals who are listed in Google's search results are also extremely reliant on Google for vital web visitors. For one poignant example, see John Battelle's book *The Search*, which describes how a small shoe merchant was devastated by a change in Google's search-ranking algorithm.[72, 73] Our dependence upon certain online services, particularly in the absence of valid competitors, puts us in a precarious situation. Dependence increases the power base of online companies and weakens our ability to resist changes and policies we don't like, such as forced migration to new versions of software.[74]

Summary

If I had to summarize the threat of our use of online tools, it would be "Power tends to corrupt; absolute power corrupts absolutely." I hope that I've convinced you that we are disclosing a great deal of sensitive information and that this is a threat. Of all the online companies, Google is arguably the most powerful because of its wide range of popular free tools, top-tier intellectual talent, nearly infinite data storage, financial resources, and information-processing capabilities. Most important, however, is the information that Google captures as we use its wide range of popular free tools. Information is slippery, and it can be lost, taken, or deliberately disclosed. This book is really about information—how you disclose it and how it can be linked, aggregated, mined, and exploited. This problem isn't isolated to Google—it applies to any company we provide information to. Information stockpiles of this magnitude have not gone unnoticed by marketers, corporate competitors, law enforcement, and governments worldwide. These entities covet the data and the power it brings, and we will pay the price unless we are aware of the problem and take action.

When we invite Google and other online companies into our lives, we gain the short-term advantage of free tools and services. But this relationship causes dependence. When we live in Google's world, we are bound to it. Publicly held companies are legally required to act in the best interests of their shareholders, not necessarily their users. Conflicts will certainly arise between these two, often competing, goals. Google isn't evil, but it isn't alone. The deeper the relationship we have with Google and other online companies, the less ability we have to control where our data resides and who has access to it.

A key part of the problem is that, today, there is no cure-all for web-based information disclosure. Of course, you always have the option not to use these services, even if online companies are giving them away for free. Technically, abstinence would solve the problem, but at the cost of being excluded from the wired word. Denying yourself access to these tools and the power they provide is not the solution. Likewise, ignoring the problem will not solve anything. We are placing too much power into the hands of too few companies. One day we will pay for our naïveté.

Promising solutions are developing, however—systems such as Tor[75] help provide anonymous browsing, privacy-enhanced browsers help manage cookies, online companies are promising to anonymize some of their logs, and policy makers are debating more stringent protections for web users. I cover more in Chapter 9, "Countermeasures." The most important thing, and a key goal of this book, is to raise awareness to the problem and suggest directions that we can pursue, jointly with online companies, to allow these companies to flourish but still protect us from the threat.

ENDNOTES

1. Definition of *google. Merriam-Webster Online Dictionary.* www.m-w.com/
   dictionary/google.

2. "Passwords Revealed by Sweet Deal," BBC News, 20 April 2004.
   http://news.bbc.co.uk/1/hi/technology/3639679.stm, last accessed 28 October 2007.

3. Some progress has been made. In 2007, Google announced that it would start
   anonymizing its search logs after 18 to 24 months. See http://blog.wired.com/
   27bstroke6/2007/03/google_to_anony.html. Note that the policy makes no mention
   of anonymizing logs from any of its other tools and services.

4. Google Privacy Policy, Google, 14 October 2005. www.google.com/
   privacypolicy.html, last accessed 26 May 2008.

5. SSL is the protocol designed to encrypt web communications. You have certainly
   used it when you've entered your credit card number online or whenever you've seen
   the padlock in the corner of your browser. SSL is the underlying encryption mechanism for secure web browsing (HTTPS).

6. Google doesn't support SSL for search, but it does support SSL for other services,
   such as Gmail.

7. "HIPPAA News Archives," HIPPAA Advisory.com, January 2003. www.
   hipaadvisory.com/News/newsarchives/2003/jan03.htm, last accessed 28 October
   2007.

8. Andrew Orlowski, "Phishing with Google Desktop," *The Register,* 3 December 2005.
   www.theregister.co.uk/2005/12/03/google_desktop_vuln/, last accessed 28 October
   2005.

9. Data mining is the science of extracting useful information from large data sets or
   databases. See http://en.wikipedia.org/wiki/Data_mining for a quick overview.

10. See the World Wide Web Consortium's "A Little History of the World Wide Web,"
    www.w3.org/History.html, for more information.

11. Matthew Gray, "Web Growth Summary." www.mit.edu/people/mkgray/net/
    web-growth-summary.html, last accessed 3 September 2007.

12. Mark Ward, "How the Web Went Worldwide," BBC News, 3 August 2006.
    http://news.bbc.co.uk/1/hi/technology/5242252.stm, last accessed 3 September 2007.

13. "The Size of the World Wide Web," Pandia Search Engine News, 25 February 2007.
    www.pandia.com/sew/383-web-size.html, last accessed 3 September 2007.

14. The surface web consists of traditional web pages that are easily indexed by search engines. The deep web, on the other hand, is far more difficult to index because it includes such things as password-protected, multimedia, and dynamically generated content.

15. Peter Lyman and Hal R. Varian, "How Much Information?", 2003. School of Information Management and Systems, University of California Berkeley, 27 October 2003. www.sims.berkeley.edu/how-much-info-2003, last accessed 3 September 2007.

16. Sharon Gaudin, "The Digital Universe Created 161 Exabytes of Data Last Year," *Information Week,* 7 March 2007. www.informationweek.com/news/showArticle.jhtml?articleID=197800880, last accessed 3 September 2007.

17. "Internet Usage Statistics—The Big Picture," Internet World Stats, www.internetworldstats.com/stats.htm, last accessed 3 September 2007.

18. Suzy Bausch, "Nielsen//NetRatings Reports Topline U.S. Data for July 2007," Nielsen//NetRatings, 13 August 2007. www.netratings.com/pr/pr_070813.pdf, last accessed 3 September 2007.

19. Suzy Bausch, "Nielsen//NetRatings Announces July U.S. Search Share Rankings," Nielsen//NetRatings, 20 August 2007. www.netratings.com/pr/pr_070820.pdf, last accessed 3 September 2007.

20. Steve Bryant, "Google Crowned World's Most Visited Site," Google Watch, 25 April 2007. http://googlewatch.eweek.com/content/google_strategy/google_crowned_worlds_most_visited_site.html, last accessed 3 September 2007.

21. "GOOG: Key Statistics for Google," Yahoo! Finance. http://finance.yahoo.com/q/ks?s=GOOG, last accessed 4 September 2007.

22. "Total GDP 2006," World Bank. http://siteresources.worldbank.org/DATASTATISTICS/Resources/GDP.pdf, last accessed 4 September 2007.

23. Saul Hansell, "Google Answer to Filling Jobs Is an Algorithm," *The New York Times,* 3 January 2007. www.nytimes.com/2007/01/03/technology/03google.html?ex=1325480400&en=e71cadb22a20a3c4&ei=5088, last accessed 4 September 2007.

24. John Markoff and Saul Hansell, "Hiding in Plain Sight, Google Seeks More Power," *The New York Times,* 14 June 2006. www.nytimes.com/2006/06/14/technology/14search.html?ex=1307937600&en=c96a72bbc5f90a47&ei=5088&partner=rssnyt&emc=rss, last accessed 4 September 2007.

25. Here I'm assuming a machine with an Intel Xeon processor (3.6GHz, 2MB L2 Cache, 800MHz bus) capable of 13 gigaflops (floating-point operations per second).

26. "29th TOP500 Supercomputer List," Top 500 Supercomputer Sites, June 2007. www.top500.org/lists/2007/06, last accessed 4 September 2007.

27. "Conversation with Eric Schmidt—Hosted by John Battelle," Web 2.0 Expo, 17 April 2007. www.google.com/press/podium/web_expo_2007.html, last accessed 4 September 2007.

28. John Battelle. "The Web Time Axis." Searchblog, 13 April 2004. http://battellemedia.com/archives/000573.php, last accessed 2 August 2008.

29. Google Labs, "Passionate About These Topics? You Should Work at Google." http://labs.google.com/, last accessed 5 September 2007.

30. "Language Tools—Use the Google Interface in Your Language," Google.com. www.google.com/language_tools, last accessed 5 September 2007.

31. "Language Tools—Visit Google's Site in Your Local Domain," Google.com. www.google.com/language_tools, last accessed 5 September 2007.

32. "United Nations Member States," United Nations, 3 October 2006. www.un.org/members/list.shtml, last accessed 6 September 2007.

33. Even at a large company such as Microsoft, which offers its own search engine, employees favor Google. See http://it.slashdot.org/it/06/06/22/029243.shtml for more information.

34. I've excluded some of Google's more tongue-in-cheek languages here, including Bork, bork, bork!, Elmer Fudd, Hacker, Klingon, and Pig Latin.

35. Google Investor Relations, "Google Code of Conduct." http://investor.google.com/conduct.html, last accessed 2 September 2007.

36. It is important to note that judges aren't the only officials authorized to issue a subpoena. Any officer of the court, including lawyers, can do so.

37. In August 2006, AOL posted 24 million search queries of 650,000 AOL users on the web.

38. Michael Barbaro and Tom Zeller. "A Face Is Exposed for AOL Searcher No. 4417749," *The New York Times*, 9 August 2006. www.nytimes.com/2006/08/09/technology/09aol.html, last accessed 1 November 2007.

39. The Sobiesk Information Disclosure Metric is named after its creator, security researcher Dr. Edward Sobiesk.

40. Vlad Constandes, "On Gmail and Google Talk Privacy," Softpedia, 10 December 2007. http://news.softpedia.com/news/On-GMail-and-Google-Talk-Privacy-73395.shtml, last accessed 27 May 2008.

41. Nicholas Carlson, "eBay Resumes Google Advertising," InternetNews, 22 June 2007. www.internetnews.com/ec-news/article.php/3685126, last accessed 30 May 2008.

42. Sarah Schafer, "With Capital in Panic, Pizza Deliveries Soar," *Washington Post,* 19 December 1998. www.washingtonpost.com/wp-srv/politics/special/clinton/stories/pizza121998.htm, last accessed 1 November 2007.

43. This strategy is sometimes called the Four Horsemen of the Infocalypse; see http://en.wikipedia.org/wiki/Four_Horsemen_of_the_Infocalypse.

44. We are also seeing a dramatic increase in network storage.

45. Candace Lombardi, "Study: Shoppers Will Pay for Privacy," CNET News, 7 June 2007. http://news.cnet.com/Study-Shoppers-will-pay-for-privacy/2100-1029_3-6189380.html, last accessed 29 May 2008.

46. Declan McCullagh and Elinor Mills, "How Search Engines Rate on Privacy," CNET News, 13 August 2007. http://news.cnet.com/2100-1029_3-6202068.html, last accessed 29 May 2008.

47. "Wire and Electronic Communications Interception and Interception of Oral Communications," Cornell University Law School, Legal Information Institute, U.S. Code collection, Title 18, Part I, Chapter 119. www.law.cornell.edu/uscode/18/usc_sup_01_18_10_I_20_119.html, last accessed 28 May 2008.

48. Paul Kiel, "D'Oh: House Panel Screw-Up Reveals Whistleblower E-mail Addresses, *TPM Muckraker,* 26 October 2007. www.tpmmuckraker.com/archives/004576.php, last accessed 1 November 2007.

49. *A Chronology of Data Breaches,* Privacy Rights Clearinghouse, 25 October 2007. www.privacyrights.org/ar/chrondatabreaches.htm, last accessed 1 November 2007.

50. "Google Privacy Policy Highlights," Google.com, 14 October 2005. www.google.com/intl/en/privacy.html, last accessed 2 October 2007.

51. HIPPAA News Archives, HIPPAA Advisory.com, January 2003. www.hipaadvisory.com/News/newsarchives/2003/jan03.htm, last accessed 28 October 2007.

52. "Info on 3.9M Citigroup Customers Lost," CNNMoney.com, 6 June 2005. http://money.cnn.com/2005/06/06/news/fortune500/security_citigroup/, last accessed 1 November 2007.

53. Roy Mark, "VA Data Breach Stirs Washington," Internetnews.com, 23 May 2006. www.internetnews.com/bus-news/article.php/3608411, last accessed 1 November 2007.

54. "Phishing with Google Desktop." www.theregister.co.uk/2005/12/03/google_desktop_vuln/.

55. Liam Tung, "Gmail Cookie Vulnerability Exposes User's Privacy," CNET News, 27 September 2007. http://news.cnet.com/2100-1002_3-6210353.html, last accessed 27 May 2008.

56. Jim Finkle. "Hackers Steal U.S. Government, Corporate Data From PCs." Reuters, 17 July 2007. www.reuters.com/article/domesticNews/idUSN1638118020070717, last accessed 2 August 2008.

57. Companies are very hesitant to report such incidents because it erodes consumer trust and confidence. You wouldn't put your money in an online back that announced it had just been broken into.

58. Bugtraq Mailing List, SecurityFocus.com. www.securityfocus.com/, last accessed 1 November 2007.

59. "Robert Philip Hanssen Espionage Case," Federal Bureau of Investigation press release, 20 February 2001. www.fbi.gov/libref/historic/famcases/hanssen/hanssen.htm, last accessed 1 November 2007.

60. "Aldrich Hazen Ames," Federal Bureau of Investigation. www.fbi.gov/libref/historic/famcases/ames/ames.htm, last accessed 1 November 2007.

61. Nate Anderson. "Do Google and YouTube have ethical responsibility for their video services?" Ars Technica, 27 November 2006. http://arstechnica.com/news.ars/post/20061127-8289.html, last accessed 1 November 2007.

62. "Yahoo! 'Helped Jail China Writer,'" BBC News, 7 September 2005. http://news.bbc.co.uk/2/hi/asia-pacific/4221538.stm, last accessed 1 November 2007.

63. *ACLU* v. *Alberto R. Gonzales,* United States District Court—Northern District of California, 25 August 2005. www.google.com/press/images/subpoena_20060317.pdf, last accessed 28 May 2008.

64. Thomas Claburn, "Justice Department Subpoenas Reach Far Beyond Google," *InformationWeek,* 29 March 2006. www.informationweek.com/news/showArticle.jhtml?articleID=184401156, last accessed 1 November 2007.

65. Nicole Wong, "Response to the DoJ Motion," The Official Google Blog, 17 February 2006. http://googleblog.blogspot.com/2006/02/response-to-doj-motion.html, last accessed 28 May 2008.

66. Xeni Jardin, "DoJ Search Requests: Google Said No; Yahoo!, AOL, MSN Yes," *Boing Boing*, 19 January 2006. www.boingboing.net/2006/01/19/-doj-search-requests.html, last accessed 1 November 2007.

67. Michael Arrington, "Hit Pause on the Evil Button: Google Assists in Arrest of Indian Man," *Tech Crunch*, 18 May 2008. www.techcrunch.com/2008/05/18/hit-pause-on-the-evil-button-google-assists-in-arrest-of-indian-man/, last accessed 26 May 2008.

68. BondGamer, "Thousands of ICQ Numbers Deleted," Slashdot.org, 11 May 2007. http://slashdot.org/articles/07/05/11/0138251.shtml, last accessed 1 November 2007.

69. It is technically possible, although, in some cases, illegal, to precisely deny services to specific individuals, companies, or even nations.

70. "Google Threatens to End E-mail Service in Germany," *Spiegel Online*, 25 June 2007. www.spiegel.de/international/germany/0,1518,490492,00.html, last accessed 1 November 2007.

71. This idea comes from the Alt Search Engines blog, which asked people to go for a day without using one of the five major search engines: Google, Yahoo!, MSN, AOL, or Ask. See http://altsearchengines.com/2007/06/10/a-day-without-google/ for more information.

72. Ryan Singel, "How Google Got Its Groove On," *Wired*, 9 September 2005. www.wired.com/science/discoveries/news/2005/09/68792, last accessed 1 November 2007.

73. A worse case would be to be delisted altogether. You would, for all intents and purposes, disappear from the Internet.

74. Juan Carlos Perez, "Microsoft Delivers Hotmail Upgrade," *PCWorld*, 7 May 2007. www.pcworld.com/article/id,131615-page,1/article.html, last accessed 1 November 2007.

75. "Tor: Anonymity Online," Tor Project, 25 October 2007. www.torproject.org/, last accessed 1 November 2007.

Information Flows and Leakage

Every time someone sits down at a computer and accesses the web, that person actually trusts a great many people and organizations with his or her personal information, before even reaching the servers of Google or some other online company. To understand how online companies fit into the equation of web-based information disclosure, we must first understand this end-to-end big picture. The best way to understand this is to follow the flow of information from an end user's computer through its communication across the Internet until it reaches the servers of Google or another online company. Information is a slippery thing—once you lose control of it, it could end up in places and be used in ways you didn't intend or even have knowledge of.[1]

Although data can be created in many ways, here I'm focusing on individual users creating information via their personal computers. This process occurs both offline, as in the creation of a word processing document, or online when employing the tools of Google. Personal computers are very complex machines built from millions of lines of code and myriad chips and other electronic components. A security breach in any of these components can impact whether the information is kept confidential, altered without consent, or available when needed. Even if every piece of hardware and software is entirely trustworthy, computers still leak information like a sieve, through such things as network protocols (such as DNS or DHCP), automatically updating software (such as Windows Update), or automated bug reports being sent to software companies.

The vulnerabilities do not end with individual computers; they also include network communications. Numerous network service providers carry out your communications with Google and other online companies; any of these might be attempting to eavesdrop or alter your communications. Finally, once the information reaches its destination, it may simply be logged, but more likely it will be heavily data-mined and used to create profiles of users. After being logged, the information might be retained forever, shared, copied, leaked, or intentionally (or unintentionally) destroyed.

In this chapter, we examine these issues to understand the flow of information from your PC across the Internet to the servers of online companies. Along this path, we look at key ways your information can be viewed or changed without your knowledge. My intent here is to provide the appropriate context for the many faceted risks surrounding web-based information disclosure. The rest of the book focuses on Google as the primary consumer of your personal information, but the information you provide by using online products and services isn't necessarily available only to Google. Anyone who has compromised your personal computer or the network between you and Google could have access to the same information. In other words, the threat includes far more than the databases of Google. Google is the impetus for generating and transmitting the information, but the full spectrum of threats includes much more than a single, albeit powerful, company.

THE DATA, INFORMATION, KNOWLEDGE, WISDOM HIERARCHY

At its heart, this book is about information disclosure via the World Wide Web. To understand information disclosure, we need to understand the idea of information. However, the word *information* can mean many things to many people. Information theorists[2] look at information as part of a hierarchy from raw data to refined knowledge: data, information, knowledge, and wisdom. The *Random House Unabridged Dictionary* provides the following definitions:

- Data is used to describe individual facts, statistics, or items of information.
- Information applies to facts told, read, or communicated that may be unorganized and even unrelated.
- Knowledge is an organized body of information, or the comprehension and understanding consequent on having acquired and organized a body of facts.
- Wisdom is a knowledge of people, life, and conduct, with the facts so thoroughly assimilated as to have produced sagacity, judgment.

In general, users disclose data and information as they use online tools. Knowledge, and perhaps wisdom, can be gained through profiling, data mining and human analysis.

In most instances, information flows only to legitimate destinations. As I show throughout this book, even legitimate destinations, such as online companies, pose a significant risk. Unfortunately, we cannot always assume that just legitimate destinations receive the information or even that we are aware of all "legitimate" destinations because of fine-print usage agreements, legal compulsion, and third-party sharing.

A MATTER OF TRUST

Whenever you are confronted with a complex information-processing system, a useful analytic approach is to follow the flow of information through creation, storage, processing, and communication. This analysis should consider both flows inside a computer and devices in its immediate vicinity because, as the computer processes information, it communicates with internal devices soldered to the motherboard, devices connected to internal busses (think graphics cards), and external peripherals. The section, "Data Communication on the Network," covers flows that extend across the Internet.

Every time you use your computer, you trust a lot of people and organizations. If any one of these trusted parties violates your confidence, either through deliberate action or by accident, your security is at risk. Consider the main components of your computer, from the individual chips on the motherboard to its system and application software. Table 2-1 illustrates some of the people and organizations you must trust.

Table 2-1 A Look at the Many Programs and Hardware Devices You Trust Every Time You Use Your Computer

Item	Examples	Representative Manufacturers	Number of Manufacturers
Electronic chips	CPU, RAM, video, sound, and network chips	AMD, Intel, Texas Instruments[3]	Moderate
Motherboard	Personal computer, PDA, laptop	ABIT, Asus, Gigabyte	Low
BIOS[4]	Included on most computer motherboards	AMI, Award, Phoenix Technologies	Low
Operating system	Linux, UNIX, Windows, Macintosh	Apple, Microsoft, various open source developers	Low
Other internal hardware	Graphics cards, sound cards, network interface cards, hard drives	ATI, PNY, Creative, Maxtor, Western Digital	High

continues

Table 2-1   Continued

Item	Examples	Representative Manufacturers	Number of Manufacturers
Peripherals	Printers, scanners, USB key rings, external hard drives, keyboards, mouse devices, monitors, webcams, digital cameras, microphones, MP3 players	HP, Xerox, Corsair, Kingston, PNY, Logitech, Kensington, Microsoft	High
Device drivers[5]	Webcam, printer, monitor, keyboard, mouse, MP3 player drivers	Microsoft, Apple, HP, Brother, Canon, Logitech, open source developers	High
Applications	Word processors, firewalls, media players, spreadsheets, system utilities	Microsoft, Nullsoft, Zone Labs, open source developers	Very high
Plug-ins	Media players for browsers, extensions to blogging software	Adobe, Apple, Sun, open source developers	Moderate
Security and other patches to operating system and applications	Operating system service packs, patches for web server security	Microsoft, Oracle, open source developers	Moderate

When a computer is turned on, each step while booting up requires trust of the preceding one. If any breakdown occurs along this chain, the computer is at risk. To make matters worse, most of the functionality of your computer happens behind the scenes, and it is difficult, if not impossible, to determine whether something is amiss. The boot-up process starts with the central processing unit (CPU) executing the Basic Input/Output System, which initializes the primary hardware devices the computer depends on to function, such as the hard drive or CD-ROM drive. During this stage, you are trusting that all the chips on the motherboard, including the CPU, are behaving appropriately. Chip manufacturers have a positive track record for reliability and trustworthiness,[6] but chips are the ideal location to place malicious logic, particularly when they are manufactured.[7] For the prudent security professional, any chip should be considered suspect. Although the primary manufacturer of a given piece of hardware might be entirely trustworthy, one of its subcontractors (or a subcontractor's subcontractor) might not. The same is the true for motherboard manufacturers or system integrators, who rely on third-party hardware and software. Note also that chips exist in virtually every electronic component, even those with no traditional software, so this threat is potentially very far reaching. Programmable chips, such as Field Programmable Gate

Arrays (FPGAs), are particularly vulnerable because they can be programmed (and reprogrammed) with a language such as the Very High Speed Integrated Circuit Hardware Description Language (VHDL). For example, researchers have demonstrated that placing malicious logic in a VHDL design is within the capabilities of a computer science student.[8] The BIOS is another location where malicious code could reside, particularly because it can be rewritten or *flashed* with a new program. Because of this, some security experts believe that the BIOS is a growing target of attack.[9] We've already seen the Chernobyl virus, sometimes called CIH, which can corrupt the BIOS.[10]

Based on its settings, the BIOS hands off control to a bootable device that contains the primary operating system. Typically, this handoff occurs when the BIOS passes control to the code found in a hard drive's Master Boot Record (MBR)[11], which then passes off execution to the *boot sector,* the portion of the disk responsible for loading and executing the operating system, starting with the *kernel,* the central component of the operating system. The kernel initializes the device drivers, allowing the operating system to communicate with additional hardware devices, both internal and external. These hardware devices, whether internal, such as expansion cards, or external, such as keyboards, represent another important component of trust. Hardware devices such as these can easily operate in an untrustworthy manner, such as a keyboard that contains an embedded keystroke logger.

The kernel is another high-payoff target for attackers. Because the kernel controls the information that is fed to programs and system utilities, a successful compromise of the kernel can defeat all trust in a system. Attackers have been quite successful in this regard.[12] Because kernels implement most of the security in the operating system, they are hardened against misuse; however, the device drivers they load are another mechanism by which an attacker can compromise a system. Kernels are heavily scrutinized pieces of code, and often come from established operating system vendors, however, device drivers come from a wide range of sources, including relatively unknown manufacturers and developers. Again, attackers have successfully targeted device drivers, and security experts believe these attacks will continue to rise.[13]

After the kernel completely initializes the system, a user can log on and begin running application programs. In most cases, these application programs run in *user space,* a region of memory designed to hold user applications. When these applications need access to computer resources, they make *system calls* to the kernel, which checks the validity of the request, mediates between competing requests, and provides access to authorized resources. The protection the kernel provides is insufficient to guard against malicious or insecurely written applications. Many forms of malicious software bypass these protections and can infect computing systems.[14] Whether the malicious code was added during official production, because of an undetected virus, or even because of a malicious compiler, the threat exists.[15]

If you are beginning to think your computer is a lot like Swiss cheese, you are correct. Any breakdown in the chain of trust from the hardware to the software will destroy the security of your system.[16] Although the act of procuring hardware or software from a reputable firm and the fact that source code is available for an application are helpful, neither guarantees that a given application or component is trustworthy.

The threat to electronic devices is widespread; in many ways, little difference exists between a traditional desktop computer and other computing devices, such as cell phones, PDAs, network routers, and your Internet-ready toaster. This section covered places where your trust might be violated;[17] the next section covers how information can leak from your computer, intentionally or unintentionally.

INFORMATION FLOWS AND LEAKAGE ON A PC

Imagine drawing a circle with a piece of chalk around your computer and considering information that flows across this boundary, either outbound or inbound (see Figure 2-1).[18] Why such a holistic approach? I believe that a comprehensive model such as this helps push the boundaries of your thinking and prevents surprises. I'm sure that you are aware that information flows across networks, perhaps via a network cable or wireless connection, and that someone could walk off with your hard drive, but it is a useful exercise to attempt to consider *everything* that crosses that boundary you drew in chalk. Your computer communicates with the outside world in a number of ways: USB, serial and parallel ports, connections to your monitor, and rewritable CDs and DVDs. Even something as simple as a USB port opens up a multitude of ways that information can leak from your computer.[19] Similarly, this model is a useful way to consider the emanations from your computer, which leaks electromagnetic energy—and, hence, information—like a sieve. What you *deliberately* disclose is only part of the equation. What you *actually* disclose is another matter.

Many things can and do cross this boundary, some you might not have thought of. Of course, people and physical items, such as USB drives and DVDs, do. A network connection is designed to communicate information, but information also leaks in the form of acoustic energy (sound) and electromagnetic radiation. The double-ended arrows in the figure are deliberate: A computer might radiate information deliberately, as in the case of a wireless network connection, or unintentionally, but also in response to outside stimuli. A great example is a passive RFID tag. Most of the time, the tag lies inert, but when bathed with an RF signal of the right frequency and strength, the tag transmits a response.[20] Each of the vectors in the figure operates similarly. Each inbound border crossing can trigger a response in the computer. For example, a surge of electricity across a power line might destroy a component in the computer or commands (in the form of electric pulses) coming across the network can be used to compromise a computer's operating system. Note that these examples include two different levels, a physical level where inbound energy generates an effect based on the laws of nature and the other at a logical level in which energy, usually in the form of inbound information, triggers the computer to disclose information or otherwise alter the security state of the computer. This inbound information can also cause the human to disclose information, as is the case of a phishing e-mail or free online tool that might appear innocuous but is actually designed to trick or subtly encourage the human to disclose valuable information.

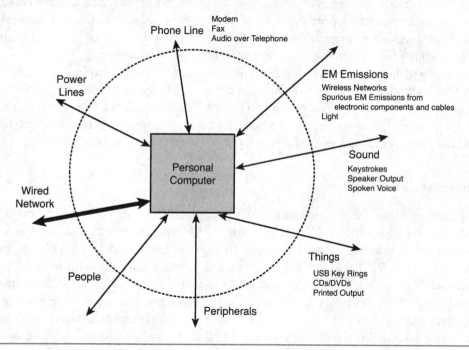

Figure 2-1 Imagine drawing a circle in chalk a few meters in diameter around your computer. Information flows across this boundary in myriad ways, some desired and some undesired.

NETWORKS

Consider the networks that computers can connect to, including wired, wireless, and telephone networks. This is where information is supposed to flow, both inbound and outbound. They also offer extremely high bandwidth.[21] Networks are the lifeblood of the connected world; without them, there is no Internet. Because network connections are how you surf the web, they are the biggest threat vector for web-based information disclosure, but they also generate a great deal of unintentional leakage. Attackers constantly probe the Internet for vulnerable machines, but eavesdropping on networks reveals a great deal. Simply turning on a typical computer initiates a number of networking protocols and applications that disclose sensitive information, such as the Address Resolution Protocol (ARP), DNS, file-sharing protocols, and e-mail or instant messaging clients set to run automatically. Myriad programs, including antivirus software and browsers, "phone home" to download updates.

For best visibility on wired networks, eavesdroppers require physical access to the network via a nearby network port, cable, or compromised computer, switch, or router. For wireless networks, computers are deliberately broadcasting their traffic, so attackers need only be within a few hundred meters; physical access isn't required.[22, 23]

It is also worth considering rogue (unofficial or unauthorized) wireless access points, fax machines, and modems when evaluating network leakage. Nonmalicious users set up such devices to work around technical and policy restrictions they find inconvenient. Malicious users who have a degree of physical access to a given network also set up these devices to allow remote access and a surreptitious channel of communication.

PERIPHERALS

Computers are designed to communicate with the outside world, and modern motherboards include USB, serial, parallel, video, audio, PC Card, FireWire (IEEE 1394), and network ports. Computers communicate both internally and externally via busses such as PCI, IDE, AGP, SCSI, and PCI Express. The busses themselves allow communications to external devices such as hard drives and scanners, and internal devices such as graphics cards, hard drives, network interface cards, and modems. The key idea here is that computers communicate at a very high data rate to devices integrated into the motherboard, internal but also removable components such as hard drives, and external devices. Many of these devices, in turn, facilitate additional communications via cabling and wireless media. Virtually all of these communications emit RF energy perceptible outside the device packaging or cabling itself. (More on this in a second.) One notable exception is fiber-optic cable that does not emit light outside a properly shielded cable.[24]

Peripherals, such as webcams and microphones, worsen the situation because an attacker can use them to further collect information in the environment surrounding compromised machines. It is important to also consider personal digital assistants, which can contain microphones, cameras, and a great deal of sensitive information, because they can be connected directly or indirectly to the Internet. They, too, pose a significant risk.[25] Technically, cell phones represent a similar risk because they all contain microphones and many include cameras. Little publicly available information exists about the capabilities of cell phone surveillance, but the risk should be considered.[26]

EM RADIATION

All electronic circuits emit some amount of *electromagnetic (EM) energy,* self-propagating waves in space. The EM spectrum is continuous and includes radio bands, television bands, microwaves, infrared light, visible light, ultraviolet light, x-rays, and gamma-rays. Some of these emissions are deliberate and others not, but many can be detected from great distances. The most common deliberate application is radio; where electromagnetic energy is transmitted by one station and received by another, as is the case with a home wireless network. The "Networks" section of the chapter already covered wireless networks; this section covers unintentional EM radiation.

You might think that the unintentional EM radiation a typical PC generates isn't anything to worry about, but it doesn't take much information (even as little as 1 bit— something happened or didn't happen) to yield useful information. An excellent example of the significance of a single bit of information is that of a radar detector detector. Police use such devices to determine whether a car has an operational radar detector. Such a detector looks for the emissions of a certain type of local oscillator that indicates the presence of a radar detector.[27] If you are in a state that outlaws radar detectors, that one bit of information (the presence or absence of a radar detector) might be of great interest to a police officer.

On most motherboards, information flows as low-voltage electric pulses via *traces,* conductive pathways, between chips.[28] Traces also connect to expansions slots and ports designed to communicate with both internal and external devices. These devices might simply store information locally or they might further communicate the information to external peripherals or other computers through copper, fiber optic, USB, FireWire, serial, and parallel cabling, as well as wireless transmissions. It is important to note that these are the intended flows of communication to desired recipients. In almost all cases, chips and cabling emit RF energy. These emissions are the bane of computer and communications engineers, causing interference between devices and communication channels, limiting the speed at which devices can operate and channels can pass information. These same emissions pose a security risk because they can be detected with specialized interception equipment. Security professionals have long recognized this problem but have never completely solved it. However, programs attempt to mitigate the threat, most notably TEMPEST, which outlines emission standards for the U.S. government.[29, 30]

The problem isn't just with motherboards: Computer monitors can emit electromagnetic energy that reveals the contents of their screens. Wim van Eck pioneered the technique of eavesdropping on CRT displays, and the general field of study is now commonly called *Van Eck phreaking.* Similarly, devices used to eavesdrop on video displays are called *Van Eck devices.*[31]

Researchers have extended van Eck's work by demonstrating that certain types of LCD displays are also vulnerable.[32] Van Eck phreaking requires close physical access to the target machine, but it shouldn't be discounted. Dutch voting machines were decertified because researchers demonstrated that official voting machines could be eavesdropped upon.[33, 34] The U.S. government feels strongly enough about EM radiation to shield sensitive rooms with protective copper screening and alert systems.[35]

Another wireless threat, although not technically unintentional but probably overlooked, is that of wireless keyboards and mice. These devices broadcast every keystroke and mouse movement, and present a significant, albeit localized,[36] eavesdropping threat. Attackers have demonstrated that it is possible to intercept certain current models of Microsoft keyboards.[37] Wireless Bluetooth devices have shown similar vulnerabilities.[38, 39]

The visible light and infrared (IR) portions of the EM spectrum are another potential vector. Of course, attackers could simply *shoulder-surf* (look over a user's shoulder) as they type or use a video recorder with a zoom lens to observe a screen or keyboard from a distance, but there are more subtle approaches. Many laptops and personal digital systems can send and receive information via IR ports. Additionally, it seems as if every computing device has LEDs connected to it.[40] Researchers have also found that blinking LEDs can leak information.[41] Light-based threats of this sort are fundamentally a localized phenomenon; near–line of sight to the target machine is required.

SOUND

Sounds emanating from your computer, its peripherals, and your interactions with them also contain valuable information that can be detected from a distance. The most obvious are sounds coming from speakers and through your speech interactions using voice recognition. You might think that it is difficult to detect relevant sounds from a distance, but advances in sensor technology, such as parabolic microphones, can detect sounds from the distance of hundreds of yards. In some cases, microphones might not be necessary. For example, *Wired Magazine* documented the skills of three blind Israeli brothers who could hear the dialing of a phone call, understand and remember the tones (including calling cards and credit card numbers), and later used the information to commit crimes.[42]

Also, because sound does not travel far, you should not rule out the issue of bugging your workspace.[43, 44] Trojan horse programs or spyware can be surreptitiously installed on your computer and cause it to transmit sound from an external or internal microphone to an attacker across the network. Similarly, because they contain both a microphone and a transmitter, cell phones have long been suspected of having the capability to be turned into monitoring devices by law enforcement, working in conjunction with mobile telephone operators.[45] Even more exotic monitoring attacks are possible. For example, the CIA allegedly surgically altered cats during the 1960s to put microphones and transmitting devices inside the felines.[46, 47] Others have used laser beams to capture noises emanating from inside buildings.[48]

Sure, if you use voice recognition to tell your computer a password or if you use a touch-tone keypad to enter a credit card number, it shouldn't be that much of a surprise that an attacker could overhear and use the information. However, significant, more subtle attacks based on nonspeech acoustic emanations are still possible. Researchers have proven that even innocuous-seeming sounds can contain valuable security-related information. For example, security researchers were able to detect, with high accuracy, words typed into a keyboard by both sound and timing characteristics.[49, 50] Similar vulnerabilities have been found in hard drives and central processing units.[51]

POWER LINES

Power lines are another way information can cross the boundary surrounding your computer or other electronic device. It is unlikely that your computer is inadvertently spilling a great deal of information across its electric cord; a PC's power supply includes filtering circuitry that makes this unlikely. However, in general, it is possible to communicate information across electrical wiring. Power line networking is a proven, albeit not widely adopted, technology for communicating information across household electrical wiring, with data transfer rates of at least 10Mbps.[52, 53] Researchers have also discovered *power analysis attacks,* which yield information by monitoring power consumed by a device, such as secret keys contained in tamper-resistant hardware.[54]

HUMANS AND THE THINGS THEY CARRY

For sure, humans cross the boundary and have long been the source of information leakage.[55] Beyond just what is in their head, humans may take with them analog (think computer printouts) and digital storage devices containing a great deal more information.

For example, a number of printers and copiers from major manufacturers surreptitiously encode the serial number and manufacturing code on every document they produce.[56, 57]

One of the more obvious ways information can flow out of your computer is via media designed for just this purpose, such as CDs, DVDs, and USB key rings, and external hard drives. Internal hard drives should also be considered in this threat category, as should PDAs, cell phones, digital cameras, MP3 players, and BlackBerries.[58] All of these can contain gigabytes or more of data and can also contain malicious code. For example, USB key ring drives can be infected with software that automatically runs when inserted into a personal computer.[59] But you shouldn't exclude toys—think of the Furby, which the National Security Agency banned because it could record conversations, and other consumer electronics, such as digital picture frames, which attackers could use to install malicious code.[60, 61] In short, you should consider any item that is portable and can contain information as a risk. Thanks to their physical nature, all of these devices require a human to carry the device away from the machine.

This section covered a wide range of ways information can flow into and out of your computer (see Table 2-2). This model should help you understand the big picture of information flows in the immediate vicinity surrounding your computer. For purposes of web-based information disclosure, the main communication vector to be concerned with is the Internet, which is the subject of the next section.

Table 2-2 Comparing the Properties of Information Disclosure Vectors

Category	Medium	Bandwidth	Likelihood of Leakage	Inbound Logical Attack Risk	Risk Distance
Wired network	Copper/fiber	Very high	High	High	Remote
Telephone network	Copper	Moderate	Low	Low	Remote
Wireless network	Air	High	Very high	High	Local/remote
Peripherals	Copper/air	Variable	Moderate	Low	Local
EM emissions	Air	Low	Very high	Very low	Local
Sound	Air	Low	Moderate	Very low	Local
Power lines	Copper	Varies	Very low	Very low	Local
People	Humans	Low	Varies	Varies	Varies
Things	Varies	High	Moderate	Low	Varies

DATA COMMUNICATION ON THE NETWORK

The preceding section, "Information Flows and Leakage on a PC," provided a comprehensive look at ways information can unintentionally emanate from a computer and its nearby environment. This section focuses on intentional web-based information disclosure across the most significant of those vectors, the Internet, and analyzes the threats of eavesdropping, alteration, and accessibility of communications with online companies.[62]

Interactions with the servers of online companies require trusting a number of organizations, including local ISPs, long-haul Internet backbone providers, the Domain Name System, the makers of all hardware and software on every device transited or interacted with, and, of course, the online company itself.[63] To make matters worse, even if all of these organizations, applications, and devices are entirely trustworthy, an attacker with access to communication links could threaten the confidentiality, integrity, and availability of the communication stream. Remember also that the infrastructure of the Internet is run by computers that suffer many of the security risks described in the preceding section. The chain of security and privacy is only as strong as its weakest link. Even if you have an extremely secure computer or network, it is essentially worthless if a single component is compromised.

INFORMATION FLOWS AND LEAKS ON THE INTERNET

Your computer reaches web sites such as Google through links between network devices—usually routers—that are smart enough to route your messages to the correct destination web server. The communications begin with a connection from your computer to the first such device in the chain, then across 10 to 20 more such devices, and ultimately arrive at the correct web server (see Figure 2-2). As illustrated in the preceding section, information can flow from individual computers in many unexpected ways. The same applies to this chain of network devices. In the figure, the dotted line extends the idea of the "chalk circle," discussed earlier, to include the entire communication path.

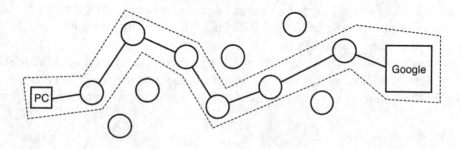

Figure 2-2 Flow of information from your personal computer across a number of intermediate routers before ultimately reaching a Google server. Any point in this chain is potentially eavesdropped upon.

Anyone with access to any of these devices can attempt to eavesdrop, alter, redirect, slow down, or block your communications. Whether you are browsing the web, reading your mail, communicating via instant messaging, or using online mapping, your requests and responses must traverse the network, and all are potentially vulnerable. Many of these services are "in the clear"—that is, no encryption is used to protect you from eavesdropping. For example, using a network monitoring tool, such as Wireshark, to sniff any of the links, you can easily see such activity. The following HTTP request was created when I searched Google for "surveillance," and I captured it using Wireshark, just as an eavesdropper could. Note that the search term (bolded) is clearly visible in the payload.

```
GET /search?hl=en&q=surveillance&btnG=Google+Search HTTP/1.1
```

Even if you protect your communication with unbreakable encryption across the Internet,[64] it is still vulnerable, in its unencrypted form, at either endpoint. For example, Secure Sockets Layer (SSL) is the most widely deployed cryptographic mechanism of all time[65] and is used to secure communications from your web browser to a destination web server. Most online businesses use SSL to protect sensitive communications from eavesdropping, such as when banking or entering a credit card number. Your browser lets you know that SSL is being used by displaying a small padlock icon in your browser. Google uses SSL when you log into your Google Account or read your Gmail. After login, Gmail doesn't use SSL by default, but it can be configured to do so. "By default" is a key phrase; because most users will never reconfigure their account, they are vulnerable to eavesdropping and may, perhaps, lose control of their account.[66] Unfortunately, many of Google's services do not offer an SSL option. For example, if you attempt to access Google using SSL, https://www.google.com/, you are automatically redirected to the unprotected http://www.google.com/. I do not fault Google for this. The fact is, cryptography requires significantly more processing power than unencrypted equivalents. If all of Google's services were protected with cryptography, either you would face significantly slower response times or Google would face prohibitively expensive costs to upgrade its processing infrastructure.

To see how many network devices, primarily routers (devices that determine the correct route across the Internet for your communications), you use when you access Google, try the Windows tracert command or UNIX traceroute command.

```
c:\tracert www.google.com[67]
```

Tracing route to www.l.google.com [64.233.169.104] over a maximum of 30 hops:

```
 1 <1 ms <1 ms <1 ms 192.X.X.X
 2 8 ms 6 ms 10 ms 10.X.X.X
 3 6 ms 7 ms 7 ms 24.X.X.X
 4 7 ms 7 ms 7 ms 24.X.X.X
 5 8 ms 9 ms 10 ms 24.X.X.X
 6 * * 11 ms 24.X.X.X
 7 10 ms 10 ms 11 ms pop2-new-P4-0.atdn.net [66.X.X.X]
 8 10 ms 9 ms 10 ms bb1-new-P3-0.atdn.net [66.X.X.X]
 9 121 ms 201 ms 203 ms bb1-ash-P14-0.atdn.net [66.X.X.X]
10 15 ms 15 ms 16 ms pop1-ash-S0-0-0.atdn.net [66.X.X.X]
11 17 ms 18 ms 17 ms Google.atdn.net [66.X.X.X]
12 16 ms 18 ms 18 ms 216.X.X.X
13 17 ms 19 ms 17 ms 64.X.X.X
14 20 ms 31 ms 23 ms 72.X.X.X
15 19 ms 19 ms 19 ms yo-in-f104.google.com [64.X.X.X]
```

From this example, you can see that it took 15 hops to get from my computer to www.google.com. You will get different results if you try tracert from your computer, but you should find that it takes between 10 and 20 hops to get to the servers of most online companies. Any of the devices along this path or along each link can be configured to eavesdrop on you, both legally or illegally. Legal eavesdropping is a contentious subject and one worth studying. A good start is by examining the Communications Assistance for Law Enforcement Act (CALEA)[68] and the counterarguments at the Electronic Frontier Foundation[69] and the Electronic Privacy Information Center.[70]

Even if Google used SSL (or some other form of cryptography) for every single transaction, SSL does not provide any protection at the endpoints because both you and Google are the trusted partners in the communication. SSL was designed to protect your communication from being eavesdropped upon, but it does nothing to protect you from each other. So if your computer is infected with malicious software or Google is compromised, or was itself malicious, your personal information is vulnerable.[71] We can see here that there is a distinction between what is visible to a network eavesdropper on the Internet and what is visible to Google .

Not shown in the figure but worthy of note are the Address Resolution Protocol (ARP) and the Domain Name System (DNS). ARP is a common protocol that occurs unbeknownst to most users and broadcasts requests for a host's low-level Media Access Control (MAC) when all that is known is an IP address. ARP requests occur only on localized portions of a network. The next step, DNS, communicates more broadly. DNS is the Internet-wide service that maps domain names, such as www.google.com, that humans prefer dealing with, to IP addresses, such as 64.233.169.104, that the Internet Protocol requires to deliver packets. When local DNS servers do not have a cached copy of a given domain name–to–IP address mapping, they must recursively look up the correct address from a chain of third-party DNS servers. Although this is not necessarily a tremendous information leak, trusting third-party servers represents a significant threat nonetheless. If an attacker compromises the DNS system, users can be silently redirected to other sites that might spoof a legitimate web site or contain malicious content. An excellent example of the power of DNS is the Site Finder controversy caused when VeriSign, the .com and .net top-level domain operator, redirected all traffic to unregistered domains to a Verisign site laden with advertisements. In other words, instead of receiving a traditional error message when a user mistyped a URL, he was instead directed toward VeriSign's site, creating a storm of controversy. VeriSign benefited from an inflated number of page views of its advertisements. This is a perfect example of a company using the power that its vantage point on the network offers it to coerce a "service" onto the Internet that many people didn't want.

Another important risk associated with DNS is its dependence on 13 *root servers*, which answer and redirect domain name requests for the Internet.[72] Because of the risk, DNS root servers are heavily defended, but they must endure near-constant attack.[73] More localized forms of attack are possible. *DNS cache poisoning* is an attack that exploits a flaw in DNS software and allows an attacker to redirect web surfers to domains of his choosing. Nation-states have also been accused of manipulating DNS for their own advantage .[74]

GOOGLE VERSUS AN ISP

The threat of web-based information disclosure doesn't just include Google, or even all online companies; it also includes Internet service providers (ISPs)[75] and *Internet backbone providers,* companies that supply long-haul communications between ISPs.[76] The key difference between Google and these network providers is that network providers transfer information from your computer to destination web sites. Google and other online companies provide the free tools and services at the destination of the connection. Their tools and services provide the *impetus* for disclosing sensitive information. This book provides a service-by-service analysis of the type of information people disclose. Each of these disclosures is vulnerable to eavesdropping by a network provider, unless there is encryption between the browser and the destination web site.[77]

A key difference between network providers and Google is one of vantage point (see Figure 2-3). Google sees a portion of activity from about half of the world's 1 billion Internet users. ISPs can see all unencrypted activity from their relatively smaller number of subscribers. In the United States, the largest ISP has 17.9 million subscribers, and 12 ISPs have 1 million or more subscribers (not tiny, by any means, but an order of magnitude less than Google). Twenty-three ISPs control 75% of the U.S. market.[78] ISPs have one very important piece of information that makes them different from online companies. They assign network addresses to their customers and maintain records between a given IP address and a real-world subscriber's account. More important, ISPs must be able to bill for access, so they know the name, street address (they had to run a cable to each home, after all), and possibly credit card number of each customer. Online companies might pick up this information via online disclosures, but ISPs *require* such information before service is ever provided. Internet backbone providers share most of the risks concerning communications via ISPs, although some notable differences exist. Backbone providers lack detailed billing records of end users, as well as the mappings of IP address to user account that ISPs possess,[79] but they have visibility on users from many different ISPs .

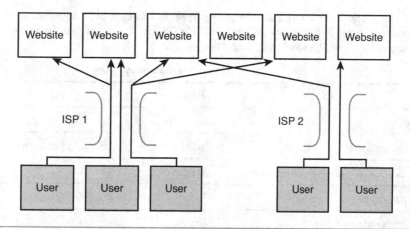

Figure 2-3 Simplified diagram of information flows across the Internet. Unless encrypted, ISPs have full visibility on their subscribers' activities, while Google has access to a fraction of these activities, but from a larger number of users across many ISPs.[80]

Unless a user employs some sort of countermeasure, such as SSL, an ISP has visibility on every web site that its subscribers visit on the web[81] and all its unencrypted communications. This concerning degree of visibility that a given ISP has over its subscribers becomes opaque, however, as its subscribers travel or relocate to a new areas and employ a different ISP. However, Google and other online companies don't suffer from this problem. If a user has a registered account or fails to delete cookies, Google can identify a user after a move to Seattle or when surfing from a hotel in Japan while on holiday. Note that some industry analysts believe Google is seeking to become an ISP because of its unused fiber-optic network, significant participation in the FCC wireless spectrum auction, and pilot wireless programs in San Francisco and Mountain View, California. Google denies these rumors.[82] A combined Google/ISP would combine the risks of both, greatly magnifying the threat.

It is useful to compare the differing motivations and resources of online companies and networking providers (see Table 2-3). Google and its competitors care deeply about the information users provide, to maximize their advertising revenues and improve user experiences. Google's mission is to organize the world's information and make it universally accessible and useful, after all. Google is organized around this mission, including the world-class data-mining expertise and information-processing resources detailed in Chapter 1, "Googling." On the other hand, ISPs and Internet backbone providers are largely concerned, again because of their business model, to provide network access for a fee.

Table 2-3   Comparison of the Information-Gathering Threat by Large Online Companies and ISPs. Both Present a Significant Threat, but the Online Companies That Compel You to Disclose Sensitive Information Have the Greatest Ability and Motivation to Data-Mine It.

	Online Company	ISP
Visibility	Global	Regional
Encryption (SSL)	Ineffective	Effective
Access to online activities	Partial	All unencrypted traffic
Ability to track your web surfing destinations	Variable[83]	Total[84]
Incentive to data-mine	High	Moderate
Ability to uniquely identify users	Variable	High
Analytic capability	High	Low

Another useful comparison between large online companies and networking providers is that of data retention. Complete, long-term logging of online activity by an ISP or other networking provider does not directly support current business models. However, the primary business model of Google and its competitors is based on providing free, high-quality, customized services that are supported by advertising. In this case, data mining and data retention are natural extensions of this model. In fact, one need only browse the advertisements for Google Labs vacancies[85] to note the emphasis. A better understanding of each user supports targeted advertising and, hence, increased advertising effectiveness and revenues. Logging of interactions instead of complete online activity is far more efficient and within reach with current storage and processing technologies.

Currently, networking providers do not have the same motivation and capability to data-mine their customers' online activities as does Google. In the future, this might change.[86] In today's environment, most web users expect that networking providers won't alter their inbound or outbound communications. However, simply providing network communications is becoming increasingly competitive, reducing profit margins of networking providers. Some providers are experimenting with modifying communications that traverse their networks and inserting advertisements.[87] Security researcher Dan Kaminsky calls this activity the Times Square Effect.[88] (When New York City's Times Square is shown in movies, the brilliantly lit advertising signs are often replaced with those of other advertisements.) Because of the potential profitability of this practice, be prepared for future threats to the integrity of online communications.[89, 90] The subject of advertising is too broad to cover here, but Chapter 7, "Advertising and Embedded Content," covers advertising risks in great detail.

Regardless of whether you perceive either a networking provider or an online company as a potential threat (or both), remember that the information that you disclose, intentionally and unintentionally, creates the risk. If you imagine the combination of access of your networking provider and the online companies, you should see that you reveal most all of your online interactions with a third party. The end result is a chilling combination. This information disclosure, and ways you can mitigate it, is the focus of the rest of the book .

SUMMARY

The first chapter outlined the many types of information users disclose when using Google's free online tools and services. This chapter places those disclosures in context by examining the many people and organizations users must trust, whether they want to or not, every time they sit down at their computers. We also examined how information flows intentionally and unintentionally from individual computers and network devices, and analyzed the potential eavesdropping risks posed as information flows across the Internet to the servers of Google.

We face a hierarchy of threats. Although all computers inadvertently disclose information via electromagnetic radiation, it is unlikely that this information is actually being monitored except in very specific circumstances, such as with law enforcement surveillance or industrial espionage. Wireless networking technologies are a more significant problem. Wireless-enabled computers and wireless access points actively broadcast networking information with a range of meters to miles, but although this is important, the phenomenon is still localized to a relatively small geographic area. The most significant information disclosure occurs as web-based interaction traverses network and computing devices under the control of external parties, most likely including an ISP and Internet-backbone provider before eventually ending up on the servers of Google. Ultimately the siren song of the free online services entices us to reveal tremendous amounts about our personal, corporate, and organizational lives.

ENDNOTES

1. Unfortunately, "losing control" of information is a very easy thing to do. As a great example, in September 2007, MediaDefender (www.mediadefender.com/), a company specializing in Internet piracy prevention (or peer-to-peer network poisoning, depending on your viewpoint), lost control of 700MB of embarrassing internal e-mails. The entire collection was distributed on the Internet via BitTorrent—see http://arstechnica.com/news.ars/post/20070916-leaked-media-defender-e-mails-reveal-secret-government-project.html.

2. If you are interested in digging deeper into the field of information theory, a great place to start is Claude Shannon's seminal paper "A Mathematical Theory of Communication," at http://cm.bell-labs.com/cm/ms/what/shannonday/paper.html. I also recommend John Pierce's *An Introduction to Information Theory* (Dover, 1980) for a gentle introduction.

3. For a list of more than 125 chip manufacturers, see www.chipdocs.com/manufacturers/list.html.

4. The Basic Input Output System (BIOS) is the small program that resides on a personal computer's motherboard and helps identify and initialize hardware before passing control to the primary operating system, such as Windows or Linux.

5. Device drivers are typically provided by the hardware manufacturer and allow the operating system to communicate with the device. Most device drivers are relatively small, but there is a trend toward very large installation packages that include, often unneeded, bundled software. Kodak's EasyShare software comes to mind.

6. Errors do occur. A popular Intel Pentium processor was found to contain a floating point flaw, one that affected certain types of calculations and yielded inaccurate results. See http://support.intel.com/support/processors/pentium/sb/CS-013007.htm.

7. The threat of malicious hardware has existed for many years, but there has been a surge in both real-world incidents and awareness in the security community. See http://hsdailywire.com/single.php?id=6065 for one recent example.

8. Samuel King, Joscph Tucek, Anthony Cozzie, Chris Grier, Weihang Jiang, and Yuanyuan Zhou, "Designing and Implementing Malicious Hardware," First Usenix Workshop on Large-Scale Exploits and Emergent Threats (LEET), 2008. Available online at www.usenix.org/event/leet08/tech/full_papers/king/king.pdf.

9. Robert Lemos, "Researchers: Rootkits Headed for BIOS," *Security Focus,* 26 March 2006. www.securityfocus.com/news/11372, last accessed 16 December 2007.

10. "CIH Virus," Gibson Research Corporation, 25 June 2004. www.grc.com/cih.htm, last accessed 16 December 2007.

11. The MBR has long been a target for attack because carefully corrupting the MBR allows malicious code to be executed before the primary operating system is booted. Early viruses commonly attacked the MBR, but very recently researchers have discovered modern MBR rootkit infections. See www.prevx.com/blog/84/MBR-Rootkit-new-tricks-added.html for one example.

12. Anne Saita, "New Trojan, Kernel-Level Rootkit Have 'Frightening Capabilities,'" *SearchSecurity,* 21 March 2006. http://searchsecurity.techtarget.com/originalContent/0,289142,sid14_gci1174522,00.html, last accessed 16 December 2007.

13. "Device Drivers at Risk," *Dark Reading,* 12 July 2006. www.darkreading.com/document.asp?doc_id=98989, last accessed 16 December 2007.

14. There have been numerous instances of legitimate software becoming infected with a virus and being shipped, shrink wrapped, to consumers.

15. David Maynor, "The Compiler As Attack Vector," *Linux Journal,* 5 January 2005. www.linuxjournal.com/article/7839, last accessed 25 December 2007.

16. For two seminal papers on trust in computing, see Ken Thompson's "Reflections on Trusting Trust" and William Arbaugh, David Farber, and Jonathan Smith's "A Secure and Reliable Bootstrap Architecture." These papers are available online at http://cm.bell-labs.com/who/ken/trust.html and http://www.cs.umd.edu/~waa/pubs/oakland97.pdf, respectively.

17. For more on trusted computing, see the resources at the Trusted Computing Group, www.trustedcomputinggroup.org/.

18. Technically, this chalk circle should be a sphere, but you get the idea.

19. Small USB storage devices are available in wristwatches, mock sushi, and even thumbnail-size micro drives. See Johnny Long's "Death of a Thousand Cuts—Finding Evidence Everywhere!" talk from Black Hat Europe, 2006, for an excellent survey of possible storage devices.

20. The recent inclusion of RFID chips in passports has given rise to a cottage industry of RF-shielded wallets and other gear.

21. This isn't true, of course, for modems that are limited to about 56K. Telephone modems are a dying breed, but I'm including them here for completeness.

22. With specialized antennas, attackers can be far more distant, on the order of miles. The wireless world record is at least 125 miles, http://compnetworking.about.com/b/2005/08/18/world-record-for-wi-fi-wireless-distance.htm.

23. Erratasec makes available a free tool called Ferret, by Robert Graham and David Maynor, which sniffs wireless networks and gathers information leakage (www.erratasec.com/ferret.html).

24. Fiber-optic cable can still be tapped. See M. E. Kabay's "Tapping Fiber Optics Gets Easier," www.networkworld.com/newsletters/sec/2003/0303sec1.html.

25. Mike Elgan, "Opinion: The Stalker in Your Pocket," *ComputerWorld,* 20 July 2007. www.computerworld.com/action/article.do?command=viewArticleBasic&articleId=9027438&pageNumber=1, last accessed 27 December 2007.

26. For one analysis, see http://lauren.vortex.com/archive/000202.html.

27. "Radar Detector Detector (RDD)." http://radar.757.org/VG2.htm, last accessed 27 December 2007.

28. In addition, researchers are experimenting with using light to communicate inside computers.

29. NSTISSAM TEMPEST/2-95, "Red/Black Installation Guidance," 12 December 1995. http://web.archive.org/web/20070408221244/cryptome.org/tempest-2-95.htm, last accessed 27 December 2007.

30. "Tempest Certification Program," National Security Agency. www.nsa.gov/ia/industry/tempest.cfm, last accessed 27 December 2007.

31. You can download Wim van Eck's seminal paper "Electromagnetic Radiation from Video Display Units: An Eavesdropping Risk?" at http://citeseer.ist.psu.edu/311647.html.

32. Markus Kuhn, "Electromagnetic Eavesdropping Risks of Flat-Panel Displays," Workshop on Privacy Enhancing Technologies, May 2004. Available online at www.cl.cam.ac.uk/~mgk25/pet2004-fpd.pdf, last accessed 28 December 2007.

33. "Dutch Voting Computers Decertified," *Wij vertrouwen stemcomputers niet,* 7 November 2007. www.wijvertrouwenstemcomputersniet.nl/Wij_vertrouwen_ stemcomputers_niet, last accessed 28 December 2007.

34. A video of the voting computer attack is available at www.youtube.com/ watch?v=B05wPomCjEY.

35. Michael McCarthy, "The Pentagon Worries That Spies Can See Its Computer Screens," *Wall Street Journal,* 7 August 2000, p. A1. See also http://technews.acm.org/ articles/2000-2/0807m.html#item1.

36. The probable intercept range is about 50 feet, but it could be as far as a mile with specialized intercept gear and a low noise environment. See www.schneier.com/ blog/archives/2007/12/microsofts_wire.html.

37. John Leyden, "Microsoft Wireless Keyboards Crypto Cracked," *The Register,* 3 December 2007. www.theregister.co.uk/2007/12/03/wireless_keyboard_ crypto_cracked/, last accessed 28 December 2007.

38. Bruce Schneier, "Eavesdropping on Bluetooth Automobiles," Schneier on Security, 2 August 2005. www.schneier.com/blog/archives/2005/08/eavesdropping_o.html, last accessed 28 December 2007.

39. A video of such an attack is available at www.remote-exploit.org/max/ automated.html.

40. Mike Elgan, "We the People Demand a Gadget Bill of Lights," *Computerworld,* 11 May 2007. www.computerworld.com/action/article.do?command= viewArticleBasic&articleId=9019163&source=rss_news10, last accessed 27 December 2007.

41. Robert Lemos, "Researchers: Blinking LEDs Leak Info," CNET News, 7 March 2002. www.news.com/2100-1001-854946.html, last accessed 27 December 2007.

42. Michael Kaplan, "Three Blind Phreaks," *Wired* 12.02, February 2004. www.wired.com/wired/archive/12.02/phreaks.html.

43. Note that all speakers can act as, albeit inefficient, microphones. See http://www.zyra.org.uk/sp-mic.htm.

44. For a list of different bug types, see www.brickhousesecurity.com/about-telephone- wiretaps-cellphone-recording-bugs.html.

45. Mark Odell, "Use of Mobile Helped Police Keep Tabs on Suspect and Brother," *Financial Times.* www.ft.com/cms/s/4239e29e-02f2-11da-84e5-00000e2511c8.html.

46. Charlotte Edwardes, "CIA Recruited Cat to Bug Russians." www.telegraph.co.uk/ news/main.jhtml?xml=/news/2001/11/04/wcia04.xml

47. Squirrels have also been charged with espionage—see www.washingtonpost.com/wp-dyn/content/article/2007/07/19/AR2007071902453_3.html.

48. Kevin Murray, "Laser Beam Eavesdropping—Sci-Fi Bugs," Murray Associates. www.spybusters.com/Laser_Beam_Eavesdropping.html, last accessed 27 December 2007.

49. Niall McKay, "'Whispering Keyboards' Could Be the Next Attack Trend," *SearchSecurity News*, 11 May 2004. http://searchsecurity.techtarget.com/originalContent/0,289142,sid14_gci963348,00.html, last accessed 27 December 2007.

50. "Snooping On Text by Listening to the Keyboard," Schneier on Security, 13 September 2005. www.schneier.com/blog/archives/2005/09/snooping_on_tex.html, last accessed 27 December 2007.

51. Adi Shamir and Eran Tromer, "Acoustic Cryptanalysis: On Nosy People and Noisy Machines," Preliminary Proof of Concept Presentation. www.wisdom.weizmann.ac.il/~tromer/acoustic/, last accessed 27 December 2007.

52. Matt Lake, "What Is Power-Line Networking?" *CNET Reviews*, 13 November 2002. http://reviews.cnet.com/4520-3243_7-5021351-2.html?tag=arrow.

53. Jeff Tyson, "How Power-Line Networking Works," Howstuffworks. http://computer.howstuffworks.com/power-network2.htm, last accessed 28 December 2007.

54. Paul Kocher, Joshua Jaffe, and Benjamin Jun, "Differential Power Analysis," *Lecture Notes in Computer Science* 1666 (1999): 388–397. Available online at www.cryptography.com/resources/whitepapers/DPA.pdf, last accessed 28 December 2007.

55. At the risk of sounding exceptionally paranoid, you should also consider information flows directly into and out of the human mind. Although not considered feasible with today's science, at some point, the electrochemical emanations (or some other mechanism yet to be discovered) of your mind might be able to be read and understood.

56. Jason Tuohey, "Government Uses Color Laser Printer Technology to Track Documents," *PC World*, 22 November 2004. www.pcworld.com/article/id,118664-page,1/article.html, last accessed 28 December 2007.

57. Donna Wentworth, "Is Your Printer Spying on You?" Electronic Frontier Foundation, 24 July 2005. www.eff.org/deeplinks/2005/07/your-printer-spying-you, last accessed 28 December 2007.

58. With a little practice, it takes only about 60 seconds to remove an internal hard drive from a server.

59. Will Dormann, "The Dangers of Windows AutoRun," Vulnerability Analysis Blog, Computer Emergency Response Team, 24 April 2008. www.cert.org/blogs/vuls/2008/04/the_dangers_of_windows_autorun.html, last accessed 6 June 2008.

60. "Furby a Threat to National Security?" CNN.com, 13 January 1999. www.cnn.com/US/9901/13/nsa.furby.ban.01/, last accessed 28 December 2007.

61. Robert Lemos, "Malware Hitches a Ride on Digital Devices," *SecurityFocus,* 9 January 2008. www.securityfocus.com/news/11499, last accessed 6 June 2008.

62. The security community commonly calls these three facets: confidentiality, integrity, and availability.

63. The online company could rely on a third-party web hosting service or ISP as well, but I assume here that this is not the case.

64. Completely unbreakable encryption is nearly impossible in practice. Most cryptanalysts consider encryption techniques to provide protection only for a given period of time, but they will eventually be rendered obsolete as computer processing power increases.

65. Whitfield Diffie, "Information Security: 50 Years Behind, 50 Years Ahead," *Communications of the ACM* 51, no. 1 (January 2008): 55–57.

66. Robert Vamosi, "Researcher: Web 2.0 Vulnerable to Cookie Theft," CNET News.com, 2 August 2007. www.news.com/8301-10784_3-9754204-7.html, last accessed 30 December 2007.

67. To anonymize the results, I've replaced some of the address values.

68. "Communications Assistance for Law Enforcement Act (CALEA)," Federal Communications Commission. www.fcc.gov/calea/, last accessed 1 September 2007.

69. "Communications Assistance for Law Enforcement Act (CALEA): The Perils of Wiretapping the Internet," Electronic Frontier Foundation. www.eff.org/Privacy/Surveillance/CALEA/, last accessed 1 September 2007.

70. "Wiretapping," Electronic Privacy Information Center. www.epic.org/privacy/wiretap/, last accessed 1 September 2007.

71. Google could employ encryption on its local file system, but keys would still need to exist and are thus still subject to compromise.

72. Root Server Technical Operations Association, 2 December 2007. www.root servers.org/, last accessed 30 December 2007.

73. "DNS Attack Factsheet 1.1," Internet Corporation for Assigned Names and Numbers, 8 March 2007. www.icann.org/announcements/announcement-08mar07.htm, last accessed 30 December 2007.

74. "China in the Habit of Copying and Redirecting U.S. Sites," Slashdot.org, 18 November 2007. http://slashdot.org/articles/07/11/18/1824230.shtml, last accessed 30 December 2007.

75. Other organizations, such as universities, large companies, and governments, also provide ISP-like connectivity. They fall into the same category of ISPs for this analysis.

76. Here I'm deliberately assuming that your computer's operating system isn't compromised. If Microsoft was collecting information surreptitiously in some way, I believe it would be detected. Detecting eavesdropping on the Internet is very difficult to detect.

77. Tor is another mechanism for encrypting Internet connections; it is discussed in Chapter 9, "Countermeasures."

78. Alex Goldman, "Top 23 U.S. ISPs by Subscriber: Q3 2007," *ISP-Planet*, 13 December 2007. www.isp-planet.com/research/rankings/usa.html, last accessed 31 December 2007.

79. This is true unless the backbone provider also provides ISP-like service to an end customer.

80. Note this simplified diagram only shows the user's ISP. After exiting each ISP, the user's traffic will transit numerous links across Internet backbone providers and the ISPs of the destination websites.

81. SSL protects the contents of network communications but doesn't protect IP header information, such as IP addresses. Similarly, SSL does not protect DNS lookups.

82. Eli Milchman, "Google Denies ISP Rumors," *Wired,* 30 June 2006. www.wired.com/techbiz/it/news/2006/06/71293, last accessed 31 December 2007.

83. Online companies with advertising networks or web traffic analytics services have visibility on a user's websurfing destinations, even if the company doesn't control the destination server directly, see Chapter 7.

84. One exception to an ISP's "Total" access is when the user employs a countermeasure such as an anonymization proxy. Chapter 9 will cover such techniques in greater detail.

85. See http://labs.google.com/ for more information.

86. In the UK, this is already changing, with the Phorm advertising system (http://www.phorm.com/), in which the ISP tracks the user's browsing habits to target advertisements. British Telecom (BT) has come under criticism for testing this system on users without their consent, see http://www.theregister.co.uk/2008/03/17/bt_phorm_lies/.

87. "Rogers accused of hijacking other web pages." CBC News, 11 December 2007. http://www.cbc.ca/technology/story/2007/12/11/tech-rogers.html, last accessed 31 December 2007.

88. Dan Kaminsky. "Black Ops 2007: Design Reviewing the Web." BlackHat USA, 2007.

89. "Will ISP Web Content Filtering Continue to Grow." Slashdot.org, 10 December 2007. http://yro.slashdot.org/yro/07/12/10/1812245.shtml, last accessed 31 December 2007.

90. Nate Anderson. "MPAA head: Content filtering is in ISPs' best interests." Ars Technica, 5 December 2007. http://arstechnica.com/news.ars/post/20071205-mpaa-head-content-filtering-in-isps-best-interests.html, last accessed 31 December 2007.

Footprints, Fingerprints, and Connections

Whether simply browsing the web or using the most complex of online tools, users leave behind a distinct trail in the logs of each server they interact with. Sometimes these logs are discarded, but in the case of large online companies, logs are aggregated, mined, and used to create user profiles to help target advertising. These are core points of this book, but what exactly do these logs contain, how is the data captured, and how can users be uniquely identified? This chapter answers these questions by covering how logs are created when using web-based applications and the primary pieces of information they can contain, including information provided by network protocols, software applications (such as web browsers), and users. It also addresses profiling and fingerprinting users. The more information users disclose, the more likely the online company will be able to uniquely identify them on subsequent visits, profile their activities, determine their real-world identity, and tie differing activities to other individuals and groups. The first step in this analysis is to examine how web browsers request and receive web pages, images, and other media from web servers.

BASIC WEB INTERACTION AND DATA RETENTION

Central to the problem of web-based information disclosure is the interaction of web browsers and web servers. At the web's most basic level, web surfers request web pages and other objects by typing in a *uniform resource locator (URL)* into the address bar of their browser or clicking on a link contained within a web page. A URL is a global address to any publicly available document or other object on the web. The URL is a simple but elegant concept, in that it allows web pages and web-based applications to easily request any object on the web. For example, the URL for the Google logo is http://www.google.com/intl/en_ALL/images/logo.gif. Web browsers and web servers communicate using the lingua franca of the web, the HyperText Transfer Protocol (HTTP). (Note the "http" in the preceding URL.) HTTP defines the rules for requesting and receiving web content. Figure 3-1 shows a basic interaction, in which a web browser uses an HTTP Get command to request a given URL. If all goes well, the web server responds by sending the desired content to the web browser, most likely a web page in Hypertext Markup Language (HTML). The web server commonly keeps a log of all URL requests. In the case of a single HTML document, a web server generates a single log entry.[1]

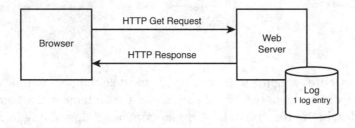

Figure 3-1   A simple browser request for a web page generates a single log entry.

Real web pages almost always contain more content than a single HTML document, usually in the form of embedded images and other media. After loading an initial page,[2] the web browser examines the HTML for these URLs and downloads the additional objects without any user interaction. Figure 3-2 shows this more realistic scenario, a web page containing images. The browser downloads the original HTML page and then downloads two images. The end result is three HTML Get requests, one for the HTML page and one for each of the images. In this case, the destination web server makes three log entries. Normally, the web server is the same for each of these files, but this doesn't have to be the case. A web page could include media from any number of third-party sites (see Figure 3-3). Online advertisers exploit this behavior by placing advertisements on web pages across the web that all point to the advertiser's server. The main HTML pages are downloaded from the sites a user requests to visit, but the user's browser also downloads the advertisements from a large advertiser's servers, enabling the advertiser to track the user's activity across large portions of the web. Chapter 7, "Advertising and Embedded Content," discusses the risks associated with downloading third-party content in more detail.

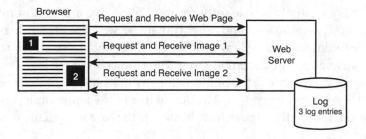

Figure 3-2 A more realistic web page includes embedded media, resulting in multiple log entries.

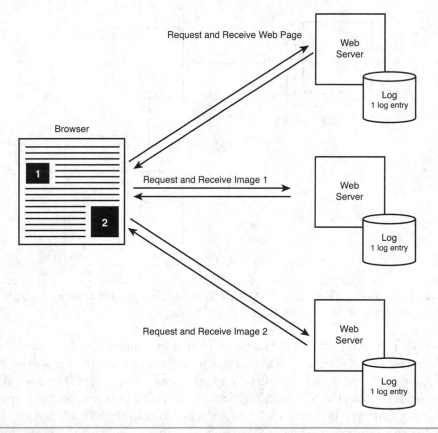

Figure 3-3 Media embedded in a web page can come from any web server across the Internet, leaving log entries on multiple servers.

A web server is a relatively simple software application; it contains a number of documents, such as web pages, images, and other content, as well as a private log on a computer accessible to the Internet.[3] Many visitors can come and make HTTP requests for the publicly available content documents, but who has access to the log? Two basic scenarios exist. In the first scenario, the online company manages the web server directly and controls the logs (see Figure 3-4). The dotted line in the figure indicates the boundary of privileged access to the logs. Private hosting is the case with many medium and large companies.

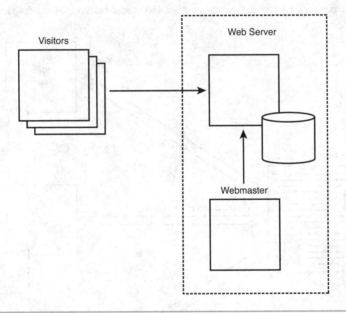

Figure 3-4   In many cases, a webmaster has physical control of a machine and does not share privileged access to the server's contents, including its logs.

In the other scenario, smaller companies will often pay for hosting by a third-party web hosting service (see Figure 3-5).[4] Securely managing an e-commerce web server is a tricky proposition, and because smaller companies (and many large companies as well) have limited resources, they often find it more cost effective to outsource the responsibility of hosting their web presence. Unfortunately, bringing in the web site hosting company makes the log accessible by both the original online company and the employees of the hosting service, creating another potential disclosure vector. To make matters worse, the lowest-cost hosting option usually is shared hosting, in which many web sites are hosted on the same physical server. Although webmasters from these other sites don't have direct access to the other logs, they do have privileged access to the shared server and are in a better position than an outside attacker to attempt to gain unauthorized access to the other hosted sites' logs. The end result is an increasingly larger group of people who must be trusted not to attack or misuse sensitive log data.

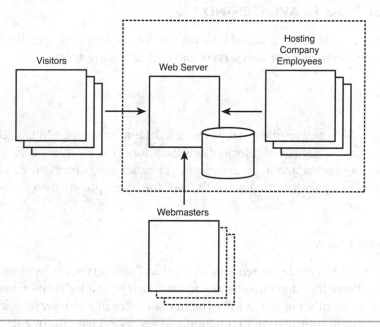

Figure 3-5   When a third party hosts the web server, many additional people must be trusted not to violate the security and privacy safeguards of the server.

The Domain Name System is another component to consider when examining information-disclosure vectors associated with even the most basic web surfing. The Internet Protocol requires IP addresses to communicate with a distant server. So when a user types a URL such as www.google.com into the browser's address bar, the operating system must determine the correct IP address to use. It does so using DNS. In this example, at least two packets contain DNS traffic. The first, from the end user, contains a DNS query requesting the IP address of www.google.com and is sent to the local name server. The second packet is the response from the local name server that contains the IP address to use for communications to www.google.com[5]—in this case, 64.233.169.99. After the requesting computer receives the DNS response, it uses this IP address for a period of time (often 24 hours) and makes a new request at that time.[6] The key idea here is that DNS activity generates another trail of records indicating web surfing destinations, outside the direct web surfer and online company communication channel.[7] However, it is important to note that DNS requests include only host names, not URLs.

THE TRAIL YOU LEAVE BEHIND

Now that we've reviewed the basics of how the web works, let's look specifically at the tracks left behind in the logs of web servers and end-user computers.

NOTE

Even the simple act of setting a web browser's default home page to Google, or any other web site, is a nontrivial information-disclosure risk. By doing so, every time the browser is run, the action automatically generates a log entry on the server of the default home page, creating a heartbeat of the user's presence on the web.

WEB SERVER LOGS

So far, this chapter has made reference to an abstract "web server log" without dealing with specifics. These logs don't involve any magic. Each time a web browser accesses a web page, image, or other object, it leaves behind an entry in a web server log.[8] The web server knows certain information to function and saves key elements in a text log or, potentially, a more robust database. The following is an example of a log entry from my www.rumint.org site.

```
86.X.X.X - - [02/Dec/2007:04:49:28 -0700] "GET / HTTP/1.1"
200 15384 "http://www.google.co.uk/search?hl=en&q=RUMINT
&meta=" "Mozilla/4.0 (compatible; MSIE 6.0; Windows NT 5.1;
SV1; .NET CLR 2.0.50727)"
```

In this example, a web surfer searched Google for the keyword "RUMINT" and clicked one of the search results, which brought him to my web site. This interaction provided each of the elements in the log entry: The network address was required to communicate across the Internet, and my server recorded the local date and time, as well as the visitor's HTTP GET request. His browser passed along the referring URL and details such as the web browser version and his computer's operating system. Table 3-1 breaks down each of these elements from the log.

Table 3-1   Breakdown of a Typical Web Server Log Entry

86.X.X.X	IP address of the device making the request. (I've anonymized the address here.)
02/Dec/2007:04:49:28 -0700	The date and time of the request.
GET / HTTP/1.1" 200 15384	The HTTP request. Here the user requested the root directory (/) of www.rumint.org. The default page, index.html, of size 15,384 bytes, was successfully returned, as indicated by an HTTP status code of 200.[9]
http://www.google.co.uk/ search?hl=en&q= RUMINT&meta=	The referring URL, the link the user clicked to go to my site. Here the user searched Google for "RUMINT." Note that Google has classified the visitor as an English (hl=en) speaker.
Mozilla/4.0 (compatible; MSIE 6.0; Windows NT 5.1; SV1; .NET CLR 2.0.50727)	Environment values passed by the web browser. In this case, the visitor claimed to use Microsoft Internet Explorer 6.0, with Security Version 1 (e.g., it is running on a system with at least Windows XP Service Pack 2). The string also reveals the client operating system version and the fact that .NET is installed.

This is just a simple example, but note that even the download of a single web page generates a significant amount of information. Now imagine the thousands to millions of such log entries people have created since they began using the web, and you'll start to get the picture of the trail each user leaves behind. The following sections describe the details and implications of each of the major elements found in web server logs.

IP ADDRESSES

IP addresses were designed to uniquely identify computers on the Internet and are used to address packets that all Internet computers send and receive as they communicate. Packets are the fundamental unit of communication on the Internet and are somewhat similar to letters in the traditional postal system. Each packet contains addressing (think sender and destination mailing addresses) and control information to help ensure that the packet will successfully reach its destination, as well as a packet payload, which contains the content of the communication itself (think the body of the letter). As web users employ an online service, their web browsers and the destination web servers send and receive many packets. Each one of the packets emanating from the user's browser leaks two IP addresses, the address of the user and the address of the destination.

Today most of the Internet uses IP Version 4, which allocates 32 bits for the source IP address and 32 bits for the destination IP address. This means there are 2^{32} (4,294,967,296) theoretical IP addresses available on the Internet. Initially, 4.3 billion seemed more than enough addresses to cover all potential computers hooked to the

Internet. However, the explosion in personal and mobile computers quickly caused a shortage, which forced people to find ways to share or otherwise conserve IP addresses. This sharing helps provide a degree of anonymity by breaking the direct link between a given computer and its IP address. Common forms of sharing include Network Address Translation (NAT) and dynamic allocation of IP addresses using a technique called the Dynamic Host Configuration Protocol (DHCP). NAT devices translate the IP addresses found on an internal network to a single IP address, or a small number of IP addresses, on the public Internet. The key idea is that hundreds, thousands, or even more computers could reside on the internal network, all sharing a single IP address on the Internet itself. The NAT device keeps track of inbound and outbound connections and converts IP addresses on the fly from the internal network to the Internet, and vice versa. The end result is a significant reduction in the total number of unique IP addresses directly connected to the Internet. DHCP also allows IP addresses to be shared, but in a slightly different manner. Using DHCP, computers are allocated an IP address when they request one. When the address is no longer in use, the DHCP server can allocate the address to a different computer. By sharing a pool of addresses, ISPs can maximize their finite number of public IP addresses. Because of the constantly changing nature of IP address assignments, DHCP also helps add a degree of uncertainty (from the perspective of the online company) between a given computer and its public IP address—the larger the pool of possible addresses and the shorter the duration of assignment, the better.

Whereas IPv4 may be running short of IP addresses, IPv6 is designed to overcome this limitation. Instead of 32 bits, IPv6 allocates 128 each for the source address and destination address, for a total of 2^{128} (3.4×10^{28}) possible addresses. However, IPv6 has been looming for many years but has yet to be widely adopted because of the potential cost and risks of the transition. In today's environment, most corporate networks employ both NAT and DHCP. Home ISP users typically receive their IP address via DHCP and might use NAT as well, if they employ a cable/DSL router, such as those made by Linksys. See Table 3-2 for a comparison of the IP addressing techniques.

Table 3-2   Common IP Address Allocation Techniques

Static IP	Fixed IP address directly entered into operating system; rarely used by home ISP users; frequently used by government, industry, and academic networks.
Dynamic IP	Allocated by a DHCP server; duration of assignment can vary from hours to months, depending on configuration.
Network Address Translation	NAT devices allow many computers on a private network to share a single public Internet IP address.

You might think that an IP address provides some degree of anonymity, and it does, but each IP address can ultimately be tied to an individual computer and, hence, the end user if the networking provider keeps records. Typically, tying an IP address back to an end user requires at least two steps. First, the IP address must be tracked back to the organization that is authorized to use it. Blocks of IP addresses are allocated to ISPs and larger companies, so legitimate IP addresses all belong in one of these group allocations. In most cases, IP address allocations are publicly available.[10] For example, if 172.128.32.16 appears in a server log[11], a visit to the ARIN WHOIS Database (http://ws.arin.net/whois/) reveals that the IP address belongs to AOL.

```
OrgName:    America Online
OrgID:      AOL
Address:    22000 AOL Way
City:       Dulles
StateProv:  VA
PostalCode: 20166
Country:    US

NetRange:   172.128.0.0 - 172.191.255.255
CIDR:       172.128.0.0/10
NetName:    AOL-172BLK
NetHandle:  NET-172-128-0-0-1
Parent:     NET-172-0-0-0-0
NetType:    Direct Allocation
NameServer: DAHA-01.NS.AOL.COM
NameServer: DAHA-02.NS.AOL.COM
NameServer: DAHA-07.NS.AOL.COM
Comment:    ADDRESSES WITHIN THIS BLOCK ARE NON-PORTABLE
RegDate:    2000-03-24
Updated:    2003-08-08

RTechHandle: AOL-NOC-ARIN
RTechName:   America Online, Inc.
RTechPhone:  +1-703-265-4670
RTechEmail:  domains@aol.net

OrgAbuseHandle: AOL382-ARIN
OrgAbuseName:   Abuse
OrgAbusePhone:  +1-703-265-4670
OrgAbuseEmail:  abuse@aol.net

OrgNOCHandle: AOL236-ARIN
OrgNOCName:   NOC
```

```
OrgNOCPhone:  +1-703-265-4670
OrgNOCEmail:  noc@aol.net

OrgTechHandle: AOL-NOC-ARIN
OrgTechName:   America Online, Inc.
OrgTechPhone:  +1-703-265-4670
OrgTechEmail:  domains@aol.net

# ARIN WHOIS database, last updated 2008-01-15 19:07
# Enter ? for additional hints on searching ARIN's WHOIS database.
```

The ISP or company authorized a given block then allocates IP addresses to individual machines, as AOL did in this example. However, AOL and other ISPs don't publicly reveal which user accounts are assigned which IP addresses under normal circumstances; still, it is a safe bet that they maintain detailed records. As with any records maintained by online companies, these records can be subpoenaed, shared, stolen, or lost.

IP address information can also be used to help determine a user's physical location. In most cases, ISPs can pinpoint the exact location of their wired subscribers and locate wireless subscribers with a lesser degree of accuracy. However, geolocation information is also publicly available, with reduced accuracy. A number of companies, such as MaxMind,[12] have developed IP geolocation databases that can pinpoint a user's geographic region with reasonable accuracy. Some estimate that country-level geolocation from publicly available databases is 95% accurate; city-level geolocation is between 50% and 80% accurate. As an example, Table 3-3 shows city-level geolocation for the top 10 visitors to my www.rumint.org site.

Table 3-3 Example of City-Level IP Geolocation

Location	Visitors	Percentage
Sunnyvale, California, United States	2,918	18.59
Unknown	2,209	14.08
New York, New York, United States	1,140	7.26
Beijing, Beijing, China	592	3.77
Mountain View, California, United States	512	3.26
Oslo, Oslo, Norway	482	3.07
Taipei, T'ai-Pei, Taiwan	324	2.06
Paris, Ile-De-France, France	277	1.77

Location	Visitors	Percentage
San Jose, California, United States	249	1.59
San Diego, California, United States	220	1.40

Third parties have sought to increase this accuracy by collaborating with web sites on which users enter a physical location or postal code.[13] Table 3-4 shows zip code based geolocation for the top ten visitors to the same web site.

Table 3-4 Example of Zip Code-Based IP Geolocation

Location	Visitors	Percentage
Unknown	8,061	47.77
94089, Sunnyvale, California, United States	2,903	17.20
10001, New York, New York, United States	1,082	6.41
94035, Mountain View, California, United States	481	2.85
10996, West Point, New York, United States	210	1.24
95101, San Jose, California, United States	209	1.24
92101, San Diego, California, United States	189	1.12
98052, Redmond, Washington, United States	177	1.05
12008, Schenectady, New York, United States	145	0.86
75207, Dallas, Texas, United States	86	0.51

In short, although IP addresses appear to be a shield to hide behind, they offer little privacy protection. If the owner of a given block of IP addresses turns over logs containing which user account was issued a given IP address at a time of interest, protection is lost. In addition, consider that Google, which receives millions of unique visitors each month, could build a massive activities database associated with each address.

NOTE

Network communications disclose a web surfer's IP address and can reveal the specific operating system in use.[14, 15]

BROWSER HEADER FIELDS

Web browsers must communicate with web servers to request and receive the web contents their users desire. To perform these tasks, the web browser complies with the HTTP standard. Although IP addresses are required to communicate across the Internet and are in the headers of packets, these HTTP communications are contained in the payload of packets. Each browser behaves slightly differently, but the following tables illustrate the behind-the-scenes communications occurring from browser to server (see Table 3-5) and the response from server to browser (see Table 3-6).

Table 3-5   Headers Sent from a Firefox Browser to the Google Web Server

GET / HTTP/1.1	The HTTP request.
Host: www.google.com	The host where the request is being made.
User-Agent: Mozilla/5.0 (Windows; U; Windows NT 5.1; en-US; rv:1.8.1.11) Gecko/ 20071127 Firefox/2.0.0.11	Information about the application and operating system making the request.
Accept:text/xml,application/xml,application/ xhtml+xml,text/html;q=0.9,text/plain;q=0.8, image/png,*/*;q=0.5	Media types the browser will accept in response.
Accept-Language: en-us,en;q=0.5	Preferred language of the requested content.
Accept-Encoding: gzip,deflate	Encoding formats the browser will accept.
Accept-Charset: ISO-8859-1,utf-8; q=0.7,*;q=0.7	Character sets the browser will accept.
Keep-Alive: 300	The number of requests that the browser supports. Here, it is 300 requests per connection.
Connection: keep-alive	A request to allow the client to make multiple requests over a given connection, to increase performance.
Cookie:PREF=ID=0a0661ceb826a27d:TM= 1199309328:LM=1199309328:S= ZoVTNgAwhwr1s3IY	Sending name/value pairs contained in a cookie Google issued during an earlier visit.

Table 3-6 Response from the Google Web Server to the Firefox Browser

HTTP/1.1 200 OK	The status code for the request. In this case, the code is 200, indicating success.
Cache-Control: private	The response is for a single user and shouldn't be placed in a shared cache.
Content-Type: text/html; charset=UTF-8	The media type of the response.
Content-Encoding: gzip	The type of encoding used on the object sent in response.
Server: gws	Information about the destination web server. In this case, gws probably stands for Google Web Server.
Content-Length: 2333	Size of the object sent in response to the request.
Date: Wed, 02 Jan 2008 21:35:03 GMT	Time of the response.

Browsers disclose a great deal of information as they visit web sites, some of which is necessary, such as the specific HTTP request, but much of which isn't necessary for most web transactions. Table 3-5 illustrated the type of information that a browser discloses with each transaction using Firefox. Browsers will reveal even more information if requested—or, in some cases, by default. The BrowserSpy web site (http://gemal.dk/browserspy/), shown in Figure 3-6, is designed to probe browsers and display the information it retrieves. Results vary by browser but can include operating system, browser version, CPU, screen size, plug-ins, presence of a sound card, local date and time, Google Toolbar version, Visual Basic Scripting version, preferred language, media player versions, cookies, and referrer values, among many others. The preceding section demonstrated that IP addresses are required for web browsing and can be used as a way to track user disclosures; it is trivial to gather information from browsers and add it to the record associated with each IP, creating a much more comprehensive picture of web site visitors. To get a feel for the magnitude of browser-based disclosure, try visiting BrowserSpy with a variety of web browsers. The following sections explore two particularly significant forms of browser disclosure, cookies and referer[16] values.

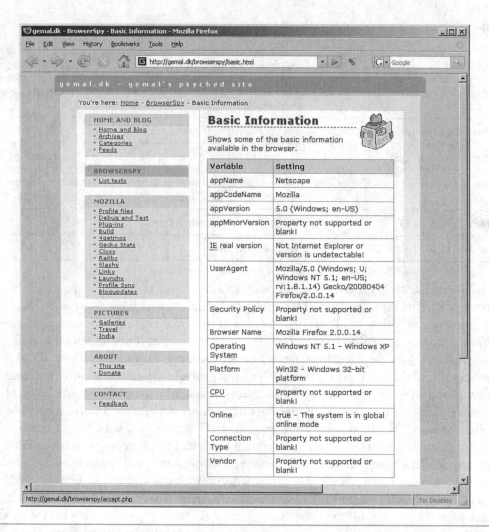

Figure 3-6   The BrowserSpy web site. This site demonstrates how much information a browser reveals, including operating system, preferred language, screen size, local date and time, and whether the browser accepts cookies.

COOKIES

Cookies are like the tracking darts scientists shoot into wild animals on nature documentaries. Web servers use cookies to mark web browsers with identifying information. This process isn't necessarily as sinister as it sounds. The primary protocol of the web,

HTTP was designed to be stateless. That is, the web server treats each command independently, without keeping track of information about previous interactions. By being stateless, web servers can operate much more efficiently because they do not need to maintain potentially huge histories of other transactions. This approach works in many instances, but it becomes problematic when a web server needs to remember something about a given user or session. For example, users can personalize their Google home page. The web server needs to recognize when this person returns, to format the web page correctly. Similarly, when users log into an account to fill a shopping cart or use a service, they do not want to reenter their password multiple times as they move about the site. By providing web browsers with unique cookies, the web server can then identify users and provide the appropriate service to each user without these hassles.

Two main types of cookies exist, persistent cookies and session cookies. Persistent cookies can exist for many years in a user's browser cache, repeatedly identifying the user to the issuing web site across many visits. Session cookies exist only for the duration of a single online visit. Cookies are issued either by the web server of the site a browser is visiting (first-party cookies) or by a third party when a given page includes embedded content, such as an advertisement or video, provided by a third-party server.

Cookies are helpful for providing a seamless browsing experience. Usability aside, however, persistent cookies are specifically designed to uniquely identify users on return visits to web sites, often over the course of years. In terms of anonymity, this is bad. Advertisers have found innovative ways to exploit cookies to track users as they visit web sites that contain their ads or other content. The larger the advertising network, the greater the risk.

Cookies are small pieces of data that are passed to and stored by the browser by a given web site. When needed, such as on a repeat visit, the cookie is passed back to the web server to uniquely identify the user. Figure 3-7 shows an example of a cookie being passed to a Google server. Although it is possible to set a web browser to block cookies, doing so breaks many online applications. For example, Google's basic web search works while blocking cookies, but Gmail does not.

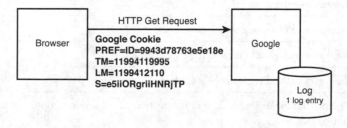

Figure 3-7 A Google cookie being passed to a Google server. It contains a number of name/value pairs that uniquely identify the visitor.

Modern browsers enable you to block cookies, but many popular sites will not function without them. Figure 3-8 is an example of a Google cookie, shown using the cookie-management option in the Firefox web browser.

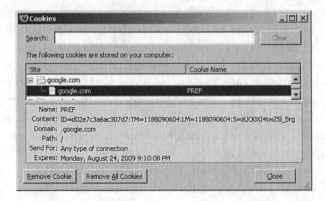

Figure 3-8   An example cookie issued by Google. Cookies are simple pieces of data that a web server passes to a web browser. Although you can set your browser to not accept cookies, most major online services will stop working if you do so.

The generic structure of cookies is useful to understand. Each cookie can contain a number of subelements.[17] The Google cookie in Figure 3-8 illustrates several of the most important (see Table 3-7).

The Content field mentioned in Table 3-7 is particularly interesting. Google cookies contain four name/value pairs: ID, TM, LM, and S. Google hasn't published details about these values, but Table 3-8 contains their likely function.[18]

Table 3-7   Main Elements of a Typical Google Cookie

Subelement	Description
Name	The name of the cookie
Content	A series of values, along with an identifier
Domain	The domain allowed to request the cookie
Path	The server path where the cookie applies
Send For	Whether the cookie should be sent on any type of connection or only on encrypted connections
Expires	The expiration date of the cookie

Table 3-8 Name/Value Pairs of a Typical Google Cookie

Name	Probable Function	Example	Notes
ID	Unique identification field	9943d78763e5e18e	Changes with each new cookie issued.
TM	Time of original cookie issuance	1199411995	Time is in UNIX time since epoch format. This value equates to 3 January 2008 at 8:59 PM.[19]
LM	Time of last preference change	1199412110	Changes when the user sets or changes preference settings. This value equates to 3 January 2008 at 9:01 PM.
S	Possibly a checksum	S=e5iiORgriiHNRjTP	Changes when other values change.

Note that cookies can be sent only to the domain that issued them.[20] That is, if you visit www.google.com and then visit www.microsoft.com, the Microsoft site cannot view any cookies that Google issued. This is an important protection because it prevents other web sites that you visit from illicitly requesting sensitive information (such as a cookie that verifies that you are logged into your web mail account). However, an important loophole exists. If you visit a web site that includes third-party content, such as advertisements, the advertiser's domain can issue you a cookie because, technically, your browser visited its domain.

Although cookies are unique in most cases, they don't necessary uniquely identify an individual. Each browser on a given computer, such as Firefox, Internet Explorer, or Opera, maintains a separate set of cookies. In addition, most operating systems maintain a separate profile for each user of the browser, each with its own distinct set of cookies. That being said, cookies uniquely identify a browser/user account combination that a given individual likely uses frequently. Because cookies are tied to a browser and user account but not an IP address, the protections NAT and DHCP provide have little value. In fact, the same cookie used from different IP addresses would allow an online company to map the networks of different domains that the user frequents, perhaps including home, workplace, school, and travel destinations. Alternatively, differing cookies from the same IP address would allow an online company to map the population inside a NAT-protected network.

Cookies themselves aren't capable of storing a great deal of sensitive information. Browsers must support only 4,096 bytes (see Table 3-9); however, cookies don't need to be large. They must merely contain a unique identifier that can be used to reference profiles stored on databases maintained by online companies.

Table 3-9 Minimum Cookie Support Required of Web Browsers According to RFC 2965, "HTTP State Management Mechanism"

Minimum total cookies	300
Minimum bytes per cookie	4096
Minimum cookies per unique host or domain name	20

The lifespan of cookies is another important aspect when considering the risk associated with cookies. The longer the expiration date, the longer the period an online company, or any domain, can track a given cookie. Major search engines vary in the duration of their cookies—Google 2 years, Yahoo! 29 years, Ask 2 years, MSN Live 13 years, and AOL Search 1 year. Google initially issued cookies that expired in the 2038 but now expires cookies after 2 years, citing a desire to increase user privacy.[21] On the surface, this may seem like a significant improvement, but in practice, the change will do little to alter the risk. Many web users change browsers and, perhaps, computers every two years, so decreasing a cookie's lifespan from approximately 30 years to 2 likely will do little to alter Google's information-collection capabilities. In addition, Google cookies are autoextended with each visit to Google. So a user would have to fail to visit Google for two continuous years before the cookie would be discarded by the web browser, an unlikely scenario.

HTTP REFERER DATA

Another source of information disclosure built into the infrastructure of the web is the HTTP referer value. When a user clicks a link in a web page, it makes a request to the appropriate web server for the desired object. All common browsers also pass a referer value, which indicates the page the user is browsing from. Figure 3-9 shows an example. In this case, the user clicked a link on a main page of www.rumint.org to a page on the Creative Commons web site (www.creativecommons.org). The user's browser contacts the Creative Common's server and passes along the source page (www.rumint.org) in the referer field.

Referer values might sound innocuous, but they allow online companies to pinpoint entry points to their web sites and link these sources to specific users via IP addresses and cookies. More important, because Google embeds search queries in the URL that users click, the destination web site receives the search queries in addition to the user's IP address. Consider these examples of referer values culled from my rumint.org site.[22] Notice the search queries in bold.

http://www.google.cz/search?q=**rumint**

http://www.google.cz/search?q=**rapidshare+Greg+Conti**

http://www.google.com/search?q=**rainfall+rumint**

http://www.google.com/search?q=**chinese+information+warriors**

http://www.google.com/search?q=**rumint+homepage**

http://www.google.com/search?q=**netork+attacks**

http://www.google.com/search?q=**visual+pcap+file**

http://www.google.ca/search?q=**china+creates+cyber+warfare+corp**

http://www.google.ca/search?q=**network+my+pvr**

http://www.google.com/search?q=**military+intelligence+ppt**

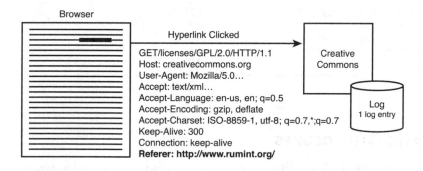

Figure 3-9 When web surfers click a link in a web page, their browser informs the destination server of where they browsing from via an HTTP referer value. Referer values allow web sites to monitor where their traffic is coming from.

Referer values, even if they don't include items like search terms, are significant because each allows the destination web site to link each visitor's IP address with the web site he or she is coming from. In some cases, the referer value indicates the specific news article or blog entry the visitor was reading. Table 3-10 shows the top referrers for www.rumint.org; note the significant presence of Google traffic. In other words, for each of the billions of successful searches Google empowers, the users' search queries are passed on, along with identifying information, to the destination web server.[23] Thus, each web search that a user conducts on Google is disclosed twice: once when the user conducts the search on Google and again to the destination site when the user clicks a search result link.

Table 3-10 Examples of Referers Passed to a Web Site

Referer	Visits	Percentage
www.astalavista.com/index.php	6,981	26.20
www.google.com/search	5,905	22.16
www.astalavista.com/	3,027	11.36
astalavista.com/index.php	2,832	10.63
www.google.co.in/search	1,304	4.89
www.google.cn/search	887	3.33
www.hvaonline.net/hvaonline/posts/list/5557.hva	643	2.41
www.stumbleupon.com/refer.php	615	2.31
www.honeynet.org/papers/individual	448	1.68
www.google.co.uk/search	415	1.56

SEMANTIC DISCLOSURES

Thus far, we've seen the identifying trail left by users as they visit the web sites of online companies, including information provided at the network level, such as IP addresses, and information disclosed by their web browser, such as cookies, referer values, operating system, CPU, screen size, software, and plug-in versions. However, we only touched upon the information leaked by users themselves through their interactions and how this information can be personally identifying. Chapter 1, "Googling," (particularly Table 1-2) provided an overview of the types of sensitive information users provide when they use Google's tools and services, including search queries, geographic locations of interest, word-processing documents, and e-mails. The core chapters of the book explore each of these specific forms of semantic disclosure. For example, the next chapter, "Search," provides hundreds of real-world search queries culled from web server logs. Here I examine two other examples that are broadly applicable: registered user accounts and web site navigation.

REGISTERED USER ACCOUNTS

Almost by definition, registering for a user account identifies you uniquely to an online company. I say "almost" here because you could always share the account with others, but let's assume that you share your account rarely, if at all, and that you don't post your user ID and password on a web site or something. Registered users are valuable to online companies because they allow precise targeted advertising. Many online services seek to find compelling reasons for you to go through the hassle of creating an account, such as by providing access to additional services or allowing you to personalize their interactions. Google is no exception. For example a Google account (see Figure 3-10) is required to use Gmail and Google Calendar, as well as save customized maps in Google Maps.

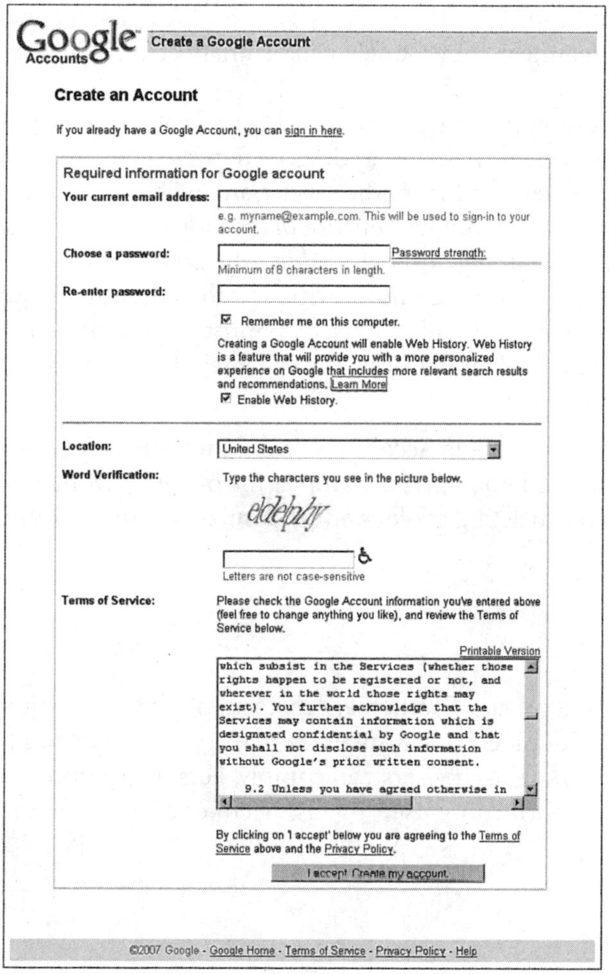

Figure 3-10 Creating a Google account

As you examine Figure 3-10, there are several important things to note. First, you are required to enter an e-mail address. During my testing, Google verified my address by sending a follow-up confirmation e-mail with a link to click before the account was activated. This process ensures a valid e-mail address. (Remember, you've also disclosed your IP address and likely been tagged with a cookie). Second, by leaving Remember Me on This Computer checked, I am automatically logged in as I use Google's services. Similarly, Enable Web History is selected by default. Web History is a Google Service that keeps track of a user's activity and helps personalize service. Users can delete information from their web history, but the "Privacy FAQ for Web History" makes it very clear that a separate log maintained by Google will be unaffected (emphasis mine):

> You can choose to stop storing your web activity in Web History either temporarily or permanently, or remove items, as described in Web History Help. If you remove items, they will be removed from the service and will not be used to improve your search experience. *As is common practice in the industry, Google also maintains a separate logs system for auditing purposes and to help us improve the quality of our services for users.* For example, we use this information to audit our ads systems, understand which features are most popular to users, improve the quality of our search results, and help us combat vulnerabilities such as denial of service attacks.[24]

In short, by creating a Google Account, you uniquely identify yourself every time you log in, whether it be from home, via a laptop at the office, or from a cybercafe in Bangalore. Obsessively deleting cookies or randomizing your IP address is of no assistance once you log in.

NOTE

Personalization is a privacy anathema. Any form of personalization allows an online company to uniquely identify users. The more compelling the personalization features, the more likely users will comply. Personalization requires an online company to uniquely identify users, by using either a cookie or a registered user account.

WEB SITE NAVIGATION

Even the simple act of browsing a web site or clicking a link reveals sensitive information. Navigation between web sites (inter–web site navigation) can be tracked via third-party advertising networks (such as Google's AdSense and DoubleClick services), web analytics services (such as Google Analytics), and click-through monitoring that reveal browsing habits useful for targeted advertising and user profiling. Similarly, how a user navigates within a web site (intra–web site navigation) is easily retrieved from server logs and provides insight into the information that user is seeking and the speed of the network connection, and perhaps helps identify that user because of unique behaviors. Likewise, Google Analytics and advertising networks might reveal what people are clicking on in a given site. Although Google does not publish the exact numbers of web sites running Google Analytics, AdSense, or DoubleClick services, hundreds of thousands of sites and millions of users likely are being tracked without realizing it.

NOTE

Asynchronous JavaScript and XML (AJAX), a web development paradigm for creating highly interactive web applications, is transforming the web from relatively static, low-interaction pages (think filling in a form and clicking Submit) to highly interactive, user-friendly web applications, such as a web-based collaborative word processor. With the increased interactivity of online applications, there exists a far greater potential to monitor and fingerprint a user's interactions.

Inter–Web Site Navigation

Many ways of tracking a user's surfing between web sites exist, including these:

- HTTP referer data reveals the previously visited web site to the destination web site.
- Third-party advertising networks reveal a user's visits to any site serving ads from the same advertiser.
- Web-analytic services such as Google Analytics can track user's movements across any site in the analytics network.
- Web bugs, small 1×1 transparent GIF images, placed by cooperative web masters, allow logging of user activities by third-parties.
- Embedded third-party content, such as videos and maps, allows content providers to monitor a user's visits to any site including their content.

- Click-through monitoring reveals which link a user clicked on a web page and, hence, that user's next destination.

The risks of HTTP referer data were covered earlier in the chapter. Third-party advertising is a big topic and is covered in Chapter 7. Click-through tracking, however, is worth discussing now.

During normal web browsing, when a user clicks on a link in a web page, such as shown in Figure 3-9, the current web site has no way of knowing whether a user clicked a given link. However, modern web browsers support the JavaScript programming language, which allows additional programming logic to be embedded in web pages. Creative JavaScript programming allows the current web server to detect which link the user clicked on a given page, which is normally not possible using traditional HTML. Google employs this technique,[25, 26] which ties together users' search queries with the links they click. If JavaScript is turned on in the user's browser, which is frequently the case, the actual links Google returns point back to Google, but JavaScript displays the real target link to the user on mouseover.[27] Click-through tracking gives Google invaluable feedback for fine-tuning the quality of its search algorithm, but can also provide a significant information disclosure risk. For example, if you searched for "video chat" and clicked a link to an adult service, you've told Google one thing; if you click on a link to a popular video teleconferencing tool, you've revealed another intent. Google's "Privacy FAQ" has the following to say about click-through tracking:

> When you click on a link displayed on Google, the fact that you clicked on the link may be sent to Google. In this way, Google is able to record information about how you use our site and services. We use this information to improve the quality of our services and for other business purposes. For example, Google can use this information to determine how often users are satisfied with the first result of a query and how often they proceed to later results. Similarly, Google can use this information to determine how many times an advertisement is clicked in order to calculate how much the advertiser should be charged.[28]

Google clearly gives itself the right to perform click-through monitoring, and, from my experience it does so. However, it is impossible to say that Google does this for all web interactions.[29] Google could turn on click-through tracking for any or all of its users on a whim.

The following is an example. First a user visits the main Google search page, types in the query "rumint," and clicks Enter. Google dutifully returns search results (see Figure 3-11).

Figure 3-11 Links clicked on Google search result pages can be tracked using click-through tracking.

On a normal web page, when a user clicks an external link, the user's browser immediately requests the object, with no further contact with the current web site (see Figure 3-9). Therefore, the current web site cannot determine the link the user clicked, but click-through tracking sends the browser back to Google before sending the browser to the intended destination (see Figure 3-12). Note that hovering the mouse over a hyperlink normally indicates the URL that will be contacted when the link is clicked, but this is not the case when Google employs click-through tracking.

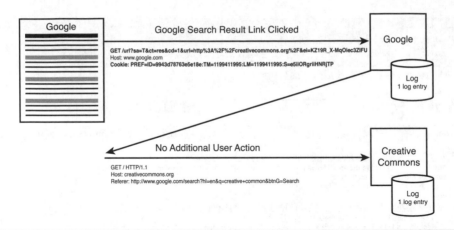

Figure 3-12   Click-through tracking allows Google to log the search result links a user clicks.

Google's use of click-through tracking is easily confirmed by sniffing the actual network packets sent and received when a user clicks a link. For example, clicking the first search result in Figure 3-11 should result in an immediate request for www.rumint.org, but instead the user is sent back to Google with the following HTTP request:

```
HTTP GET /url?sa=T&ct=res&cd=1&url=http%3A%2F%2F
www.rumint.org%2F&ei=Jgl7R-P3CqSyevCXvEQ HTTP/1.1
```

The request was sent to IP address 64.233.169.103, which a reverse IP address lookup confirms as Google, instead of www.rumint.org:

```
Search ARIN WHOIS for: 64.233.169.103
Top of Form
Bottom of Form
OrgName:    Google Inc.
OrgID:      GOGL
Address:    1600 Amphitheatre Parkway
City:       Mountain View
StateProv:  CA
PostalCode: 94043
Country:    US

NetRange:   64.233.160.0 - 64.233.191.255
CIDR:       64.233.160.0/19
NetName:    GOOGLE
NetHandle:  NET-64-233-160-0-1
```

```
Parent:      NET-64-0-0-0-0
NetType:     Direct Allocation
NameServer: NS1.GOOGLE.COM
NameServer: NS2.GOOGLE.COM
NameServer: NS3.GOOGLE.COM
NameServer: NS4.GOOGLE.COM
Comment:
RegDate:     2003-08-18
Updated:     2007-04-10

RTechHandle: ZG39-ARIN
RTechName:   Google Inc.
RTechPhone:  +1-650-318-0200
RTechEmail:  arin-contact@google.com

OrgTechHandle: ZG39-ARIN
OrgTechName:   Google Inc.
OrgTechPhone:  +1-650-318-0200
OrgTechEmail:  arin-contact@google.com

# ARIN WHOIS database, last updated 2008-01-01 19:10
# Enter ? for additional hints on searching ARIN's WHOIS database.
```

Intra–Web Site Navigation

Long a staple of web site analytics, intra–web site navigation consists of a user's browsing patterns on a single domain, where the user is easily logged. Such activity reveals users' desired goals, and repeated instances of similar browsing patterns can help a given online company uniquely identify a user. Figure 3-13 shows an example, in which a user browses a sequence of web pages (1 to 7) while leaving other pages unvisited. Normally, a web site contains a relatively small number of pages, but Google's myriad online tools and affiliated web sites allows very complex interaction patterns to be logged and mined.

Navigation within a given web site can reveal a user's desired goals and could help uniquely identify him or her.[30] The following sequence from a www.rumint.org log occurred 44 times over the course of a year. The starting location is the root index.html file, and the visitor ends by visiting outfile.txt.

/index.html
/feedback.html
/readings.html
/software/rumint/changelog.txt

/software/rumint/developer_notes.txt

/software/rumint/developer_help.txt

/software/rumint/release_notes.txt

/software/rumint/faq.txt

/software/advancedfrequencycounter/outfile.txt

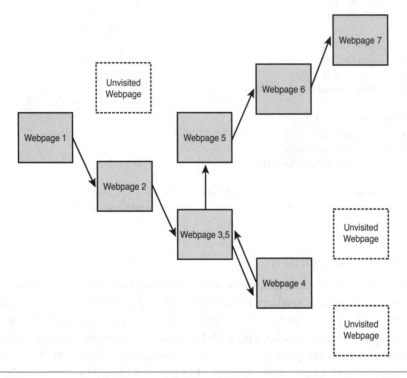

Figure 3-13   Example of a user's navigation through a web site.

Many users exhibit unique or at least uncommon navigation behaviors that uniquely identify them. This can be particularly true when the process is automated, as is the case when a user writes custom scripts or the visitor is an automated browsing script such as a web bot. Now examine the following example, which occurred only twice over the course of a year:

/feedback.html

/feedback.html

/readings.html

/readings.html

/software/rumint/changelog.txt

/software/rumint/changelog.txt

/software/rumint/developer_notes.txt

/software/rumint/developer_notes.txt

/software/rumint/developer_help.txt

/software/rumint/developer_help.txt

/software/rumint/mailinglist.txt

/software/rumint/mailinglist.txt

/software/rumint/release_notes.txt

/software/rumint/release_notes.txt

/software/rumint/faq.txt

/software/rumint/faq.txt

/software/advancedfrequencycounter/outfile.txt

/software/advancedfrequencycounter/outfile.txt

Notice that the visitor loaded each page twice, an unlikely occurrence for a human. Most likely this visitor was a misconfigured web bot.

UNIQUENESS AND BEHAVIORAL TARGETING

So far, this chapter has covered the myriad ways users disclose information to online companies, either by deliberately typing in the information directly or by having their browser and operating system do so indirectly. Table 3-11 summarizes the highlights. With this information in hand, an online company can uniquely identify a user, profile his or her activities, and possibly tie this cluster of activity to a real world identity.

Table 3-11   Common Forms of Web-Based Information Disclosure

Type of Identifying Information	How Used	Examples
IP addresses	Required to communicate on the Internet	64.X.X.X
Cookies	Issued by web server, returned on request by browser	ID=0a0661ceb826a27d:TM= 1199309328: LM=1199309328:S= ZoVTNgAwhwr1s3IY
Browser header fields	Information passed by a browser to a web server	Referer, preferred language, operating system, browser version
User accounts	Required to access some forms of online tools	Google account user ID and password
Semantic information	The actual information users disclose as they use online tools	Search queries, mapping locations, e-mails

BEHAVIORAL TARGETING

No discussion of web-based information disclosure would be complete without covering *behavioral targeting,* sometime called user profiling, which uses web interaction data to categorize a user's interests and allow targeted advertising.[31] Behavioral targeting aims to place exactly the right advertisement in front of each user at the right time to support sales. An excellent example is Tacoda, which claims the "first and largest behavioral targeted advertising network reaching more than 120 million people every month." It uses web-based interaction data to profile and categorize users. The following are example profiles from the Tacoda web site, along with top interests:[32]

- **Active Gamer**—PC console gaming, gaming, sports fantasy, and online gaming.
- **Auto Enthusiast**—SUV, passenger compact car, sports car, passenger midsize, passenger luxury
- **Auto Intender**—Pickup truck, used, midsize passenger, used compact passenger, full-size passenger
- **Business Decision Maker**—Business news, business, dining, business strategy, television
- **Career Watcher**—Careers, obituaries, shopping, news, home real estate

It is easy to imagine additional, more sensitive categories, including breast cancer survivors, recovering alcoholics, cheating wives of government leaders, political activists for the EFF, AIDs victims living in SOHO, new parents at the Fort Hood military base, college professors conducting research at Berkeley, and African-American Baptist ministers living in South Carolina. The possibilities are endless but are unlikely to appear on a company web site's marketing materials. Given Google's capabilities, Tacoma's profiles likely pale in comparison to what Google could create.

It is useful to consider profiling as an early step along the spectrum of data mining associated with web-based information disclosure. Each disclosure a user makes provides useful information that offers insights into that user's personal and professional lives that then allows him or her to be grouped with other similar users. Farther along the spectrum is fingerprinting which allows a user to be uniquely identified amid many other similar users. For example, I might be profiled as a generic "college professor" more easily than "Greg Conti, Assistant Professor at West Point."

UNIQUENESS

Of course, using the same cookie or registered user account uniquely identifies a user, but even if a user rigorously deletes cookies and never logs in with a user ID and password, fingerprinting is still possible. For example, if a user employs many Google services over time from a home computer and purchases a new laptop to use only while traveling, this new laptop will always appear from a different IP address and its cookies will not match those on the home computer. However, over time, the user will disclose significant information that will converge into unique forms of behavior, thus identifying the user of the laptop and the home computer as the same individual with an ever-increasing degree of accuracy. Figure 3-14 illustrates a simplified example. In this case, the user frequently uses search, mapping, e-mail, and news services on both machines. Information disclosed via each of these services will increase over time.

Eventually, the user will disclose enough information that his or her activities are uniquely identifiable when compared to activities from other, initially anonymous, computers on the Internet, such as home and work computers. Figure 3-15 shows the total information disclosed to an online company over time from two online users. Notice the dotted line labeled "Fingerprinting Threshold." When a user's information disclosure crosses this boundary, that user has provided enough information to be uniquely identified, as is the case with User 1 in the figure. The location of the fingerprinting threshold is a bit arbitrary because there is little published research on the exact number of disclosures required to fingerprint a user, but I argue that it is entirely possible to uniquely identify a user given enough disclosures. Note that the fingerprinting threshold slopes downward over time because of an assumption that Google's capability to fingerprint users will improve. As you examine the figure, notice User 2. If this user discloses less information, perhaps because he employs privacy countermeasures such as deleting cookies, he might never provide enough information to be uniquely identified. That being said, it doesn't take much information to be fingerprinted.[33] For example, consider how many searches a user must enter before creating a unique pattern. Note also that fingerprinting isn't really the matter of a simple pass/fail threshold; instead, fingerprinting should be considered a spectrum that ranges from no similarity (this user is indistinguishable from any other user) to a near certainty that the user is the same.

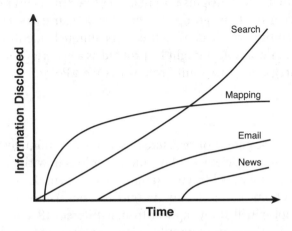

Figure 3-14   Information disclosed to Google over time for a notional user, by type of activity.[34]

NOTE

It is very likely that most users hit the fingerprinting threshold quickly. If a user employs privacy countermeasures, he or she delays hitting the threshold. Never reaching the threshold is unlikely over time, except for the extremely paranoid who are willing to continually employ a wide range of sometimes painful anonymous browsing countermeasures.

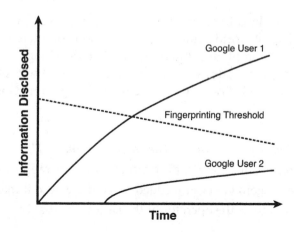

Figure 3-15 Total information disclosed to Google for two users. After a certain amount of information is disclosed, users can be uniquely identified even if they appear on another computer at another location.

Such uniqueness needn't come just from search queries, but the sum total of all activity. E-mail addresses, physical locations, pseudonyms, real-world names, hobbies, new interests, use of advanced Google features (think Google's word definition or calculator functions), commonly misspelled words, language preferences, and stock portfolios are among the many disclosures that can be aggregated around an IP address, even one used for a short period of time, and can be used to link the user to other activity on different machines or across IP address transitions.

> **NOTE**
>
> Intel tried unsuccessfully to embed a unique serial number in its Pentium III processors that could be revealed across the Internet.[35] Intense user backlash, and the subsequent public relations fiasco, resulted in Intel phasing out the program.[36]

CONNECTIONS

The traces people leave behind provide the means to link together individual users, and their profiles, across multiple computing platforms and networks, as well as across communities of users who share the same attributes. Virtually any characteristic can be used to perform the linkage, including cookies, registered user accounts, browser header data, IP addresses, physical location, computing platform, and semantic information, as well as information provided by other users (think another user's search for the combination of a pseudonym and a real-world name) and information collected by Googlebot from web pages. Something as simple as submitting a URL to the Google search engine (www.google.com/addurl/) creates a very strong link between a web site and a given user. Also consider the quote from Google CEO Eric Schmidt regarding Google's acquisition of YouTube (emphasis mine):

> *People are using videoclips everywhere. They're sharing them. They're building communities around them.* YouTube's traffic continues to grow rapidly. Video is something that we think is going to be embedded everywhere. And it makes sense, from Google's perspective, to be the operator of the largest site that contains all that video. [37]

Figure 3-16 shows an example of an individual user who works using six computing platforms. In this case, the user can be linked across most of these devices based on unique characteristics of application, network, and semantic information that the user and the machines leak. Note that creating a linkage is not guaranteed (e.g., the information disclosed is below the fingerprinting threshold), as shown by the isolated Internet Café node.

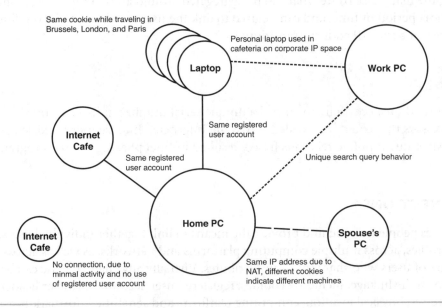

Figure 3-16   Example of ways to link the same user across multiple computing platforms. Link strength may vary from weak (thin dotted line) to moderate (dashed line) to strong (solid line).

Now consider how many different users can be linked based on these and similar characteristics (see Figure 3-17). Notice that it doesn't take much information to link a given pair of nodes. For example, if two users simply read the same blog, they create a link due to this shared attribute.[38] Much stronger links are possible if two users both search for rarely sought after data, communicate via Gmail or come from the same IP address block, among many other possibilities.

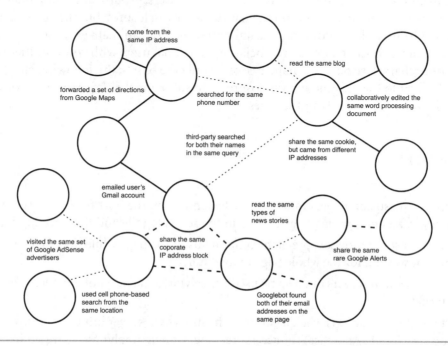

Figure 3-17 Linking many users based on characteristics of their online activities. Link strength may vary from weak (thin dotted line) to moderate (dashed line) to strong (solid line).

SUMMARY

Previous chapters examined the tremendous power of Google and how googling fits into the big picture of Internet use. This chapter covered the fingerprints left behind by using the offerings of Google and other online tools, including IP addresses, cookies, browser header fields, and user accounts. It also included an overview of the semantic data users disclose during their use of the tools themselves, such as search queries, e-mail contents, mapping locations, and preferences. Each of these disclosures reveals sensitive information, and it is safe to assume that online companies will log what can be logged. It takes only one unique aspect of these revelations to tie them together and create a profile of a user. Initially, this cluster will be anonymous, but over time, often a very short period of time, the sum of these can reveal the identity of users themselves or uniquely identify them when they appear on another, previously unused computing device. The end result is the capability to create comprehensive dossiers on users, groups, and companies. What the dossiers can contain depends on the nature of the disclosures, but they can include everything from health conditions, marital status, age, educational level, and social network. The same concept applies to associating individual users with communities that share some characteristic. This chapter covered only the basics; the following chapters delve deeply into the information disclosures, and subsequent risks, associated with many of Google's core tools and services.

ENDNOTES

1. Some requests might generate multiple log entries on the hosting web server. For example, an entry might be generated in the access log file and the error log file.

2. Note that some browsers prefetch components of the page while the page is loading, without waiting for the whole page to load fully.

3. Of course, web servers can also be used on networks that are not connected to the Internet.

4. Yet another scenario is when a company hosts its own server but uses a third party (such as Google Analytics) for access tracking. Google Analytics is covered in Chapter 7.

5. This assumes that the local name server has a cached copy of the www.google.com record.

6. "How to Disable Client-Side DNS Caching in Windows XP and Windows Server 2003," Microsoft Knowledge Base Article 318803, 12 October 2007. http://support.microsoft.com/kb/318803, 7 January 2007.

7. Security researcher Dan Kaminsky used the fact that local name servers maintain a cached copy of recently visited sites to analyze the spread of the Sony Rootkit; see http://portal.acm.org/citation.cfm?id=1132503.

8. Of course, a web server can be configured to not log such accesses, but such configurations are uncommon.

9. For a full list of HTTP status codes, see www.w3.org/Protocols/rfc2616/rfc2616-sec10.html.

10. See the Internet Assigned Numbers Authority's registry at www.iana.org/ipaddress/ip-addresses.htm and the WHOIS Database at http://ws.arin.net/whois/.

11. AOL members are often assigned 172.128.X.X IP addresses; see http://webmaster.info.aol.com/proxyinfo.html.

12. MaxMind. www.maxmind.com/, last accessed 15 January 2008.

13. "Geolocation: Determining the Location of an IP Address," DNSstuff.com. www.dnsstuff.com/info/geolocation.htm, last accessed 15 December 2007.

14. Chris Trowbridge, "An Overview of Remote Operating System Fingerprinting," *SANS GIAC GSEC Practical,* 16 July 2003. www.sans.org/reading_room/whitepapers/testing/1231.php, last accessed 18 January 2008.

15. Michal Zalewski, "The New p0f." http://lcamtuf.coredump.cx/p0f.shtml, last accessed 18 January 2008.

16. Note that *referer* is deliberately misspelled. The official HTTP specification uses this misspelling, and *referer* has become the common usage when discussing HTTP referer values.

17. For more information on cookies, see the "Unofficial Cookie FAQ" at www.cookiecentral.com/faq/. The full specification of cookies is documented in RFC 2965, available at http://tools.ietf.org/html/rfc2965.

18. "Google's Cookie," *Google-Watch,* 16 July 2007. www.google-watch.org/cgi-bin/cookie.htm, last accessed 19 January 2009.

19. You can perform similar conversions at www.unixtimestamp.com/index.php.

20. This isn't entirely true. Several workarounds can create cross-domain cookies. See www.15seconds.com/issue/971108.htm.

21. Peter Fleischer, "Cookies: Expiring Sooner to Improve Privacy," The Official Google Blog, 16 July 2007. http://googleblog.blogspot.com/2007/07/cookies-expiring-sooner-to-improve.html, 19 January 2008.

22. I've edited these a bit for clarity.

23. If the user never clicks a link on Google's search result list, there is usually no disclosure.

24. Google, "Privacy FAQ for Web History," www.google.com/history/whprivacyfaq.html, last accessed 1 December 2007.

25. Cory Doctorow, "Google Stealthily Monitoring Clickthroughs from Search Results," *Boing Boing,* 22 August 2005. www.boingboing.net/2005/08/22/google-stealthily-mo.html, last accessed 21 January 2008.

26. "Is Google Click-Tracking Regular Search Results?" Mboffin Blog, 22 August 2005. http://mboffin.com/post.aspx?id=1830, last accessed 21 January 2008.

27. When JavaScript is turned off, Google displays the correct target links all along and does not track your click-through. Unfortunately, turning off JavaScript for general web surfing breaks many online applications.

28. "Google Privacy Center: Privacy Policy." www.google.com/privacy_faq.html, last accessed 21 January 2008.

29. The AOL dataset contained a great deal of click-through information associated with user searches.

30. For one approach to user classification using an analysis of web page accesses, see Xerox's patent #559355, "User Profile Classification By Web Page Usage Analysis."

31. Russell Shaw, "Behavioral Targeting 101," *iMedia Connection,* 28 April 2004. www.imediaconnection.com/content/3297.asp, last accessed 23 January 2008.

32. "Tacoda: The Home of Behavioral Targeting," Tacoda Corporate Home Page. www.tacoda.com/, last accessed 23 January 2008.

33. Gregory Conti, "Googling Considered Harmful," New Security Paradigms Workshop, October 2006.

34. From the purist's point of view, this graph might indicate that information disclosed via mapping, news, and e-mail will eventually reach saturation and level off over time, and that search disclosures will grow exponentially. This is not necessarily correct. Each user has significantly different information disclosure curves that can vary radically from those depicted. My key point here is that users will disclose, cumulatively, an increasing amount of information over time as they continue to employ web tools, and these disclosures will grow at different rates based on the services they employ.

35. "Intel Pentium II Processor—Processor Serial Number Questions & Answers," Intel, 10 December 2003. www.intel.com/support/processors/pentiumiii/sb/cs-007579.htm, last accessed 23 January 2008.

36. Michael Kanellos, "Intel to Phase Out Serial Number Feature," CNET News, 27 April 2000. www.news.com/2100-1040-239833.html, last accessed 23 January 2008.

37. Fred Vogelstein, "As Google Challenges Viacom and Microsoft, Its CEO Feels Lucky." *Wired Magazine,* 9 April 2007. www.wired.com/techbiz/people/news/2007/04/mag_schmidt_qa, last accessed 23 January 2008.

38. Recall that Google offers free blog hosting via its Blogger service and, presumably, possesses the capability to log many users as they read various Blogger blog entries.

Search

Ah, the simple search box. Over the course of our lives, we pour our successes, failures, hopes, dreams, and life events, both significant and minor, into a small text field and turn our destinies over to Google in hopes of finding the answers we seek. The information-centric nature of the web demands a way to locate web sites and relevant information. So it should come as no surprise that one of the first services available on the web was an index of web sites maintained by Tim Berners-Lee in 1991.[1] More advanced search engines soon followed in the early 1990s, including Lycos, AltaVista, and Excite. When Google emerged on the scene in 1998, the web had grown immensely and users had become discriminating search engine users, seeking out the highest-quality search results. Google quickly gained the reputation of providing the best results and, over the next ten years, has risen to clear market dominance, with about 500 million users and more than 2.7 billion queries processed per month. This chapter focuses on the significance of these 2.7 billion queries and the billions before them.

A computer scientist I greatly respect mentioned casually that, because of Google, he no longer bothers to remember things that he can easily look up. I believe he is not alone. I myself used to maintain a large personal library, but over time it has dwindled and now consists of a few books that provide content that isn't easily accessible via the Internet. These aren't isolated trends; all across the wired-world people are coming to the same conclusions.[2] Search is the key, but search is also a nearly unbounded path of information disclosure. It is the most ubiquitous of web applications and is available on every web platform, from desktops to laptops, to cell phones and MP3 players. We search from virtually everywhere for virtually everything, leaving traces behind on the devices themselves,[3] the ISPs and network providers that provide the connectivity, and, most important, for the purposes of this book, on the servers of major search providers. This isn't meant to discount the threat of these other vectors, as described in Chapter 2, "Information Flows and Leakage"—they just aren't the focus of this chapter.

This chapter covers both the depth and breadth of search, including how much sensitive information users disclose over time, illustrated with examples from the AOL dataset and the many interfaces, applications, and devices that serve as the vehicle for these disclosures. The chapter also includes additional risks associated with search, including finding the wrong (or even malicious) information in the search index, how other users might disclose information about sensitive projects and activities, and how search queries alone, independent of IP addresses and cookies, can be used to uniquely identify and profile users and groups.

WHAT'S IN A QUERY?

The notion of search revolves around the *search query,* the piece of information entered into the search box of a browser (see Figure 4-1). Search engines are often the first site that the web's nearly one billion users visit and are the primary conduit for locating desired information. After the user enters a search query, the search engine checks its search index for relevant web content and returns a hyperlinked list of search results[4] (see Figure 4-2). From here, the user scans the results and visits sites that seem to have the best source of information to meet his or her needs.

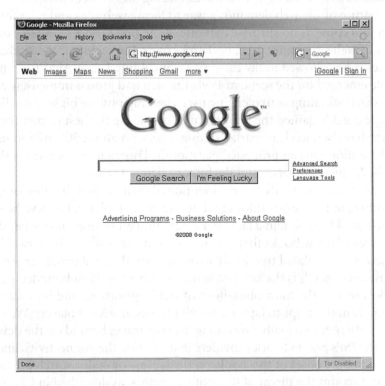

Figure 4-1   The classic Google search interface

Figure 4-2 Search results page after entering a query

At first glance, an individual search query might appear to be insignificant, but when you consider the sum of all queries over the course of years, you'll soon realize that they reveal a very complete picture. Perhaps the best examples are the queries found in the AOL dataset. Recall that this dataset contained approximately 20 million search queries of some 658,000 AOL users and was released by AOL in August 2006. The following five examples are excerpts from this dataset.

AOL User 98280[5] (see Table 4-1) illustrates many types of information disclosed during search—locations (Crosby and Dayton, Texas), religious affiliation (Lakewood Church), medical conditions (pregnancy and bipolar disorder), business plans (grocery store and gas station frachises [sic]), and hopes and dreams (what do I need to do to become an actress). Note that AOL tracked the date and time of each query, the search result link clicked (if any)[6], and the result's placement in the search result list.

Table 4-1   Searches Conducted by AOL User 98280

Query	Query Time	Clicked URL	Rank
victoria's secret	2006-03-01 18:16:32		0
premier cinemas in baytown tx	2006-03-02 18:33:47	http://www.pccmovies.com	2
ovulation calculator	2006-03-03 12:37:21	http://www.4woman.gov	1
pregnancy calculator and pictures of fetus	2006-03-07 18:17:19	http://www.paternityangel.com	1
first trimester of pregnancy	2006-03-09 16:15:58	http://www.4woman.gov	1
a drug with slang name of ice	2006-03-13 18:40:58	http://www.kci.org	5
is bipolar disorder hereditary	2006-03-20 14:56:56	http://www.bipolar.com	6
crosby tx real estate for sale	2006-03-21 12:16:49	http://www.homes.com	1
acreage for sale in crosby tx	2006-03-21 12:27:25	http://bonniebutler.homes.com	3
disorders with people owning numerous dogs	2006-03-22 14:10:19		0
symptoms of narcissism	2006-03-22 14:36:47	http://it.stlawu.edu	5
personality disorders	2006-03-22 14:55:11	http://www.4degreez.com	1
what do i need to do to become an actress	2006-03-28 17:45:37	http://experts.about.com	9
how do i get an agent for acting jobs	2006-03-28 18:16:34		0
lakewood church	2006-04-03 15:58:52	http://www.lakewood.cc	1
stories of miracles	2006-04-06 13:43:35	http://www.geocities.com	26
intercessory prayers	2006-04-07 11:07:33	http://christianity.about.com	39
grocery store gas station franchises	2006-04-12 19:03:43		0
commercial land for sale in dayton tx	2006-04-13 17:39:11		0
november birthstone	2006-04-15 23:48:01	http://www.bernardine.com	2
summer maternity clothing	2006-04-28 15:44:05	http://www.materniityapparel.com	4
format for a formal apology letter	2006-04-29 19:28:17	http://www.writeexpress.com	2
convenience store franchises in texas	2006-05-03 23:48:52	http://www.businessnation.com	4
how to start your own gasoline convenience store business	2006-05-03 23:51:19		0

Query	Query Time	Clicked URL	Rank
furlow programs	2006-05-04 15:02:09		0
definition for furlough program	2006-05-04 15:02:48	http://www.english-test.net	2
how to kill lice in hair	2006-05-09 15:07:52	http://www.walgreens.com	6

Similarly, AOL User 1963201[7] (see Table 4-2) revealed locations (Colorado County and Columbus, Texas) and a school district (El Campo Independent School District) indicative of a parent, and a number of searches indicative of a young girl (Barbie.com, Starfall.com, and Bratz.com). The spelling errors (cursiv writting [sic]) may provide insight into the user's education level and perhaps provide a unique characteristic to fingerprint her activities. Note that other terms are indicative of possibly other adult users (testicular pain), probably due to a shared family account.

Table 4-2 Searches Conducted by AOL User 1963201

Query	Query Time	Clicked URL	Rank
barbie.com	2006-03-01 20:45:35	http://www.everythinggirl.com	6
internet	2006-03-03 11:12:45		0
starfall.com	2006-03-03 21:27:47	http://www.bajada.net	3
starfall.com	2006-03-03 21:27:47	http://www.educational-freeware.com	4
bratz.com	2006-03-03 21:30:46	http://www.bratz.com	1
testicular pain	2006-03-22 10:11:34	http://www.doctorupdate.net	10
el campo independent school district	2006-03-22 10:54:47	http://www.ecisd.org	1
urology	2006-03-24 09:35:10	http://www.duj.com	2
penicillin and breast feeding	2006-04-04 12:31:39	http://www.perinatology.com	1
penguin habitat	2006-04-04 19:50:35	http://www.kidzone.ws	1
spermatic cord	2006-04-05 22:40:54	http://mywebpages.comcast.net	3
new jerusalem	2006-04-12 21:47:55	http://www.tribulation.com	5
curvy writing	2006-04-18 12:59:17	http://www.ghosts.org	9
cursiv writing	2006-04-18 13:06:36	http://www.atomicbooks.com	3

continues

Table 4-2   Continued

Query	Query Time	Clicked URL	Rank
handwriting	2006-04-18 13:08:37	http://pro.wanadoo.fr	9
cursive writting	2006-04-19 20:28:51	http://skatklub.com	8
cursiv writting	2006-04-19 20:52:58		0
cursive handwriting	2006-04-19 20:54:46	http://www.handwritingforkids.com	1
first grade bullying	2006-04-20 22:56:53	http://www.asij.ac.jp	3
texas house district 28	2006-04-24 13:22:15	http://en.wikipedia.org	4
columbus tx	2006-05-06 12:07:04	http://www.topix.net	7
colorado county sentinal	2006-05-06 12:31:00		0

Table 4-3 shows the searches of AOL user 789586.[8] Like the previous users, 789586 reveals general locations (Halifax, Hanover, and Georgetown, Massachusetts), including a precise location: Nando's Bakery on 142 Broadway, Hanover, MA 02339.[9] The searches are likely that of a gamer (World of Warcraft, WOW gold) who was searching for voice communications to use in the game (goteamspeak) and was planning a trip to New York City (top hang out [sic] in NYC).

Table 4-3   Searches Conducted by AOL User 789586

Query	Query Time	Clicked URL	Rank
haliafx ma yellow pages	2006-03-01 18:20:31		0
halifax ma yellow pages	2006-03-01 18:20:35	http://www.yellowpagecity.com	1
americas army	2006-03-06 15:32:09	http://www.americasarmy.com	1
goteamspeak	2006-03-06 16:14:28	http://www.goteamspeak.com	1
verizon wirelss	2006-03-13 07:06:54		0
verizon wireless	2006-03-13 07:06:58	http://www.verizonwireless.com	1
right here staind	2006-03-13 07:33:42	http://www.lyricstop.com	1
georgetown ma car accident tuesday	2006-03-15 11:28:23	http://cms.firehouse.com	5

Query	Query Time	Clicked URL	Rank
local news ma	2006-03-15 11:30:08		0
wow gold	2006-03-24 16:18:57		0
wow gold	2006-03-24 16:19:34		0
wow	2006-03-24 16:19:42		0
bakery halifax ma	2006-03-29 16:20:32	http://www.decidio.com	1
south shore ma bakeries	2006-03-29 16:24:18	http://boston.citysearch.com	6
nando's bakery hanover ma	2006-03-29 16:29:03		0
hanson ma golden roll	2006-04-07 17:26:24		0
department of home security	2006-04-17 09:24:01	http://www.whitehouse.gov	2
new york hot spots	2006-04-17 17:07:28	http://nyhotspots.com	1
world of warcraft	2006-04-27 15:01:11	http://www.worldofwarcraft.com	1
fox news boston	2006-04-28 17:18:05	http://www.boston.com	2
5pm fox news boston	2006-04-28 17:20:21	http://www.fox25.com	2
vampire girl	2006-05-01 18:56:20	http://www.vampgirl.com	1
top hot hang out in nyc	2006-05-20 00:26:13	http://www.villagevoice.com	6
facebook.com	2006-05-20 00:29:22	http://www.facebook.com	1

AOL user 2649647[10] is probably at a later point in life and is searching for healthcare providers (Tricare, Medicaid, hospice, and nursing homes), and is planning a second marriage, including searches for dresses (plus size wedding dresses and bridesmaid dress). She stopped her wedding preparations the day before taxes are due in the United States (15 April) to search on tax preparation (income tax and IRS). A week later, she searched for a Texas marriage license, a moving truck (Uhaul), and weight-loss information (Weight Watchers).

Table 4-4   Searches Conducted by AOL User 2649647

Query	Query Time	Clicked URL	Rank
tricare	2006-03-01 20:58:00	http://www.mytricare.com	3
bethany hospice georgetown texas	2006-03-02 08:55:32		0
medicaid	2006-03-05 11:39:14	http://www.cms.hhs.gov	2
nursing homes in texas	2006-03-05 11:47:13	http://www.carepathways.com	2
medicare	2006-03-05 11:56:10	http://www.medicare.gov	1
jobs in killeen texas	2006-03-05 20:01:47	http://jobs.jobbankusa.com	8
loveandseek	2006-03-07 19:23:48	http://www.loveandseek.com	1
days of our lives	2006-03-07 20:23:29	http://www.soapoperafan.com	1
fifties music	2006-03-11 19:05:50	http://www.fiftiesweb.com	1
jobs in humble texas	2006-03-13 00:06:36	http://www.snagajob.com	10
cvs	2006-03-13 20:51:34	http://www.cvs.com	1
walgreens	2006-03-13 20:56:19	http://www.walgreens.com	1
psychic reading	2006-03-14 23:49:45	http://www.helpself.com	5
jobs in humble texas	2006-03-15 01:04:08	http://www.sologig.com	4
christian wedding rings	2006-03-16 19:27:30	http://www.weddingclipart.com	4
wedding dresses	2006-03-16 19:30:00		0
j.c.penney bridal catlogue	2006-03-16 19:31:14		0
wedding invations	2006-03-16 21:17:14	http://weddingpoemcreations.tripod.com	8
romantic poems	2006-03-16 21:20:22	http://www.links2love.com	3
christian wedding announcements	2006-03-19 20:57:39	http://www.foreverwed.com	1
lifeway christian store temple texas	2006-03-20 21:32:22	http://www.lifewaystores.com	1
heights baptist church temple texas	2006-03-20 21:35:35	http://www.ci.temple.tx.us	4
second wedding	2006-03-22 18:12:16	http://www.idotaketwo.com	1

Query	Query Time	Clicked URL	Rank
plus size bridal suits	2006-03-26 02:09:07	http://www.womensuits.com	1
lingerie	2006-03-27 20:53:04	http://www.lingerie.com	8
bridesmaid dress	2006-03-27 21:59:42		0
wedding music	2006-03-28 21:54:01	http://www.wedalert.com	1
sexual inmacy	2006-03-29 19:40:21	http://jupiter.wpunj.edu	5
sexual relations	2006-03-29 19:41:44	http://www.fatwa-online.com	6
angie's bridal abilene texas	2006-04-04 20:48:04		0
plus size wedding dresses	2006-04-04 21:09:01	http://www.silverliningplus.com	7
apartments in porter texas	2006-04-12 21:44:01	http://www.switchboard.com	3
income tax	2006-04-14 18:38:07	http://www.irs.gov	1
irs	2006-04-14 19:02:40	http://www.irs.com	2
texas marriage license	2006-04-24 07:16:47	http://www.weddingvendors.com	4
nutri system	2006-04-24 20:06:22		0
aarp	2006-04-27 21:17:55		0
uhaul	2006-05-03 23:51:14	http://www.uhaul.com	1
weight watchers	2006-05-04 12:18:11	http://www.weightwatchers.com	2
weight watchers recipes	2006-05-04 12:21:32	http://www.angelfire.com	1

The final example, AOL user 3558174,[11] may face serious medical concerns (stage four lung cancer, fear of dieing [sic] stress) and is searching for cures (UC Davis Cancer Treatment Center, chemotherapy). At the same time, this user is planning a trip to Las Vegas (Las Vegas discounts, Rivera [sic] Hotel Las Vages [sic] deals) and is considering the purchase of a cement truck (concrete trucks for sale).

Table 4-5   Searches Conducted by AOL User 3558174

Query	Query Time	Clicked URL	Rank
las vegas discounts	2006-03-01 12:03:05	http://www.insidervlv.com	3
las vegas information	2006-03-01 12:39:13	http://www.accessvegas.com	5
surving stage four lung cancer	2006-03-01 14:03:24		0
stage four lung cancer	2006-03-01 14:34:38	http://www.cancercenter.com	3
rivera hotel las vages deals	2006-03-02 12:17:21	http://www.vegascasinos.com	7
compare flight deals	2006-03-03 13:42:53	http://www.cheapflights.co.uk	1
sick feeling in body	2006-03-07 13:06:43	http://www.cancerhelp.org.uk	3
burning pains in the body	2006-03-07 13:58:21	http://www.wrongdiagnosis.com	2
low energy	2006-03-08 11:40:18	http://thyroid.about.com	5
tired body	2006-03-08 14:53:39		0
fear of dieing stress	2006-03-08 14:55:20	http://www.healthboards.com	6
us davis cancer center	2006-03-15 16:24:14		0
uc davis cancer treatment center	2006-03-15 16:25:29	http://cancer.ucdmc.ucdavis.edu	1
uc davis medical center	2006-03-15 16:44:03	http://www.ucdavis.edu	5
new cancer drug santa rosa california	2006-03-21 11:23:03	http://www.nih.gov	3
aaa discounts	2006-03-22 14:47:29		0
advance travel deals	2006-03-22 16:34:23	http://ww2.aaa.com	4
new cemet mixer santa rosa california	2006-03-22 16:35:24		0
concrete trucks for sale	2006-03-22 17:31:14	http://www.tannerequipment.com	1
new concrete trucks	2006-03-22 17:44:33	http://www.mixertrucks.net	4
aarp medical insurance	2006-03-28 10:21:02		0
death in santa rosa california	2006-03-28 12:36:18		0
free death search in santa rosa california	2006-03-28 12:37:42		0
tp weak to stay on chemotherapy	2006-05-09 15:28:13		0

Query	Query Time	Clicked URL	Rank
chemotherapy pill	2006-05-09 15:30:31	http://www.cnn.com	9
lung cancer chemotherapy pill	2006-05-09 15:35:52		0
when to stop cemotherapy	2006-05-09 16:55:18	http://chemotherapypill.b3o3.com	18
chemotherapy pill	2006-05-09 17:54:21	http://www.rxpgnews.com	1
outsmart your cancer altogether book	2006-05-19 14:21:56		0

Previous chapters claimed the sensitive nature of search queries—here is the proof. I didn't have to look long for compelling examples such as these. From the birth of a child, to first-grade bullying, to planning a second wedding, to fighting cancer, to simply finding a good bakery, if a user conducted any number of searches, a sensitive picture emerged. I believe this is just an aspect of the human condition. Consider what the sum of your queries would reveal. Remember, as well, that search queries are just one facet of hundreds of potential web-based information-disclosure vectors.

As I write this, it is hard not to be moved by the sensitive nature of these queries; forgive me for being a bit philosophical—it is almost as if the users are communing with God. The fact that AOL made this information available to the world in a poorly executed attempt to share research data is unconscionable. But, at the same time, billions and perhaps trillions of these queries have been passed to Google and the other major search companies. Even if the world doesn't have access to these queries, online companies do. If you aren't convinced by now about the sensitivity of web-based information disclosure, you should be.

NOTE

In addition to search queries and click-throughs, search result listings allow a user to reveal other information by clicking cached links, links to similar pages, links to more results, and language-translation links.

Over Half a Million Search Engines

Billions of search queries have been disclosed to search engines large and small. Myriad search engines exist,[12] both general purpose and specialized. Too many exist to list here, but the following are the largest:[13]

- Google (49.2%[14]), www.google.com/
- Yahoo! (23.8%), www.yahoo.com/
- MSN (9.6%), www.msn.com/
- AOL (6.3%), www.aol.com/
- Ask (2.6%), www.ask.com/
- Others (8.5%)—more than 56 other monitored search engines

Each service-based chapter in the book includes a similar list; the more services a single company offers, the greater the risk. In some cases, you might not have used all of these services, but if you've been active on the web in any way, chances are, you've used some of these search engines. Each engine is broadly focused, so the risks described in this chapter apply to each. However, many more engines exist, each attempting to employ a unique spin on search, ultimately attempting to unseat Google.[15]

- **Ms. Dewey** (www.msdewey.com/)—Search by communicating with a pseudohuman[16]
- **ChaCha** (www.chacha.com/)—Search assisted by a human guide
- **Quintura** (www.quintura.com/) and Kartoo (www.kartoo.com/)—Clustering engines that present results as an interconnected cluster of related terms
- **LivePlasma** (www.liveplasma.com/)—Recommendation-based search engine that suggested related musical bands and movies
- **DogPile** (www.dogpile.com/)—Metasearch engine that searches many search engines at one time[17]
- **Search Wikia** (http://alpha.search.wikia.com/)—Wiki-based search using trusted user feedback from a community of users

Search engine companies, and the risks of web-based information disclosure aren't just an American phenomenon. In 2006, French president Jacques Chirac announced plans to create a European search engine to rival Google.[18] Another is Accoona (www.accoona.com/), an artificial intelligence–based search engine backed by the

Chinese government, which targets European and Chinese markets. Accoona even hired former President Bill Clinton as spokesman.[19] Although Accoona is important, Baidu (www.baidu.com/) is even more so. Described by *The New York Times* as "Chinese for Google,"[20] Baidu is the most popular search engine in China and Google's strongest competitor there.[21] Mozilla Online, the Chinese subsidiary of Mozilla Corporation, recently signed a deal with Baidu to ensure that Chinese editions of Firefox make Baidu available through Firefox's built-in search interface.[22] This alliance contrasts with the arrangement in North America, where Google is the default search engine for Firefox. China has a population of two billion people, a growing percentage of whom are joining the web every day. We've all heard the stories about the great firewall of China and Chinese censorship; one can only imagine the risks of web-based information disclosure in such an environment, where government censorship and access to logs is often the cost of doing business in the region.

THE MANY FACES OF SEARCH

Search is more than just the general-purpose flavor we've all encountered. Many specialized variants can assist with finding precisely the right information. The same information-disclosure risks apply with these more specific search engines, just in a narrower range of possibilities. Risk is cumulative, when a single company offers many specialized search services in addition to general-purpose search, as is often the case when a large search company attempts to leverage its foundational experience with search technologies to offer compelling new products and services. Google commonly employs this approach. Table 4-6 outlines Google's alternative search services[23] and example information-disclosure risks.

Table 4-6   Some of the Many Search Services Google Offers

Search Service	URL	Example Information Disclosure Risk
Answers[24]	http://answers.google.com/answers/	Specific questions user needs answered.
Accessible[25]	http://labs.google.com/accessible/	User may be visually impaired.
Apple	http://www.google.com/mac.html	User may be an Apple enthusiast.
Base	http://base.google.com/base/	Varied.
Blogs	http://blogsearch.google.com/	Varied.

continues

Table 4-6 Continued

Search Service	URL	Example Information Disclosure Risk
Books	http://books.google.com/	Books user is reading. E-book reader ownership.
BSD	http://www.google.com/bsd	User may be a BSD enthusiast.
Catalogs	http://catalogs.google.com/	Items user is shopping for.
Code	http://www.google.com/codesearch	User may be a programmer. Specific programming projects.
Directory	http://directory.google.com/	Varied.
Finance	http://finance.google.com/finance	User's stock portfolio and investment plans.
Groups[26]	http://groups.google.com/	Specific technical topics. Social network.
Images	http://images.google.com/	Varied.
Linux	http://www.google.com/linux	User may be a Linux enthusiast.
Maps	http://maps.google.com/	Locations of interest.
Microsoft	http://www.google.com/microsoft	Searcher may be a Microsoft software user.
Music	Appears to be retired.[27]	Musical interest.
News	http://news.google.com/	Current event interests.
Patents	http://www.google.com/patents	Organizational research initiatives.
Products[28]	http://www.google.com/products/	Items user is shopping for.
Scholar	http://scholar.google.com/	Research topics.
Trends	http://www.google.com/trends	Trends the user is tracking.
U.S. Government	http://www.google.com/ig/usgov	Government programs the user participates in.
University	http://www.google.com/options/universities.html	Schools you are considering attending or where you are an alumnus.
Video	http://video.google.com/	Varied.
Web	http://www.google.com/	Varied.

Some of these services are offered directly from Google's main page; others are nested several levels deep. Simply Google (see Figure 4-3) combines most Google search functionality on a single page and is useful for quickly exploring Google's alternative search functionality.[29]

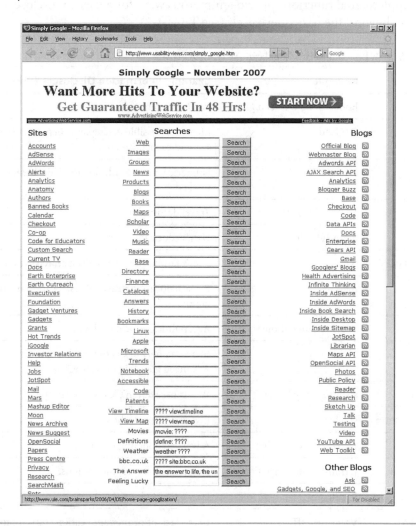

Figure 4-3 Simply Google offers a convenient one-stop location for using many of Google's search variants.

SEARCH BOX AND RELATED APPLICATIONS

Google offers a number of utilities that are accessible via Google's search box,[30] its other interface components, and its search results. Though not technically search, these utilities and supplemental functions provide numerous ways for a user to disclose additional information beyond the base query itself (see Table 4-7).

Table 4-7   Search Box and Related Applications Google Provides

Service	Example	Example Information Disclosure Risk
Books	Books Google Hacking	Reading interests.
Cache	`Cached`	Identifies possible discrepancy between existing web site and cached version.
Calculator	3.14159*5	Numeric values. Math skill level. Problems being worked.
Currency Conversion	10 USD in GBP	Travel destinations.
Definitions	define:google	User's education level.
I'm Feeling Lucky	N/A	User's familiarity with a given search's results.
Map	map:nyc	Physical location, travel plans, location of friends and family.
Movies	Movie:enemy of the state	Age, politics, education level.
Suggest	N/A[31]	Increased network activity raises user's profile. Advanced googling expertise.
Spell Checker	spell:pedagogy [sic]	Words user doesn't know how to spell.[32]
Stock Information	stock:goog	Investment portfolios.
Timeline	Defcon view:timeline	Advanced googling expertise
Translation	[Translate this page]	Languages the user understands.
Travel Information	lax airport	User's travel plans.
View as HTML	`View as HTML`	User's lack of proper application software to view file in native format. Possible removal of sensitive file from web site because HTML versions cached by Google might outlive the original's online presence.
Weather	Weather:NYC	User's location and travel plans.
Web Page Translation	N/A	Languages the user understands.

The importance of these nonsearch applications is that they disclose sensitive information that, when combined with a user's query stream, yield additional information that can reinforce or augment existing user profiles, as well as provide yet another mechanism for uniquely identifying users.

> **NOTE**
>
> The I'm Feeling Lucky option on the Google interface can quickly fingerprint users if they use it to frequently jump to rarely visited sites.

ADVANCED SEARCH OPERATORS AND GOOGLE HACKING

This isn't a book about *Google hacking*, the use of advanced Google queries to locate security vulnerabilities, or an advanced users' guide to googling; however, the use of such queries tells much about the sophistication of users and their intent. Advanced googling techniques[33] include the following:

- **allintitle**—Search for keywords contained in web page titles
- **allinurl**—Search for keywords contained in indexed URLs
- **cache**—View cached copy of web page
- **filetype**—Constrain search to desired file format
- **intitle**—Search for keyword contained in web page titles
- **inurl**—Search for keyword contained in indexed URLs
- **link**—Display pages that link to a given domain
- **n..m**—Search for numeric values in a given range
- **related**—Show web pages similar to a given URL
- **site**—Constrain search to a given domain
- **-keyword**—Exclude pages that contain a keyword
- **""**—Treat keywords as single unit (by surrounding the search in quotation marks)

Google hackers employ these techniques to rapidly identify vulnerabilities in web applications and locate sensitive documents that Googlebot collects and the Google search engine makes available.[34] Google hacking has proven to be immensely effective. See the following list for examples from the Google Hacking Database (http://johnny. ihackstuff.com/ghdb.php):[35]

- `intitle:"Index of..etc" passwd`—Find web servers that list their password file
- `filetype:xls inurl:"email.xls"`—Find Excel spreadsheets containing email in their name
- `intitle:"curriculum vitae" filetype:doc`—Locates Word-formatted vitas (resumés), which often include personal information
- `"not for public release" site:.edu`—Locates documents on the .edu domain containing the phrase "not for public release"
- `filetype:xls username password email`—Locates a spreadsheet containing usernames, passwords, and e-mail addresses

It is important to note that web users are constrained by the limitations of publicly available Google search commands. Google's internal users with access to the full database would have far more access and flexibility by using extremely powerful SQL queries and regular expressions. The publicly accessible face of Google provides only a small fraction of its capabilities to end users when compared to the internal capabilities of Google.

> **NOTE**
>
> Using techniques from the Google Hacking Database, or other web-hacking techniques, allows Google to immediately identify Google hackers. Whether Google is uninterested in tracking this activity is a subject for debate.

It is a common misconception that using the Google cache link in web search results leaves traces only on Google's servers. This is not usually the case. Viewing a Google cache document causes the user's browser to download images and other data objects, such as external JavaScript files, from the original server.[36] However, researchers such as Dartmouth's Anna Shubina and Sean Smith are studying how to use caching to support browsing anonymity.[37]

OTHER SEARCH VECTORS

A web portal isn't the only way to search Google's index. In fact, Google provides many ways to access its search index, as well as leverage its search technology on personal machines and large networks (see Table 4-8). Each of these services extends the reach of Google and raises important information-disclosure concerns.

Table 4-8   Other Search Applications Google Provides

Service	URL	Description
Alerts	http://www.google.com/alerts	E-mail updates on latest Google results
API	http://code.google.com/	Automated access to Google databases
Custom Search Engine	http://www.google.com/coop/cse/	Embedded Google search functionality in web pages
Desktop	http://desktop.google.com/	Google application to index and search the user's personal computer
Enterprise	http://www.google.com/enterprise/	Google appliances for searching and indexing enterprise networks
SMS	http://www.google.com/intl/en_us/ mobile/sms/	Search using text messages

Google Alerts

Google Alerts are e-mail updates based on a user's choice of query. In other words, a user enters a specific search query into Google Alerts and provides an e-mail address. When Google detects new information on the subject, it sends the user an e-mail with links to the new information. Google confirms the e-mail address by sending a confirmation e-mail. Google Alerts provide the powerful capability to monitor topics of interest on the web in near–real time. From a security perspective, Google Alerts is risky. Each user is uniquely identified through an e-mail address, and the act of creating an alert demonstrates a high degree of importance to the user. As the web page suggests (see Figure 4-4), Google Alerts has many handy uses (although I would call them security risks), such as monitoring a developing news story or keeping current on a competitor or industry. It is easy to imagine many alerts are used for automated vanity surfing, companies monitoring Google for news about their secret projects, and virtually any form of sensitive search imaginable. Google Alerts offers an easy-to-use interface for managing alerts *if* the user maintains a registered Google account, creating another fingerprinting opportunity. Finally, it is easy to link groups of users based on the similarity of their search queries (e.g., all users with alerts for breast cancer cures) or the domain name of the e-mail address. I wonder how many ibm.com, cisco.com, or microsoft.com addresses have active Google Alerts?

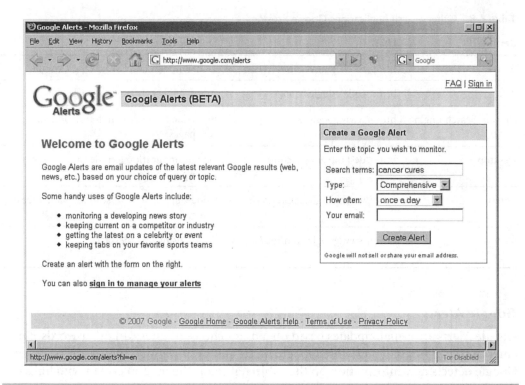

Figure 4-4 Google Alerts informs Google about extremely important topics of interest to a given user and can uniquely identify users through their e-mail addresses.

Google Alerts is one form of automated search—that is, a computer program that conducts searches on behalf of a user. But this isn't the only form of automated search. For example, some browsers automatically search the web if the user mistypes a URL or server name, revealing to the search company the destination desired, which would help a third-party search engine map an internal network, if desired. As another example, Google can instruct browsers to begin downloading content from the top search result, to speed up access, a process called *prefetching*. I believe prefetching presents a significant information-disclosure risk because it takes the decision to visit a site out of the user's hands and can result in cookies being placed in the browser or search queries being passed to these web sites without the user's knowledge and consent.[38]

Another related variation is the Google Toolbar, an application that embeds itself into the Firefox or Internet Explorer browsers and provides ready access to much of Google's search functionality. Such toolbars raise the concern of unintentional Google searches. In the latest version, Toolbar 5, the toolbar can search Google for a URL when the user attempts to navigate to a URL that does not exist. Most versions of the Google Toolbar include one or more unique application numbers that are required for Google Toolbar to work and cannot be disabled. When the Google Toolbar is installed or uninstalled, messages—including the serial number(s)—are sent back to Google. In addition, the Googlebar periodically contacts Google and requests automatic updates to the latest version. Such requests include the serial number(s) embedded in the Toolbar.[39]

The key idea is that "helpful" tools can conduct searches and pass along uniquely identifying information without deliberately asking the user. With hundreds of millions of web users, it is easy to imagine a continuous flow of sensitive sites, internal servers, and serial numbers being passed to online companies through these "helpful" features.

Google API

The original Google Application Programming Interface (API) provided a powerful way to automate search by allowing software applications to access Google services. It used the Simple Object Access Protocol (SOAP) to allow programs to send queries and receive results, which led to a wide range of innovative applications, including automated tools for testing Google hacking queries. The Google API was extremely successful. As a result, the list of Google APIs has grown significantly (see Figure 4-5)[40] and now includes APIs for generating social graphs (http://code.google.com/apis/socialgraph/), interacting with the Google Calendar tool (http://code.google.com/apis/calendar/), dynamically creating charts (http://code.google.com/apis/calendar/), embedding Google Maps in users' web pages (http://code.google.com/apis/maps/), and updating Blogger content (http://code.google.com/apis/blogger/), among many others. APIs allow incredible innovation by tapping into the creativity of developers across the planet who combine their ideas and have access to Google data and applications. Because of the wide range of potential applications, the security risks of Google APIs are hard to quantify, but the general conclusion is that each provides an additional vector for passing semantic information to Google. In addition, developers of applications are immediately obvious as they build and test new projects. Many APIs require user registration to use them to their full extent. The adoption and subsequent use of the projects will reveal to Google the tool's user base over time. Finally, each application will be designed for a specific use (such as Google hacking) and will reveal the community of users surrounding each tool and their general intentions.

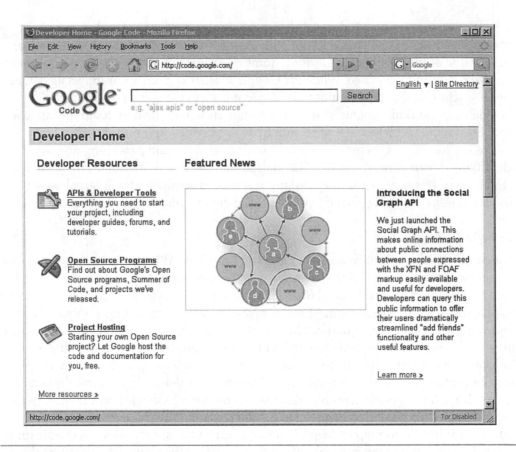

Figure 4-5   Google offers a wide range of powerful APIs that enable applications to tap Google resources; however, Google APIs provide a never-ending source of disclosure vectors.

Site-Based Search

Google enables users to create custom search interfaces for web sites, blogs, special-interest groups, and businesses, as well as nonprofit, government, and educational organizations (see Figure 4-6). A number of risks are associated with creating site-based search. The first is that each custom search engine immediately links the users who access the site. Examples from Google's featured sites page includes sites such as Expanding Your Horizons, a search engine that focuses on nurturing girls interest in science; MacWorld, a search engine for Apple enthusiasts; and GreenMaven, a search engine that focuses on environmentally friendly web sites. Besides disclosing communities of users and their queries, such customized sites could lower the defenses of someone who trusts the parent company but has concerns about Google.

Figure 4-6   Google's Custom Search Engine service allows individual webmasters to embed customized search capability in their websites.

Desktop Search

Desktop search applications bring the power of search engines to individual computers. Google's desktop search works by scanning the files on a user's computer and creating an index accessible by an interface, a process very similar to Google's web search. It also creates cached copies of files. The end result is far more powerful than traditional "find file or folder" tools built into operating systems. In short, Google Desktop enables users to leverage the power of Google search as they seek documents, e-mails, web history, and other data stored on their computer.

A number of security and privacy implications are involved when using Google Desktop or a similar tool.[41] The first is that you are installing a complete application (instead of using the tool remotely via the web); when installing software on your computer, you should have complete trust in the source. (I'll leave how much you trust Google up to you.) Google Desktop includes a unique serial number; if the user chooses Improve Google Desktop, an option provided by the tool, Google Desktop will frequently pass information back to Google. If the user chooses to configure personalization, additional communications can occur. The Google Desktop Privacy Policy enigmatically describes the process of using nonpersonal usage data to provide personalized content: "Google Desktop may send non-personal usage data to Google in order to provide personalized content, such as personalized news."[42] In some cases, the user can choose to store the entire index on Google's servers, allowing search across multiple computers—a powerful idea, but patently bad from the security and privacy perspective. Google also can automatically update Google Desktop[43]; when combined with the unique serial number, this leaves open the (albeit unlikely) possibility that a specific user or group of users can be pushed a specially crafted variant. Google Desktop also gives people who have physical access to the machine a powerful way of finding sensitive information.[44]

Even if a desktop search application behaves entirely as advertised, it can also contain security vulnerabilities. Google Desktop has not been immune to this problem and has had flaws that allowed attackers to view files or run unauthorized software on systems employing Google Desktop.[45, 46]

Ultimately, users should seriously consider the risks associated with Google Desktop before installation. Any application that indexes an entire personal computer or laptop, creates cached copies of data, allows searching across multiple computers, and can communicate with the outside world has the potential to be very dangerous.

Enterprise Search

If you believe that desktop search is very powerful and a security issue, enterprise search is several orders of magnitude more so, on both counts. Enterprise search uses specialized search appliances (i.e., hardware devices) to index the information assets of medium and large companies. Enterprise search appliances enable companies[47] to control the frequency of spidering, the appearance of search results, and which content is indexed. The end result is a powerful search capability tailored to the needs of the organization. Google appliances come in several variants, the Google Mini version for smaller businesses (prices start at around $3,000) and the Google Search Appliance designed for larger customers (prices start at around $30,000) (see Figure 4-7).[48] The Google Mini is capable of searching at least 50,000 documents in more than 200 file formats.[49] The Google Search Appliance can search up to 500,000 documents. The search appliance also supports searching all records in the corporate databases, including Oracle, SQL Server, MySQL, DB2, and Sybase.[50] Enterprise search is a competitive, growing market.[51] Google states that it has more than 9,000 enterprise search customers—I expect that number to rise significantly.[52] Microsoft entered the fray in 2007 with two appliances, the Search Server and Search Server Express.[53]

Enterprise search appliances raise many enterprise-wide security concerns. Hardware appliances are not guaranteed protection against vulnerabilities; in fact, the lack of visibility on the inner workings of the machine could make detecting security issues even more difficult. Google's search appliances have already been found to have serious vulnerabilities.[54] The concern also arises that an index of up to half a million corporate documents places too much information in a centralized location. Finally, hardware devices make it even more difficult to verify that a product is behaving as advertised, and could easily contain hidden functionality.

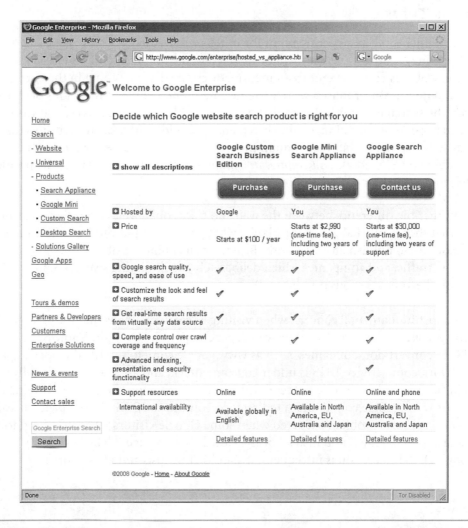

Figure 4-7 Google Enterprise's search appliances enable companies to index hundreds of thousands of internal corporate documents, presenting a prime target for attacks.

RISKS

Beyond the individual forms of search-related information described earlier in the chapter, substantial big-picture risks are associated with search. Accidental, malicious, or legally compelled disclosure is an ever-present risk, but there are many other facets to consider. The following sections cover a number of possibilities.

DRIVING TRAFFIC

Search engines serve as a starting point for much online activity. Users visit a major search engine and trust that they will be directed to the best results. This doesn't have to be the case. Users could be sent to an incorrect web site despite typing in the correct domain name, a compromised search engine could send people to malicious destinations,[55] the search engine's index could be corrupted by web sites successful at gaming the search-ranking algorithm, or the search engine could send users to web sites that appear to be legitimate but that contain malicious content. The following quote from Hellerstein and Stonebraker's *Readings in Database Systems* helps illustrate the problem of steering traffic to incorrect destinations:[56]

> Another big difference between the web and traditional, well-controlled collections is that there is virtually no control over what people can put on the web. Couple this flexibility to publish anything with the enormous influence of search engines to route traffic, and companies which deliberately manipulating search engines for profit become a serious problem.

The most fundamental concern when visiting a search engine is that it might not be the correct site in the first place. The web depends upon the Domain Name System (DNS) to convert domain names, such as www.google.com, to the IP addresses required for network connectivity. DNS is under constant attack, and attackers occasionally succeed in finding and exploiting vulnerabilities. Many users reported just such an incident when the www.google.com domain redirected people to the SoGoSearch page instead.[57] This year, a similar problem occurred when some Google visitors were redirected to the Chinese search engine Baidu instead of the Google search page.[58] The key idea is that although DNS redirection is infrequent, it shouldn't be discounted as a threat.

> **NOTE**
>
> Because of DNS vulnerabilities, it is possible to type in a correct domain name but be directed to a malicious web site.

Finding Incorrect Things (or the Perils of SEO)

Placement in search results is extremely valuable: The better the placement, the more web surfers will be driven to a given web site, resulting in online purchases and advertising revenues. Because search placement is such a valuable commodity, web site owners seek to acquire the best placement possible, often through legitimate high-quality content on their sites, but other times by seeking weaknesses in search result algorithms (sometimes called "chasing the algorithm")[59] to boost their placement, a process called *search engine optimization* (SEO).

It is difficult to estimate the value of a given placement in search results, but Google's Adwords Traffic Estimator (https://adwords.google.com/select/TrafficEstimatorSandbox) provides useful insight. Google capitalizes on the value of search result placement through its AdWords program (https://adwords.google.com), which guarantees advertising placement adjacent to top search results. For example, as of this writing, Google values mesothelioma, the form of cancer usually attributed to asbestos exposure (and the source of potential workplace lawsuits), at between $18.99 and $28.48 *per click.* Although Google carefully places advertisements to avoid confusion with search results,[60] some search engines use similar auctions to sell top positions in the search results themselves. Pioneered by companies such as Overture (initially called Goto), which Yahoo! later acquired, pay-per-placement search is another key technique for monetizing (and corrupting) web search.

Legal cases surrounding search rankings also point to the value of placement, such as the following examples:

- An online business owner threatened to sue a blogger because the blogger's Google placement was better.[61]
- An attorney threatened to sue a search engine because an online ranking system for lawyers gave him unsatisfactory placement.[62]
- An online company sued Google because Google allegedly downgraded its search-result ranking without reason or warning and resulted in a 70% fall in the site's audience and an 80% decline in revenue.[63]
- A Chinese professor threatened to sue Google and Yahoo! for removing all results with his name in China.[64]

These cases also raise two important points: A change in ranking can have a cataclysmic impact on an online business, and it is possible for search engines to "erase" the online presence of companies and individuals from that search engine. In the case of Google, such erasure would make these people essentially invisible on the web.

Google's policy is to let its confidential search algorithms determine the exact placement of sites within search results, in an attempt to provide unbiased results. However, because of the intense competition for top placement, there is significant risk in assuming that search results are accurate. In other words, search result listings might not operate in the user's best interest and might not return the highest-quality results. Google's key ranking algorithm, PageRank,[65] is based upon links contained within web pages.[66] The following is a description from the patent:[67]

> Method for node ranking in a linked database: A method assigns importance ranks to nodes in a linked database, such as any database of documents containing citations, the world wide web, or any other hypermedia database. The rank assigned to a document is calculated from the ranks of documents citing it. In addition, the rank of a document is calculated from a constant representing the probability that a browser through the database will randomly jump to the document. The method is particularly useful in enhancing the performance of search engine results for hypermedia databases, such as the world wide web, whose documents have a large variation in quality.[68]

Because links are a key component of Google's ranking algorithm, SEO marketers and others seeking to bias search results place spurious links in an attempt to skew rankings in their favor. One such approach is link farming, groups of web sites that link to each other in hopes of raising member sites' search result rankings.[69] The gaming of search results to direct searchers to the wrong destination web sites is an ongoing game of one-upmanship that will likely never cease. Google orders its results based on an ever-changing set of characteristics;[70] PageRank is just one component. Those seeking to sway results will continually adapt to these changes and seek countermeasures for their own benefit.

FINDING MALICIOUS THINGS

The power of search engines did not go unnoticed by malicious software developers, who use search engines to find virus, worm, and Trojan horse examples; bring victims to compromised or spoofed web sites; and help find potential targets. The key idea is that Google and other search companies can be exploited to aid malware and malware creators in many possible ways, including the following:

- Google hackers can use Google to find vulnerable systems.
- Some malware uses Google to find potential victims.

- Authors can use search to find malware examples.
- Search engines can send unwary visitors to compromised web sites.
- Advertising networks can send victims to malicious web sites through sponsored search results.[71, 72]
- Malware on an end user's computer can log online activities.
- Google could inadvertently host malicious code on its sites, such as Blogger.[73, 74]

The "Advanced Search Operators and Google Hacking" section already covered Google hacking, but malware developers have started creating malicious software that contains built-in functionality to conduct automated searches to better target victims. You can think of this form of attack as automated Google hacking. The following are two examples:

- A variant of the MyDoom worm used Google, Yahoo!, AltaVista, and Lycos search to locate e-mail addresses of potential targets, slowing the search engines to a crawl and facilitating its rapid spread.[75, 76]
- A variant of the Santy worm used Google to select potential victims by identifying a specific flaw in phpBB, a popular web page forum application.

Unless protected using password access or some other security mechanism, source code (and executable files) for malicious software is indexed by webbots along with most everything else publicly available on the web. More important, search engines can inadvertently drive traffic to compromised web sites that contain software that attacks users' computers through their browsers. SEO techniques are most commonly employed by companies seeking better placement in search results, but there is an interesting variation: Attackers create web pages designed to attract potential victims and use browser vulnerabilities to infect their systems with malware. Malicious sites appearing in search results isn't an uncommon occurrence; one recent study found that 1 in 25 search results was risky.[77] Google conducted a survey of 4.5 million pages and discovered that, one in 10, some 450,000 contained malicious code that could infect a user's PC.[78] Many of these risky sites were put in place for phishing scams designed to trick users into disclosing sensitive information. Phishers have traditionally used e-mail, but there is an increasing trend toward setting up web sites and letting Google bring them traffic. The sites benefit from the trust users place in Google's search results and Google's algorithmic approach to search results ordering.[79]

> **NOTE**
>
> The prevalence of malware-infected sites being available on Google led one leading security researcher, H. D. Moore, to create a malware search engine that locates live malware samples through Google queries (http://metasploit.com/research/misc/mwsearch/index.html).[80]

It is important to note that recently Google has taken admirable steps toward identifying and removing malware-infested sites from its index[81] and has removed tens of thousands of such sites.[82, 83]

THE SEARCH QUERIES OF OTHERS

Even if a user carefully avoids searching on personal data, there is no guarantee that others will not do so. The driving force is simple: The more precise a given query is, the better the search results are. Because of this, the search queries of web searchers often include additional information about other individuals and organizations. Perhaps the best example is that of the witness protection program. It is easy to imagine government employees or confidants (such as close family members) searching Google to see if anyone has caught on to the new identity. A search query such as "<old name> <new name> witness protection program" would immediately tie the old and new identities together.[84] Another example is that of a proprietary corporate project and cover name. Employees could easily search on both, providing a link between the sensitive cover name and a description of the project. Although these are somewhat extreme examples, the key idea is that the search queries of others provide unconstrained flows of information to online search, flows that are largely out of the control of the targeted individual or organization. Without having access to the logs of Google and the billions of queries it contains,[85] it is difficult to know the exact extent of the problem, but because web browsers pass along search queries to destination web sites, examining their web server logs provides useful insight. The following are examples from my www.rumint.org site:

- conti traffic
- conti secure
- author:conti intitle:a comprehensive undergraduate information assurance program
- greg conti security visualization
- conti computer systems

- gregory conti
- conti@acm.org googling considered harmful
- conti g. why computer scientists should attend hacker conferences
- gregory conti visualization
- conti computer
- gregory conti framework
- conti personal
- conti presentation
- conti lens presentation
- google considered harmful conti
- gregori conti
- gregory conti translation
- greg conti "network attack visualization" defcon 2004

Each query contains at least my last name and an additional piece of information provided by some third-party web surfer. These pieces of information reveal my e-mail address, research papers I've written, research topics I'm exploring, and the fact that I presented at DEFCON in 2004. In addition, web surfers reinforce the connection between their search and a given web site by using their human intelligence to select and click a link to a destination they believe is correct. The destination web site could then be mined to discover additional information.

Beyond this example, the ability of a web surfer to inject arbitrary pairings presents additional threats. One possible attack is one in which the attacker creates a false association by searching for terms that are not facts. For example, the attacker could use a web crawler to spoof the referer field to include fake associations in spoofed search attempts. Some sites leak their access logs, so Googlebot could collect this information and put it in the Google index. In another possible attack, a surfer uses a search engine to search for false pairings and chooses a target web site far down in the list of search results, strengthening the pairing and artificially raising the site in the search results listing.

(SELF) CENSORSHIP

Consider two important facets of censorship regarding search: self-censorship of one's own activities and censorship by the search company, at its own whim or at the behest of a governmental organization.

When a user self-censors activities because of security concerns, such as logs being turned over to a government or because he believes the searches will be used in an inappropriate way, he constrains the power that search offers. This is a very bad state—when users are conditioned to limit their exploration of knowledge, mankind will suffer. However, as outlined in Chapter 1, "Googling," web users have good cause for concern.[86] Admittedly, in today's environment, there might be no other truly effective solution than never entering a query in the first place, but as we look to the future, I believe better solutions are possible.

> **NOTE**
>
> Contrary to earlier utopian theories of the Internet, it takes very little effort for governments to cause certain information simply to vanish for a huge number of people.[87]

Censorship at the online company or governmental level is equally concerning. Perhaps the best example is Google's censorship in China[88, 89], where Google launched versions of its search and news web sites that censored content objectionable to Chinese officials.[90, 91] As a testament to the malleability of corporate policies, Google pulled its "Google does not censor results for any search term" statement from the Google Help Center.[92] Initially, Sergey Brin attempted to defend the position on grounds of greater access, that, despite censorship, the situation would be better for Chinese Web users.[93] Google later admitted compromising its principles in China.[94] Perhaps we will see improvements: Sergey Brin, one of Google's cofounders, admitted, "On a business level, that decision to censor … was a net negative."[95, 96] The key idea here is that censorship is alive and well in the twenty-first century, particularly with regard to the web and our own thoughts.[97]

FINGERPRINTING

Chapter 3, "Footprints, Fingerprints, and Connections," went into detail regarding profiling and fingerprinting users, organizations, and disparate groups based on their online disclosures. Search queries alone can allow profiling, fingerprinting, and linking, but can also be combined with other forms of semantic, application-level (including browser header fields, cookies, and log-on information), and network information to facilitate more rapid profile growth, stronger linking with other users, and unique identification of users themselves. Even if search companies completely destroy their logs, search queries might have been eavesdropped on as they transited the network, logged by destination web sites, and stored in browser-based caches on individual machines. In other words, they could persist in other locations beyond their lifespan on the servers of search companies.

> **NOTE**
>
> Because search engines include queries embedded in the referer field, it is possible for destination web sites to begin fingerprinting users based on their queries.

I believe that search queries precisely identify users over time, particularly when combined with related activities such as their use of advanced googling functions, what words they misspell, when and how frequently they search, the length of their queries, how they reformulate their queries as they use the search engine, and what links they click on in search result listings.[98] Even if a small group of users, such as a family, share the same IP address and browser, that family will exhibit unique characteristics, as will individual members of the family. In this case, I believe it is possible to tease apart the searches of each family member with a reasonable degree of accuracy. Users opting to personalize their search interface and results dramatically increase the likelihood of fingerprinting because the search engine must identify them upon each subsequent return to the site, probably by using a cookie or registered user account.

Unique identification can occur rapidly if the user repeatedly generates a set of queries that differs from other users', which I believe is often the case. Each search query allows the user to be profiled based on interests and clustered with similar users. Over time, and with enough queries, each user will exhibit characteristics, or features, to increase their uniqueness with higher degrees of precision, all without the need of cookies or registered user accounts to aid in the process.

SUMMARY

At its heart, Google is a search tool with many powerful options; unfortunately, the sum of all an individual's or organization's queries reveals a great deal of sensitive information. The elegance and simplicity of Google's search interface is an enticing gateway for Google's suite of search-oriented tools. Hundreds of millions of people use them to search for information regarding all aspects of their daily lives. Counterintuitively,

Google's interface could be too usable, tempting people to reveal information without concern, including extremely sensitive, personal, and, ultimately, uniquely identifying information. Advanced search features and search box–oriented tools accelerate the process. The end result is that even the most innocuous searches become sensitive when aggregated over time. Each search query provides a new piece of information that converges on a profile of each user and eventually provides the means to uniquely identify him, even if he starts over on a new machine and different network.

Beyond sensitive search, search engines possess many inherent risks: sending people to incorrect or malicious destinations, perhaps targeting specific users, or providing a way for third parties to reveal sensitive information about other people, groups, and companies. The end result is that users are handing over their intellectual freedom by allowing search engines to send them only to destinations that companies such as Google feel are acceptable. At the same time, users are giving away so many details of their lives that users are subject to the whims of those who run the search engines. Google has the power to make people disappear from the electronic universe, shape public perception, and blackmail world leaders and individual citizens. This power is ceded by each use of online free tools. Search is the core of Google's power and the key way we relinquish control over our destinies, one query at a time.

ENDNOTES

1. Aaron Wall, "History of Search Engines: From 1945 to Google 2007," SearchEngineHistory.com. www.searchenginehistory.com/#early-engines, last accessed 29 January 2008.

2. Clive Thompson, "Your Outboard Brain Knows All," *Wired Magazine* 15.10, 25 September 2007. www.wired.com/techbiz/people/magazine/15-10/st_thompson, last accessed 18 February 2008.

3. Have you ever searched from a computer that you don't control, such as those in a school, library, or other public place?

4. In 2006, Google was awarded a patent for the design of its search results page; see http://news.zdnet.com/2100-9588_22-6143586.html.

5. "Stalking User #98280," AOL Stalker. www.aolstalker.com/98280.html, last accessed 30 January 2008.

6. Note that any webmaster whose web site was visited could easily review the logs and identify the IP address of the visitor and his or her queries.

7. "Stalking User #1963201," AOL Stalker. www.aolstalker.com/1963201.html, last accessed 30 January 2008.

8. "Stalking User #789586," AOL Stalker. www.aolstalker.com/789586.html, last accessed 31 January 2008.

9. The address is available at www.yelp.com/biz/nandos-bakery-hanover.

10. "Stalking User #2649647," AOL Stalker. www.aolstalker.com/2649647.html, last accessed 31 January 2008.

11. "Stalking User #3558174," AOL Stalker. www.aolstalker.com/3558174.html, last accessed 31 January 2008.

12. One source, GoshMe (www.goshme.com/), suggests that more than half a million specialized search engines exist.

13. Danny Sullivan, "Nielsen NetRatings Search Engine Rankings," Search Engine Watch, 22 August 2006. http://searchenginewatch.com/showPage.html?page=2156451, last accessed 29 January 2008.

14. Percentages represent the portion of the U.S. market.

15. Instead of rediscovering fire, most of these categories and sites are drawing from Charles Knight's excellent *Top 100 Alternative Search Engines* work. See the list at www.readwriteweb.com/archives/top_100_alternative_search_engines.php.

16. I find Ms. Dewey interesting for about 15 seconds and annoying afterward. Your mileage may vary.

17. As an added bonus, with metasearch engines, you leave your queries in the logs of many online companies at one time.

18. Ben Tanner, "European Companies Develop Search Engine to Rival Google," *Digital Media Asia,* 16 January 2006. www.digitalmediaasia.com/default.asp?ArticleID= 12650, last accessed 29 January 2008.

19. "Bill Clinton Helps Launch Search Engine," MSNBC/Associated Press, 7 December 2004. www.msnbc.msn.com/id/6666890/, last accessed 29 December 2008.

20. David Barboza, "The Rise of Baidu (That's Chinese for Google)," *The New York Times,* 17 September 2006. www.nytimes.com/2006/09/17/business/yourmoney/ 17baidu.html, last accessed 29 January 2008.

21. Pete Barlas, "Baidu Is Beating Back Google, Winning Fans Among Analysts," *Investor's Business Daily,* 31 August 2007. www.rawstory.com/news/mochila/Baidu_ Is_Beating_Back_Google_Winnin_11082007.html, last accessed 29 January 2008.

22. Ryan Paul, "Mozilla Expands in China, Inks Agreement with Baidu," Ars Technica, 7 December 2007. http://arstechnica.com/news.ars/post/20071207-mozilla-expands-in-china-inks-agreement-with-baidu.html, last accessed 30 December 2008.

23. The services Google offers are a constantly shifting target; consider this list just a snapshot in time. However, after reading this chapter, you should be able to analyze the impact of future changes in the list.

24. Google Answers is no longer accepting questions, but previous answers are available via search or browsing.

25. Malicious and nonmalicious webmasters can cause their pages to rank better in Google's Accessible Search by adhering to the W3C's Web Content Accessibility Guidelines—see http://it.slashdot.org/article.pl?sid=06/07/20/1242210. Note that this capability is declared a feature, not a bug.

26. Google Groups is used to search a Usenet posting archive containing more than 700 million messages, but it also allows users to create their own groups.

27. Google Music does not appear to have a direct portal, but legacy applications can still access it via a specially crafted URL, such as http://google.com/musicsearch?q= metallica.

28. Note that the Froogle.com domain now maps to Google Products.

29. Of course, this type of service adds another attack vector because users are sending their information through a third-party site that can also collect information and, therefore, must be trusted as well.

30. You can find a comprehensive list at www.google.com/help/features.html.

31. Google Suggest (www.google.com/webhp?complete=1&hl=en) is an attempt at an autocomplete function for searches—that is, it suggests possible search queries based on each letter the user enters. These suggestions from Google to the user's browser result in increased network traffic and can disclose information before the Search button is clicked.

32. I wonder if Google could generate a reasonably accurate SAT or GRE verbal score based on a user's misspellings and search queries.

33. An excellent, comprehensive guide to advanced Google queries is available at www.googleguide.com/. Google offers a graphical user interface for employing some of these operators at www.google.com/advanced_search?hl=en, and limited textual descriptions at www.google.com/help/operators.html.

34. Google also maintains a tongue-in-cheek Google interface in *leet speak,* the jargon used by some elements in the hacking community (www.google.com/intl/xx-hacker/). I expect that many of the individuals who have visited this site have at least a passing interest in security and hacking.

35. The list goes on and on. For more information on Google hacking, I recommend reading Johnny Long's excellent *Google Hacking for Penetration Testers,* Volume 2 (Syngress, 2007), to learn more about protecting yourself. The book is available in (at least) English, Spanish, German, Korean, French, and Slovak.

36. "Don't Use the Google Cache as Anonymous Surf," The Virtual Chase, 8 December 2004. www.virtualchase.com/ask_answer/google_cache.html, last accessed 6 July 2008.

37. Anna Shubina and Sean Smith, "Using Caching for Browsing Anonymity," *ACM SIGecom Exchanges* 4.2 (Summer 2003): 11–20. Available online at www.cs.dartmouth.edu/~sws/pubs/ss03.pdf.

38. "Results Prefetching," Google Help Center, 2008. www.google.com/help/features.html#prefetch, last accessed 17 February 2008.

39. "Google Toolbar Privacy Notice," Google Help Center, 4 December 2007. www.google.com/support/firefox/bin/static.py?page=privacy.html&, last accessed 17 February 2008.

40. See http://code.google.com/ for the complete list.

41. For a comparison of desktop search applications, see www.goebelgroup.com/desktopmatrix.htm.

42. "Google Desktop—Privacy Policy," Google, 21 September 2007. http://desktop.google.com/privacypolicy.html, last accessed 17 February 2008.

43. Reports have circulated that Google Desktop's autoupdate might not function properly. Regardless, the issue of targeted autoupdating and updating large user bases with vulnerable software still exists as a general security problem.

44. Of course, anyone with physical access to the machine could just take (or copy) the hard drive, or even the entire machine, and seek out sensitive information at their leisure. Google Desktop just makes it easier.

45. Robert McMillan, "Second Google Desktop Attack Reported," *InfoWorld,* 23 February 2007. www.infoworld.com/article/07/02/23/HNsecondgoogledesktopattack_1.html, last accessed 17 February 2007.

46. John Markoff, "Rice University Computer Scientists Find a Flaw in Google's New Desktop Search Program," *The New York Times,* 20 December 2004. www.nytimes.com/2004/12/20/technology/20flaw.html?_r=1&oref=slogin, last accessed 17 February 2008.

47. For a comparison of search appliances from a variety of vendors, see www.goebelgroup.com/sam.htm.

48. Elinor Mills, "Google Unveils Enterprise Search Appliance," CNET News, 18 April 2006. www.news.com/2100-1038_3-6062593.html, last accessed 17 February 2008.

49. "Google—Mini 2.0 Review," *IT Reviews,* 28 November 2006. www.itreviews.co.uk/hardware/h1104.htm, last accessed 17 February 2008.

50. "Google Search Appliance—Universal Search for Your Business," Google/You Tube, 19 November 2007. www.youtube.com/watch?v=7NrO4Llyr0Y, last accessed 17 February 2008.

51. Microsoft has gone as far as to offer financial incentives to companies, to help increase search market share. See www.infoworld.com/article/07/03/15/HNmspayforsearchdata_1.html.

52. "Google Enterprise: Intranet Search Solutions," Google, 2008. www.google.com/enterprise/intranet_search.html, last accessed 17 February 2008.

53. J. Nicholas Hoover, "Microsoft Enters Enterprise Search Market," *Information Week,* 6 November 2007. www.informationweek.com/news/showArticle.jhtml?articleID=202802673, last accessed 17 November 2008.

54. "Google Appliances Vulnerable," *Security Focus,* 23 November 2005. www.securityfocus.com/brief/59, last accessed 17 February 2008.

55. Although it's unlikely, a search company could itself be evil and direct traffic to a malicious destination. Worsening the situation, it is technically possibly to provide correct service for most users and target individuals or even entire countries. For an illustration of some of the possibilities associated with county-specific skewing, see http://blog.searchenginewatch.com/blog/050517-135157.

56. Joseph M. Hellerstein and Michael Stonebraker, *Readings in Database Systems* (Boston: MIT Press, 2005).

57. Peter Rojas, "Google Down? Google Hacked/Not Hacked!" *Engadget,* 7 May 2005. www.engadget.com/2005/05/07/google-down-google-hacked-not-hacked/, last accessed 8 May 2008.

58. Duncan Riley, "Cyberwar: China Declares War on Western Search Sites," *TechCrunch,* 18 October 2007. www.techcrunch.com/2007/10/18/cyberwar-china-declares-war-on-western-search-sites/, last accessed 8 February 2008.

59. Brian Quinton, "BigDaddy Means Big Changes at Google," *DIRECT Magazine*, 25 January 2006. http://directmag.com/searchline/1-25-06-Google-BigDaddy/index. html, last accessed 10 February 2008.

60. A number of usability analysts argue that some users confuse Google's textual advertisements with actual search results.

61. "Bizarre Google Request," DeanHunt.com Blog, 9 December 2006. http://deanhunt. com/bizzare-google-request/, last accessed 10 February 2008.

62. John Cook, "Avvo's Attorney Rating System Draws Fire," John Cook's Venture Blog, seattlepi.com, 8 June 2007. http://blog.seattlepi.nwsource.com/venture/archives/ 116417.asp#extended, last accessed 10 February 2008.

63. "KinderStart Sues Google over Lower Page Ranking," *USA Today*, 19 March 2006. www.usatoday.com/tech/news/2006-03-19-google-kinderstart_x.htm?POE= TECISVA, last accessed 11 June 2008.

64. "Chinese Professor Suing Google and Yahoo for Making Him Disappear from Chinese Search," *Techdirt*, 8 February 2008. http://techdirt.com/articles/ 20080207/142142203.shtml, last accessed 10 February 2008.

65. Google's PageRank algorithm is elegant and powerful. U.K. researchers believe that PageRank can even help search out hospital superbugs—see www.newscientist. com/channel/health/dn13142-google-tool-could-search-out-hospital-superbugs. html?feedId=online-news_rss20.

66. Another approach is to use the "wisdom of crowds" to help verify the quality of search results—that is, by using click-through tracking to determine what results users click on and raise the ranking of the site accordingly for future searchers.

67. You can find an official article describing how Google collects and ranks results at www.google.com/librariancenter/articles/0512_01.html.

68. "United States Patent: 6285999," United States Patent and Trademark Office, 9 January 1998. http://patft.uspto.gov/netacgi/nph-Parser?Sect1=PTO1&Sect2= HITOFF&d=PALL&p=1&u=%2Fnetahtml%2FPTO%2Fsrchnum.htm&r=1&f=G&l =50&s1=6285999.PN.&OS=PN/6285999&RS=PN/6285999, last accessed 10 February 2008.

69. See the Link Farm article on Wikipedia for an interesting overview, http://en. wikipedia.org/wiki/Link_farm.

70. Saul Hansell, "Google Keeps Tweaking Its Search Engine," *The New York Times*, 3 June 2007. www.nytimes.com/2007/06/03/business/yourmoney/ 03google.html?_r=1&oref=slogin, last accessed 10 February 2008.

71. StankDawg, "Hacking Google AdWords," Defcon, 13, July 2005.

72. Malicious advertising is particularly worrying because a would-be attacker can purchase advertising like any other legitimate advertiser.

73. "Malicious Code Appears on Blogger.com," Fortinet, 14 March 2007. www.fortiguardcenter.com/advisory/FGA-2007-04.html, last accessed 10 February 2008.

74. In this instance, Google would presumably know the IP addresses of potentially infected victims.

75. David Becker and Michael Kanellos, "MyDoom Variant Slams Mailboxes, Search Engineers," CNET News, 26 July 2004. www.news.com/MyDoom-variant-slams-mailboxes%2C-search-engines/2100-7349_3-5283940.html?tag=st.nl, last accessed 5 February 2008.

76. Richard Shim and Michael Kanellos, "Google, Other Engines Hit by Worm Variant," CNET News, 26 July 2008. www.news.com/Google%2C-other-engines-hit-by-worm-variant/2100-1023_3-5283750.html?tag=st.nl

77. Jeremy Reimer, "Study Shows One in Twenty-Five Search Results Are Risky," Ars Technica, 13 December 2006. http://arstechnica.com/news.ars/post/20061213-8417.html, last accessed 11 March 2008.

78. "Google Searches Web's Dark Side," BBC News, 11 May 2007. http://news.bbc.co.uk/2/hi/technology/6645895.stm, last accessed 11 February 2008.

79. Munir Kotadia, "Phishers Lie in Wait for Google Searchers," CNET News, 1 December 2004. www.news.com/Phishers-lie-in-wait-for-Google-searchers/2100-7349_3-5473663.html, last accessed 11 February 2008.

80. Ryan Naraine, "Metasploit Creator Releases Malware Search Engine," *eWeek*, 17 July 2006. www.eweek.com/c/a/Security/Metasploit-Creator-Releases-Malware-Search-Engine/, last accessed 10 February 2008.

81. Ian Fette, "Help Us Fill the Gaps!" Google Online Security Blog, 29 November 2007. http://googleonlinesecurity.blogspot.com/2007/11/help-us-fill-in-gaps.html, last accessed 10 February 2008.

82. "Google Purges Thousands of Malware Sites," Slashdot, 29 November 2007. http://it.slashdot.org/article.pl?no_d2=1&sid=07/11/29/1318257, last accessed 10 February 2008.

83. See also Google's Safe Browsing extension for Firefox, www.google.com/tools/firefox/safebrowsing/, and web site blacklist, http://sb.google.com/safebrowsing/update?version=goog-black-url:1:1.

84. Also recall my example in Chapter 1 of revealing a hacker's real-word identity and pseudonym in a similar fashion.

85. I'm assuming here that Google's pledge to anonymize the IP addresses in search query logs does not extend to deleting search queries.

86. There is a great article on self-censorship available on Wikipedia, at http://en. wikipedia.org/wiki/Self-censorship.

87. Seth Finkelstein, "Google Censorship—How It Works," Blog Posting, 10 March 2003. http://sethf.com/anticensorware/general/google-censorship.php, last accessed 6 February 2008.

88. Researcher Seth Finkelstein has an interesting analysis of country-by-country Google censorship—see http://sethf.com/infothought/blog/archives/001014.html (#6).

89. The human-rights organization Human Rights Watch also censured Yahoo! and Microsoft for their censorship in China, stating that Yahoo! was most aggressive in its censorship activities. See www.businessweek.com/globalbiz/content/aug2006/gb20060810_220695.htm?campaign_id=rss_null.

90. Elinor Mills, "Google Bows to Chinese Censorship," ZDNET, 25 January 2006. http://news.zdnet.co.uk/internet/0,1000000097,39248911,00.htm, last accessed 6 February 2008.

91. Of course, censorship isn't limited to search queries, but is used across the entire range of communication and thought. See www.itnews.com.au/News/62931, chinese-internet-censorship-machine-revealed.aspx for an example of censorship at the nation-state level, and see www.worldnetdaily.com/news/article.asp? ARTICLE_ID=50323 for information on Google's censorship of news.

92. Lester Haines, "Google Pulls 'We Don't Censor' Statement," *The Register,* 27 January 2006. www.theregister.co.uk/2006/01/27/google_doesnt_censor/, last accessed 6 February 2008.

93. "Google Founder Defends China Portal," CNNMoney, 25 January 2006. http://money.cnn.com/2006/01/25/news/international/davos_fortune/, last accessed 6 February 2008.

94. "Google Admits Compromising Principles in China," Slashdot, 7 June 2006. http://it.slashdot.org/article.pl?sid=06/06/07/1430205, last accessed 6 February 2006.

95. "Google Admits China Censorship Was Damaging," Slashdot, 27 January 2007. http://yro.slashdot.org/article.pl?no_d2=1&sid=07/01/27/1839238, last accessed 6 February 2008.

96. Jane Martinson, "China Censorship Damaged Us, Google Founders Admit," *Guardian Unlimited,* 27 January 2007. www.guardian.co.uk/technology/2007/jan/27/news.newmedia, last accessed 6 August 2008.

97. "Censorship 'Changes Face of Net,'" BBC News, 6 June 2007. http://news.bbc.co.uk/2/hi/technology/6724531.stm, last accessed 6 February 2008.

98. Normally, search queries are sent in their entirety to search engines when the user clicks the submit button, but tools such as Google Suggest leave open the possibility of fingerprinting users based on their character-by-character typing characteristics.

5 Communications

Communication is the killer app driving the growth of the Internet. Whether it is via text, audio, images, file transfers, or video, humans and computers demand this most basic need. This chapter addresses threats associated with person-to-person communication by examining the services Google provides, including Gmail, Google Groups, Google Talk, and Google's mobile-based applications. Every one of us, including our parents and grandparents, has used these or similar offerings by other online companies, and the major information-disclosure threats associated with communication impact us all. Machine processors can understand and mine the content of the messages we send, in any electronic format, as evidenced by context-specific advertising often included when using these tools. This opens the door to not just disclosure, but the real possibility that Google can extract the information it desires from the millions of messages that pass through or reside on its servers.

E-MAIL

E-mail is one of the oldest communication mechanisms on networked computers: Ray Tomlinson invented it in its current form in 1972.[1] Beginning with simple text e-mails exchanged between professional colleagues, e-mail is now a major rival with the telephone as the dominant communication channel. More than 30 billion e-mails are sent each day—some estimates say that as much as 95% is spam, but most experts agree that at least 40% is spam.[2, 3, 4] Free web-based e-mail has been extremely successful; such services include Hotmail (now, technically, Windows Live Hotmail), Gmail, Yahoo! Mail, and Hushmail.

E-mail messages are used for almost every conceivable purpose: announcing a birth, making travel arrangements, sending sensitive documents, sending Google Alerts, providing billing receipts, conducting research … the list is as long as your imagination. The ubiquitous nature of e-mail also has led to its casual use. Recent e-discovery rules have surprised many users who assume e-mails will remain private, when, in fact, they won't.[5]

Google's Gmail has been particularly successful since its inception in 2004. For the first three years of its existence, Gmail was by invitation only. During this period, particularly in the first year, a Gmail address was a sign of elite standing in the technology community. I recall numerous discussions on hacker mailing lists of members actively seeking an invitation. I found this surprising because invitations provide Google with an immediate link between a given user and his or her social network; Gmail also requires a registered user account, which facilitates the linking of each user's e-mails with his or her searches and other online activities (see Figure 5-1).

Figure 5-1   Gmail is an extremely popular free e-mail system that offers mobile phone access and spam filtering, and encourages users to send and store large files. It requires a registered user account to access.

The knowledge of social networks, easily derived from communication records, is tremendously powerful. For example, users place a great deal of trust in e-mails that purportedly come from friends, colleagues, and family members.[6] In the case of e-mail, only a small percentage of users (somewhere between 2% and 20%) click links in spam e-mails sent from random e-mail addresses. Researchers from MIT and Indiana University discovered that 16% of the college students they tested clicked on such links (including revealing their user ID and password to an untrusted server); however, when the e-mail purportedly came from an acquaintance, 72% of participants did so.[7] Gmail, and other e-mail services, have access to detailed social network information on their users. Although I don't believe Google will be sending spam messages anytime soon, we should be uncomfortable placing valuable social network information into the hands of a third party.[8]

Google doesn't provide statistics on the number of Gmail users, but many estimates place this in the range of 50 million accounts.[9] The system is popular because it is free and powerful. As of this writing, Gmail provides spam filtering, e-mail search, integrated chat using the Google Talk network, access via mobile phones, the capability to label messages, and more than 6GB of free storage, "so you'll never need to delete another message."[10, 11] Gmail was made available to a number of countries around the world, including Europe, Africa, Japan, Australia, and Russia, before it became available globally in 2007.

> **WARNING**
>
> The popularity of a given service increases the chance that it will be a target for attackers. For example, the developer of G-Archiver (www.garchiver.com/), a tool designed to back up Gmail accounts to a user's local machine, allegedly harvested copies of Gmail user account credentials.[12]

These same advantages also raise security and privacy concerns. Gmail is nominally free but is subsidized using text ads and related links that are relatively unobtrusive to users. By analyzing the e-mails and inserting context-specific advertising, Google has discovered a profitable business model; however, this also means that a computer read the e-mail and understood it well enough to provide related advertising.[13] For example, Google is able to prevent ads from "running next to messages about catastrophic events or tragedies," which provides evidence that they can detect such events.[14]

With access to 50 million users and billions of e-mails, the capability to machine-process e-mail for content is particularly concerning. Just because Google has a stated policy that humans do not read Gmail messages to target advertising, it doesn't mean they do not have the capability to do so. Gmail's privacy document provides the following useful insights regarding e-mail:

> All e-mail services scan your e-mail. They do this routinely to provide such popular features as spam filtering, virus detection, search, spellchecking, forwarding, auto-responding, flagging urgent messages, converting incoming e-mail into cell phone text messages, automatic saving and sorting into folders, converting text URLs to clickable links, and reading messages to the blind.[15]

The document goes on to say that these features are widely accepted, trusted, and used by hundreds of millions of people every day. I couldn't agree more—the fact that such activity is widely accepted and trusted provided an impetus for writing this book. The policy also contains other useful insights, shown in Table 5-1.

Table 5-1 The Gmail Privacy Policy Contains Useful Insights into How Your Information Will Be Used

Excerpt	Analysis
"You need a Google Account to access Gmail. Google asks for some personal information when you create a Google Account, including your alternate contact information and a password, which is used to protect your account from unauthorized access. A Google Account allows you to access many of our services that require registration."	A Gmail account uniquely identifies you as you use Gmail and other Google services. Alternate contact information provides a way to link activities with other non-Google accounts.
"Gmail stores, processes, and maintains your messages, contact lists, and other data related to your account in order to provide the service to you." "Google maintains and processes your Gmail account and its contents to provide the Gmail service to you and to improve our services. The Gmail service includes relevant advertising and related links based on the IP address, content of messages, and other information related to your use of Gmail."	Google stores copies of your messages and contact lists on its servers and uses your IP address to assist in creating effective advertising.

Excerpt	Analysis
"When you use Gmail, Google's servers automatically record certain information about your use of Gmail. Similar to other web services, Google records information such as account activity (including storage usage, number of log-ins), data displayed or clicked on (including UI elements, ads, links), and other log information (including browser type, IP-address, date and time of access, cookie ID, and referrer URL)."	Google can record log-in activity, IP addresses, cookie IDs, referer URLs, and user interface elements or advertisements the user clicks.
"Residual copies of deleted messages and accounts may take up to 60 days to be deleted from our active servers and may remain in our offline backup systems."	Deletion of e-mail from "offline" backup systems isn't guaranteed.
"We do not sell, rent, or otherwise share your personal information with any third parties except in the limited circumstances described in the Google Privacy Policy, such as when we believe we are required to do so by law."	Google can provide personal information to its subsidiaries, affiliated companies, and trusted businesses or persons for the purpose of processing personal information on their behalf. Information transfer can occur if Google becomes involved in a merger or acquisition. Information can also be shared as required to satisfy any applicable law, regulation, legal process, or enforceable government request.[16]
"Google's computers process the information in your messages for various purposes, including formatting and displaying the information to you, delivering advertisements and related links, preventing unsolicited bulk e-mail (spam), backing up your messages, and other purposes relating to offering you Gmail."	The e-mails will be examined by Google's machine processors.

More worrisome is that whereas users can control who hosts their e-mail service and whom they send mail to, they have no control over who their e-mail recipients forward e-mail to. E-mail forwarding to Gmail accounts increases Google's access to a larger swath of global e-mail traffic. The key idea here is that many e-mails will eventually touch a Google-controlled server, where they will be logged and stored. In 2006, Google began offering "Gmail for Your Domain," which allows organizations to host their e-mail using Google's service.[17] This service enables companies to use their e-mail domains, such as ceo@*company.com*, which masks the fact that the destination is Gmail, so senders will likely be unaware that their messages, and those of the entire company, are presumably visible to Google. An additional risk of outsourcing organizational e-mail to Google is that, if the Internet connection goes down, the entire service goes down. Normally, locally hosted e-mail (such as with a college campus) would still function. Locally hosted e-mail gives system administrators greater control over backing up and logging. Other important points must be considered as well: Sensitive internal e-mails will transit Google's servers, and the service could change from free to cost prohibitive very quickly, creating disruption.[18] The bottom line is that any organization that is considering using such a service needs to weigh these concerns against the cost of running the service internally.

Gmail also provides easy-to-use mechanism for users to label, search, and filter their e-mail (see Figure 5-2). Such tools make locating specific messages easier. However, labeled information allows e-mails to be data-mined more effectively. For example, in the figure, this user has marked e-mails with labels such as Work, Family, Friends, and Vacation, allowing for more intelligent machine analysis on a system-wide scale.[19]

Figure 5-2   Gmail allows a user to label, search, and filter e-mail. However, these practices make potential Google data mining easier.

E-mail, in general, faces many security issues. Users configure out-of-office messages to autorespond to incoming e-mails when they are traveling or on vacation. Normally, only one such message is sent to a given party, providing only limited information. But the e-mail-hosting company has far more detail.[20] It is aware immediately when a user turns on the feature, presumably when he or she is departing, and is also aware of when the user returns and turns off the service. If the user checks mail in the interim, the company knows probable travel destinations of the user. E-mail services also strip some attachments from incoming e-mail, primarily for security reasons, or bounce e-mails if they contain unsupported formats or too-large files.[21] Both of these circumstances disclose the entire e-mail and its attachments to the destination e-mail provider; even if the e-mail is subsequently bounced or stripped of attachments, the data can still be captured and logged. Many users use free e-mail services for temporary or throwaway e-mail addresses, perhaps due to the sensitive communications they contain.[22] The online mail provider can monitor the activity on an account, and, I argue, detect "interesting" e-mail accounts from the sea of accounts created for uninteresting uses. When I say "interesting," I mean used in a way that you wouldn't want publicly known. An interesting variant is using the e-mail service as a dead drop. For example, terrorists have used Hotmail to store draft e-mails that can then be read by any number of interested parties.[23] HTML e-mail has also been exploited using web bugs. Web bugs are graphics that are embedded in HTML e-mail but that are served by another machine designed to log the IP address of the recipient when the user views his or her mail.[24]

Online e-mail services are not immune to vulnerabilities. One recent attack against the Yahoo! e-mail service used JavaScript to infect a user's computer by merely viewing the e-mail.[25] Gmail had a similar vulnerability that allowed an attacker to forward e-mails to an arbitrary e-mail account when a logged-in Gmail user clicked on a malicious link.[26] Gmail was also shown to be vulnerable to an attack in which a wireless eavesdropper could sniff session cookies and access the target's Gmail account.[27]

Large amounts of online storage represent another risk. Gmail currently offers about 6GB. This encourages users to never delete messages—not that "deleting" messages can ever be guaranteed when using an e-mail service. More important, large amounts of storage encourage users to use the service to store documents they would not normally store online, increasing disclosure. Corporate policies and the law provide some protection regarding the right of privacy for stored electronic communication,[28] but pragmatic readers should assume that a subpoena granting access to your stored documents is a real possibility.

Spam is the scourge of the Internet, and online companies provide effective mechanisms for detecting and filtering spam. For example, I once received a spam e-mail coming from someone claiming to be "Barbara Blexler." We can note several important things regarding this SPAM e-mail, and e-mail in general. In this case, the return address was *Barbara_Blexler@noipmail.com*. Noipmail.com is a free anonymous e-mail service that deliberately removes the user's IP address from the header; many more legitimate e-mail services include the user's IP address in the header. More important, spam filtering implies machine processing of the contents of e-mails—in other words, a machine reads each e-mail, looking for specific content. Machine processing of e-mails is a common practice that is also used to create context sensitive advertising and to detect malicious attachments.[29] The capability to perform automated processing of e-mail contents is a significant security threat that could be abused. See the "Computer Analysis of Communications" section later in the chapter for more information.

Typographic errors represent another significant leakage threat. The owner of a given domain name can capture all e-mails sent to it. Attackers exploit this fact by purchasing common misspellings and variations of popular domain names and harvesting mistyped e-mails.[30, 31] Similarly, even if it isn't wasn't possible to acquire an appropriate domain name—say, for a large e-mail service—an attacker could create an e-mail address on the same service (i.e., with the same domain component) and a common variant or misspelling of the local component (e.g. jimmy@fictitiousdomain.com vs. jimmi@ fictitiousdomain.com). Interesting variants of typographic errors are mailing lists and *group aliases.*

I once worked in an organization in which a pair of employees shared off-color jokes via e-mail. Inadvertently, one of these individuals typed only a partial e-mail address, which turned out to be a group alias for about one third of the organization. He then proceeded to send out the e-mail to thousands of his coworkers, a patently bad career move. Similar problems arise when mail clients helpfully autocomplete e-mail addresses based on names in the user's address book. I've received numerous accidental e-mails this way, and I suspect you have, too. A similar problem occurs when a user accidentally hits Reply to All instead of just Reply. Again, the wrong individuals receive the message, often with embarrassing consequences.

To address these problems, researchers from MIT developed an innovative technique that searches Google Images[32] and displays pictures of the people the e-mail is being sent to in the user's e-mail client. Although their system is an excellent technique to keep e-mails from being sent to unintended destinations, it has the unfortunate side effect of alerting Google to the user's e-mail recipients.[33, 34]

As a means of summarizing the information-disclosure issues surrounding Gmail and other online services, let's examine some of Gmail's marketing copy (see Table 5-2).[35]

Table 5-2   Comparing Online Marketing of Gmail and Potential Security and Privacy Implications

Stated Uses and Advantages of Google Groups	Possible Information Disclosure and Risks
"More friends are more fun. Gmail welcomes your AIM friends—now you can talk to your AIM friends using an integrated chat list right inside Gmail."	Your entire AIM social network and your AIM communications.
"Group chat—chat with multiple people without multiple windows."	More chat communications.
"Free IMAP—sync your inbox across devices instantly and automatically. Whether you read or write your e-mail on your phone or on your desktop, changes you make to Gmail will be seen from anywhere you access your inbox. Another way to use Gmail on your iPhone is through the browser."	Location and type of all your computing platforms.
"Increased attachment limit—20 MB! Now you can start share more of those home videos, large presentations, and files you just can't seem to get smaller. We have doubled the allowable attachment size to 20 MB to make your Gmail space even more useful."	Sensitive files.
"It's a Gmail party and everyone is invited! You can still invite your friends to enjoy Gmail's spam protection, 5GB free storage, and other great features."	A party, indeed—recruit your friends to disclose information.
"Get mail from other accounts. Now Gmail can check for the mail you receive at your other e-mail accounts. You can retrieve your mail (new and old) from up to five other e-mail accounts and have them all in Gmail. Then you can even create a customized 'From:' address, which lets you send messages from Gmail but have them look like they were sent from another one of your e-mail accounts."	Credentials from other e-mail accounts and all your messages. This fools others into thinking that the e-mails were not sent via Gmail.
"Get Gmail on your mobile phone—download it once, and start accessing Gmail on your phone with just a click or two."	Cell phone number.
"Voicemail—Your friends can leave you a voicemail using Google Talk. The voice message is sent to your Gmail account as an audio file that you can download or play right from your inbox."	Audio captures of your voice and that of your friends.
"Vacation auto-responder—set an auto-response so that if you're lying on a beach or taking a train across Siberia, your friends will know you won't be checking your e-mail."	The fact that you are on vacation, the frequency of your vacations, and any details contained in the autoresponse message.

continues

Table 5-2   Continued

Stated Uses and Advantages of Google Groups	Possible Information Disclosure and Risks
"Contact groups—one of our most-requested features is finally here! Now you can send messages to a group instead of having to pick out the individual addresses every time."	Logical groupings of your contacts.
"Virus scanning is here! For your protection, Gmail now automatically scans for viruses every time you open or send a message with an attachment."	Low-level analysis of your files and communications.
"Auto-save—Saves to drafts as you're composing. Never lose a half-written e-mail again."	Half-written messages before you've clicked Send.
"Customized 'From:' addresses—customize the address on your outgoing messages to display another one of your addresses instead."	Prevents recipients from easily seeing the true source of e-mail.
"Import Contacts—move all your contacts from Yahoo! Mail, Outlook, and others to Gmail in just a few clicks."	Contacts across many other communication streams.
"Signature options—From the settings page, create a signature that's automatically added to the end of all your outgoing messages."	Title, cell phone, work phone, employer, and real-world address.

Consider the power you cede to e-mail service providers. A malicious e-mail provider could do the following:

- Copy and forward any e-mail to any recipient
- Create filters to block (or allow) any e-mail from any sender[36]
- Alter the contents of any e-mail, even after arrival
- Add malicious attachments on inbound or outbound messages
- Delete any e-mail
- Send spoofed e-mail, perhaps imitating your writing style
- Allow third parties to read or modify any message
- Maintain undisclosed archives of messages

Virtually every online interaction of any magnitude generates an e-mail message, opening the opportunity to create precise social networks that can be tied together with Google accounts, cookies, e-mail addresses, IP addresses, and even the contents of the messages themselves. These networks and information flows can then be combined with other online activity, such as searches, resulting in a staggering threat.

VOICE, VIDEO, AND INSTANT MESSAGING

Voice communication has long been the mainstay of interpersonal communication. The technology of choice has been the Public Switched Telephone Network (PSTN) provided by the local telephone company. With the advent of high-speed Internet, there is an increasing trend away from the PSTN to voice over the Internet, generically called Voice over IP (VoIP).[37] Popular VoIP services include Skype (www.skype.com/), Vonage (www.vonage.com/), Apple's iChat (www.apple.com/macosx/features/ichat.html), and Gizmo (http://gizmo5.com/pc/products/desktop/). Instant messaging is another communication technique that allows users to send and receive real-time textual messages across the Internet. Popular services include AOL's Instant Messenger (http://dashboard.aim.com/aim), Yahoo! Messenger (http://messenger.yahoo.com/), and MSN Messenger (http://messenger.yahoo.com/). However, the boundaries between voice and text communication tools, as well as video, are no longer clear. Services are combining voice, text, and video into one-stop communication tools. Google Talk (www.google.com/talk/) is a great example that offers integrated instant messaging and PC-to-PC voice calls, as well as file transfers and e-mail notifications. Gmail not only offers e-mail, but also offers one click chat via the Google Talk network.[38, 39] Similarly, Google Talk includes a "chatback" service that enables web sites, including bloggers, to embed a "badge" that allows visitors to easily contact the author via Google Talk. Unfortunately, the web page source uses an HTML iframe tag to dynamically retrieve the tag from Google, as seen in the following snippet:[40]

```
<iframe src="http://www.google.com/talk
/service/badge/Show?tk=z01q6amlqlak...
```

This code allows Google to log every visitor to the website, as discussed in Chapter 3, "Footprints, Fingerprints, and Connections." The issue of including third-party content embedded in web pages as a means of tracking users represents a serious threat because it reaches far beyond just user's activity on Google's servers to virtually any web site he or she visits. Chapter 7, "Advertising and Embedded Content," covers in more detail the issue of using third-party content to broadly track user surfing.

In many ways, the information-disclosure risks associated with voice, video, and instant messaging mirror those of e-mail, including disclosure of messages and contacts.[41] The capability to attach files to outgoing messages, and the related risk of information leakage, is also common in many systems. Inbound files pose an additional risk because they may contain sensitive information disclosed by a third party or even malicious content.[42] A related risk is URLs contained in messages that point the user to malicious web sites, a threat commonly found in e-mail.

Voice, video, and instant-messaging services all use the Internet as a communication medium, which raises the specter of eavesdropping anywhere along the communication path. As a strength, Google Talk can encrypt its communications between the client and Google, but not all such systems do so.[43, 44] Although this encryption may protect against an eavesdropping threat, it does not mask the communications from Google itself.

Early synchronous communication services began life as closed networks—in other words, only members of a given instant-messenger network could communicate with like users.[45] In an attempt to increase adoption and market share, this position is changing. Most modern services allow communication to their competitor's networks. Although this trend is great for enhanced communication, it greatly magnifies the range and scope of information disclosure. For example, Google Talk allows communication directly with users of Earthlink, Gizmo Project, Tiscali, and Medai Ring, among others.[46, 47]

Google Talk use requires a registered Google account, which facilitates tying together other forms of Google activity more comprehensively than cookies or IP addresses. The Google Talk privacy policy states that Google may record information about usage, including time of communications, the contacts communicated with, as well as "information displayed or clicked on in the Google Talk interface." It further states that Google deletes activity information associated with accounts on a regular basis, but does not specify exactly what information is deleted. The policy does note that the information collected, including presumably the content of the communication themselves, "may remain on backup media" after the user has requested deletion.[48] This assumption is strengthened by the fact that Google removed "Google Talk does not archive the contents of your text or voice communications on Google's servers, and we will not archive such contents on our servers without your express permission" from its earlier Google Talk Privacy Notice.[49]

Voice and video messaging disclose far more information than traditional e-mail, including extensive samples of the user's voice and image, as well as background noise and images of the user's operating environment.[50] However, distinct differences do exist. Voice, video, and instant messaging are synchronous services that allow for immediate interaction between the two communicating parties. This strength can be a weakness because synchronous communications let an attacker test whether a given message recipient is physically at the computer. Google Talk worsens the situation by reporting whether a user is present based on workstation use—for example, after ten minutes of inactivity, Google Talk informs the user's contacts that the machine is idle.[51, 52] Typical users might dislike this feature because it promotes constant interruptions. For the security conscious, broadcasting the fact that you are away from your computer is also a bad idea.[53]

Security and privacy issues aside, the future of voice, video, and textual instant messaging is bright and getting brighter. The possibility of low-cost, or free, communications is a powerful draw, particularly in underdeveloped regions without the overhead of legacy communications infrastructure, and in the increasing number of areas offering high-speed wired and wireless Internet connectivity. Unfortunately, the increased user base just magnifies the information disclosure risks. Virtually every computing platform offers these capabilities—even the Sony PlayStation Portable.[54]

GROUPS

Although e-mail, voice, and instant messaging are often used in one-to-one communications, the Internet has long fostered the forming of groups to discuss issues ranging from the mundane to the life-threatening. Usenet, an extremely large distributed discussion forum, was the most popular of these services. In 2001, Google acquired a comprehensive Usenet archive (greater than 500 million individual messages) and made it available as part of its Google Groups service (see Figure 5-3).[55] Google Groups has proved to be extremely popular and now includes more than 10,000 groups and 800 million postings, each of which is easily searchable using Google's search technology. According to Google, its Usenet collection is "the most complete collection of Usenet articles ever assembled and a fascinating first-hand historical account."[56]

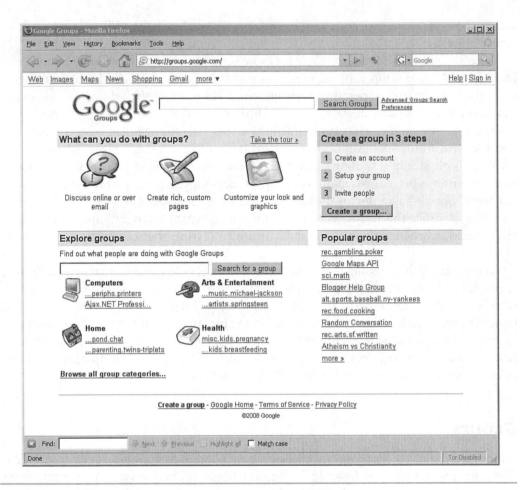

Figure 5-3   Google Groups now offers access to more than 10,000 groups.

Many downsides exist to using (and searching) Google Groups. First, users need a Google account to create a group or post comments, which, in turn, requires an e-mail address and password, providing a unique identifier for each user.[57] Second, by using the service, users disclose their e-mail address in each posting. Addresses are obfuscated in the postings themselves, but the full e-mail address can be retrieved with a simple test to identify human users (see Figure 5-4).

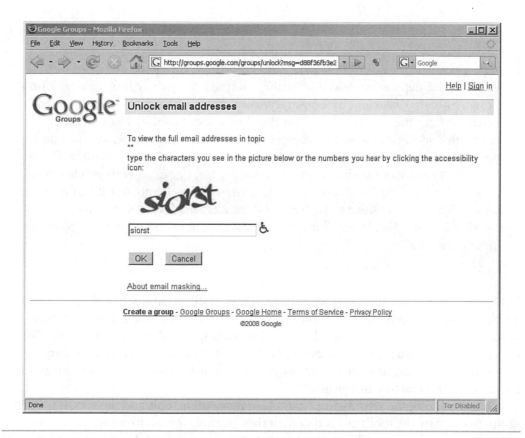

Figure 5-4 When searching or browsing using Google Groups, Google blocks access to users' e-mail addresses until the user completes a simple test.

Google blocks machine-readable e-mail addresses to prevent harvesting by webbots. Although this is a good idea, it doesn't prevent Google itself from data-mining the full addresses, along with the contents of each related message. Furthermore, spammers have successfully been able to bypass Google's CAPTCHA via automated bots and human laborers. When users create a group, they are linking themselves with some topic, as does each person that posts a message to the group, and even those that search for and view messages.

Beyond the social networks and unique identifiers disclosed by Google Groups usage, those "fascinating first-hand historical accounts" can contain extremely sensitive information about each of the authors, such as someone personally dealing with cancer or supporting someone who has it. The following is an example from the alt.support.cancer newsgroup, retrieved using Google Groups search:[58]

> **NOTE**
>
> Hello every one, I am very new here, I am very desperate right now. if any one can suggest me if there is any resource, facility, clinical trials or anything can be done for her. She was diagnosed by ovarian cancer three years back, she had developed ascites at that time, actually thats how they knew about cancer. Than total hysterectomy was done followed by chemo. She has been on chemo since, last year in Nov last session of chemo was done, and again very severe ascites ws there. Dr are saying that cancer cell are in the surrounding tissues, not in any organ. They took the sample of her fluid and did some sensitivity test for chemo, bur it turn out that these cells are not sensitive to any drug. I dont want to give up, she is my best friend, she is just 45, please tell me what to do??? I dont want to give up.. please I am begging you !

Google Groups members may also create public profiles that disclose their name, geographical location, and other information. Google servers store the contents of their postings and any files a user uploads, such as photographs, videos, and programs. The Google Groups privacy policy states that Google collects and maintains information about the groups that users join or manage, as well as lists of other members, including those merely invited to join a group.[59]

When analyzing the security implications of new online tools and services, it is often useful to evaluate the tool's marketing materials carefully for security concerns. Table 5-3, lists quotes from an online tour of Google Groups and related security implications.[60]

Table 5-3   Comparing Online Marketing of the Google Groups Service with Potential Security and Privacy Implications

Stated Uses and Advantages of Google Groups	Possible Information Disclosure
"Search or browse for information—want to learn about car repair? Have a question about computers? You can find a discussion or a group about it."	Information you are seeking. This category is very similar to the disclosure risks described in Chapter 4, "Search."
"Join a group—find something you like? Join straight away, or request an invitation if it's a private group."	Information you are seeking. Links between yourself and a given topic and group of people. Whether you know the members or are a stranger.

Stated Uses and Advantages of Google Groups	Possible Information Disclosure
"Make a group of your own—why not start your own group? For your family, your softball team … creating a group is easy—just pick a name and start inviting members."	Links between yourself and virtually any group of people sharing a common interest. By inviting members, you are stating there is such a link between you and other individuals, even if the invited member does not want to make the relationship known.
"Join in on what others are talking about—from within a group, you can reply to a message that someone else posted, or post a message or question of your own."	Specific views and questions on the topic. Frequency of communications and possibly the relationship you have with other users.
"Start a discussion in your own group—create a group of your own so you can get in touch and keep in touch with your group's members."	A topic you feel passionate enough about to form a group. Possibly a leadership role. Links between yourself and others who share this common interest.
"Discuss online or over e-mail—you can choose whether you want to read and post messages online, or to just use your current e-mail account to read and respond."	Topics of interest and relationships with other users. Contents of the messages themselves. E-mail address, including header information and/or IP address and browser header fields.
"Upload files—group members can upload files and share their work with others in the group."	Files, including potential authorship and readership. File metadata.
"Learn more about each other—each member of a group can create a profile, including a picture and quote. Now you can share information about yourself, and even find other members using search."	Whatever you decide to disclose in the profile, possibly including a photograph. Specific users you are looking for and other users searching for you.

MOBILE

Mobile devices, such as cell phones and personal digital assistants (PDAs), are a special category. They are a computing platform, as with any personal computer or laptop, but they possess unique communication characteristics. The primary function of cell phones is to provide voice communications across the telephone network. PDAs are designed to handle day-to-day information requirements such as address books, notes, to-do lists, checkbook-balancing tools, and web browsing. Both types of devices are constrained by limited battery life, small screens, small keypads, and limited processing power. However, there is a trend to combine the information-centric functionality of a PDA with the communication-centric capability of a cell phone. The results are extremely popular hybrid devices such as the BlackBerry and iPhone,[61] but there is a general trend for all cell phones to include web access (especially search[62]), e-mail, text messaging, and instant messaging. With global cell phone penetration reaching 50% (3.3 billion subscriber accounts)[63] of the world population (6.6 billion people), online companies are providing services targeted at mobile device users, such as location-based search and specially crafted web page designs. The web-surfing capabilities of mobile devices, combined with their information storage, provides an evolving, highly relevant threat vector. The following sections highlight two important concerns surrounding mobile device interaction with online companies: text messaging for access to online resources and mobile and location-based search.

ONE PHONE NUMBER FOR LIFE

In July 2007, Google announced its acquisition of GrandCentral Communications, a company that allows users to integrate all their current phone numbers and voice mail into a single GrandCentral account.[64] Using the service, users are given a single phone number that will ring their various home, work, and cell phones. The service allows users to configure which phone calls are routed to which phones and provides a number of advanced features, including the capability to screen callers, hear why someone is calling before taking the call, record calls on the fly and access recordings online, and receive voice mail via e-mail or text messaging.[65]

The service requires a GrandCentral account, which, in turn, requires alternate contact information and, in some cases, credit card and billing information. GrandCentral's servers automatically record usage activity, including calling-party numbers, forwarding numbers, time and date of calls, and duration of calls, as well as the user's IP address, browser type, date and time of web accesses, cookie ID, and referer URLs. Similar to Google's other policies, users can choose to delete their voice mail messages and recorded conversations, but the data could remain in Google's offline backup systems.[66]

If you've made it this far into the book, GrandCentral should raise some immediate security and privacy concerns. The idea of "one phone number for life" is compelling, but doing so allows Google to immediately link each user's set of formerly distinct phone numbers into a single profile, along with extensive data about the user's communications and, in some cases, recordings of the phone calls themselves. Recall also that Google maintains extensive phone number databases that can be used to turn phone numbers into real-world identities. Use of optional features raises additional concerns. For example, forwarding voice mail to e-mail addresses links the users' phones with their electronic mail accounts. In addition, GrandCentral ties users to a single phone number that they will be unwilling to change after the number is distributed to the user's social network, because of the inconvenience of broadly distributing new numbers. You should notice a trend across many "compelling" services: Users are drawn to these services for convenience, but they trade their independence and personal data in return.

TEXT MESSAGING

Though technically an independent communication technology, text messaging is most commonly seen on cell phones as an alterative to voice. *Text messaging* is an informal term for the exchange of small messages (up to 160 characters) using the Short Message Service (SMS) protocol. SMS is used most commonly between humans, but increasingly, humans use SMS to communicate with automated systems. Google offers a variety of compelling SMS-based services, including names, addresses, and phone numbers of businesses; movie showtimes; sports scores and schedules; driving directions; and weather reports[67] that can be accessed by sending a message to 46645 ("GOOGL" on the cell phone's keypad).[68] (See Figure 5-5.)

Google's SMS privacy policy is short and enigmatic.[69]

When you send a message to Google SMS, we log an encrypted version of the incoming phone number, the wireless carrier associated with the number, and the date and time of the transaction. We use this data to analyze the message traffic in order to operate, develop, and improve our services. Google will never rent or sell your phone number to any third party, nor will we use your phone number to initiate a call or SMS message to you without your permission. Your wireless carrier and other service providers also collect data about your SMS usage, and their practices are governed by their own privacy policies.

Figure 5-5 Google's text-messaging interface offers cell phone users the capability to tap Google's resources and disclose sensitive information.

From this, we can see that Google has access to the incoming phone number, the date and time of the communication, and the wireless carrier associated with the phone number. The information is logged in an encrypted form; presumably, Google has the capability to decrypt its log.[70] Left unstated is whether Google also logs the content of the message itself.

MOBILE AND LOCATION-BASED SEARCH

Mobile devices provide another computing platform from which to generate search queries. Two common interfaces are web browsers built into cell phones and Short Message Service (SMS) text messages, discussed in the preceding section. Location-based search is often used in conjunction with mobile search in order to provide location-dependent search results. For example, Google Maps[71] provides the capability to search for items in a given geographic area. Figure 5-6 shows the results for searching on "pizza" and "white house."[72]

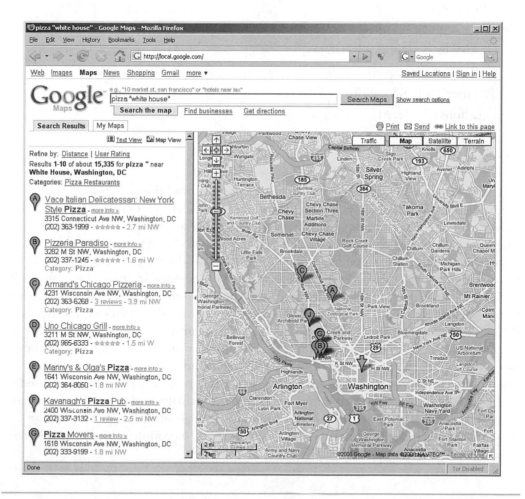

Figure 5-6 Location-based search allows a user to combine traditional search with geographic locations. Mobile devices will surely be the platform of choice for location-based search in the future.

Chapter 3 outlined many of the fingerprinting concerns associated with traditional search. Mobile communication platforms raise a host of new fingerprinting and information-disclosure concerns. According to Google Mobile's privacy policy, which is much more descriptive than its SMS privacy policy, Google may collect the following information:[73]

- Phone number
- Device and hardware identification numbers
- Device type
- Request type
- Carrier-used identification data
- Content of the request
- The user's actual location
- Locations of interest
- Personalization information and interests
- Voice samples[74]

The information disclosed via mobile search parallels traditional web-based search, but particularly concerning is the capability to uniquely identify mobile devices based on a phone number and hardware identification number. IP addresses of computers will change over time, but phone numbers change infrequently. In fact, users generally tend to avoid changing phone numbers so that their friends and family can still reach them. In addition, users change hardware devices, such as cell phones, infrequently; thus, their device-specific identification numbers will also change rarely. Therefore, it is straightforward to create unique profiles of users. The profiles can include search queries and also the user's location and voice recordings. In addition, communications from most popular mobile devices will transit the mobile service provider's network (each of these intermediate networks has its own set of security concerns and privacy policies) before reaching the servers of an online company. I expect that mobile search will grow rapidly in the upcoming years, increasing the impact of these security disclosures. For example, Google recently struck a deal with Nokia to provide Google on several of its popular phone models. These phones will be used in more than 100 countries and in 42 different languages.[75]

RISKS

Communication is at the heart of information disclosure. E-mail, instant messaging, and text messaging, as well as voice and video chat, are all communication vectors that provide the opportunity to share information with individuals, employers, groups, *and* online companies. The preceding sections in this chapter outlined specific issues associated with each type of communication technology. However, important risks are associated with communications in general.

DEPENDENCY

Communication requires an address to reach a desired party, such as a phone number, e-mail address, or instant messaging handle. Despite the concerns that addresses allow unique fingerprinting, users rarely change their addresses and service providers. Why? Addresses are sticky; changing an address requires users to inform the people (and perhaps computers) they want to remain in contact with of the change. This is a hassle that most people want to avoid.[76] As a result, people often resist changing their addresses. As an example, people felt so strongly about keeping their cell phone numbers that the Federal Communications Commission stepped in and regulated telephone number portability.[77] As an added risk, the act of communicating a change of address often takes place via the old communication channel, such as using an old e-mail account to inform friends and family of a new address. This discloses the link between the two addresses to eavesdroppers and the company providing the e-mail service.

Dependency is more than changing addresses, however. By relying on a third party for communication, users and organizations become dependent on that party's policies, procedures, and whims. This risk is even more significant when large organizations transition en mass from local resources to those of a third party, such as when using Google's Gmail for Your Domain service. Overnight, a free service can become prohibitively expensive to use. Back-up procedures can vary wildly, and users could find that their data was lost or will be costly to restore, with little recourse. Corporate strategies are just as subject to change, at great risk to their user base. For example, Google threatened to shut down the German version of its Gmail service, ironically, to resist invasive surveil-lance legislation.[78] The problem of dependency has no clear-cut solution, although one potential approach is to purchase your own domain name and possibly host your own e-mail (and other servers).

TRAFFIC ANALYSIS

Traffic analysis is the study of *message externals,* information about the communication, but not the contents of the message, to deduce useful information. Message externals can include sender, recipient, size of the message, power used, communications rate, time sent, timing of communication, location, and medium used, among others. Most forms of communication, including those described in this chapter, are susceptible to traffic analysis, even if the message itself is encrypted. Traffic analysis is extremely powerful and can reveal social networks, command and control structures, routine and emergency sit-uations, and sometimes suspicion of eavesdropping and negotiations.

ARCHIVING OF MESSAGES

To enhance user productivity, back up organizational communications, meet regulatory requirements, or enhance system performance, many online companies and other busi-nesses archive e-mail and other forms of communication employed by their user bases. Google's Gmail and Google Talk privacy policies are circumspect regarding the archiving of messages. Google Talk's policy states, "On a regular basis, [Google] deletes activity information associated with your account,"[79] but it provides little other information. Gmail's policy states the following (emphasis mine):[80]

> You may organize or delete your messages through your Gmail account or terminate your account through the Google Account section of Gmail settings. Such deletions or terminations will take immediate effect in your account view. Residual copies of deleted messages and accounts may take up to 60 days to be deleted from our active servers *and may remain in our offline backup systems.*

Gmail's policy brings up two important points: The user's view of stored information might differ from what is actually stored on Google's servers, and deleted e-mail may remain in Google's offline backup systems for an indeterminate period of time after the user attempts to delete the information. Such long-term existence of e-mails or other messages presents a high-value target for lawyers,[81] governments, and attackers. Stories of leaked, stolen, or legally acquired messaging archives are frequently in the news, such as the class-action lawsuit against Microsoft for its Vista Capable marketing scheme, which compelled Microsoft to produce sensitive internal e-mails.[82] In the United States, one congressman was forced to resign over inappropriate text messages.[83]

EAVESDROPPING, FILTERING, AND ALTERATION

Unless protected with powerful cryptographic mechanisms, communications across the Internet are subject to eavesdropping and alteration. Even when protected by appropriate technology, communications can be filtered[84] by network and online service providers. Chapter 2, "Information Flows and Leakage," described these threats in detail, but they are particularly concerning regarding communications. The most popular communication protocols began life as unencrypted applications; any eavesdropper with access to the network's path of communication could easily see and alter the communications. Network providers and online companies exploit this visibility to delete inbound spam messages with varying degrees of success. The legacy of unencrypted communication protocols, such as e-mail and instant messaging, combined with difficult-to-use encryption techniques,[85, 86] has resulted in many communication systems being unencrypted to this day. Combined with an increasing trend of network providers to alter, slow, or deny certain types of traffic across their networks, this means that this is a significant risk for virtually all information flows, both inbound and outbound.[87, 88]

LANGUAGE TRANSLATION DISCLOSURES

In most cases, human communication occurs between parties using the same language. When languages differ, the parties typically turn to human language translators. However, human translators are becoming increasingly obsolete, due to the recent progress in machine translation. Perhaps best known by AltaVista's Babel Fish Translation service (http://babelfish.altavista.com/), machine translation is becoming more accurate, is gaining acceptance, and is becoming directly integrated into the communication applications themselves. For example, Google made its machine translation service directly accessible from within Gmail and Google Talk.[89] The service is accessed by communicating with a "chat-bot," which translates the text and sends the translation as a response. The service is also available via the Google Talk client for BlackBerry.[90] Google offers a free translation service as part of its search result listings. Although on-demand free translation is a powerful aid to facilitate communications, relying on a third party instead of a standalone application on one's personal computer discloses the contents of the communication to a potentially untrusted third party.

CONVERGENCE

No longer are e-mail, instant messaging, and other communication technologies independent applications. There is now a trend toward consolidated communication portals, in which many forms of communication are integrated into one application. Consolidating these applications creates a single point of failure: One exploited vulnerability or successful subpoena will reveal all of a user's communications. We've already discussed the blending of Google Talk and Gmail. Another example is the humble address book. Comcast recently advertised a universal address book with the following announcement:

> Great news! Now there's a simple solution for accessing all of your contact and calendar information. Comcast's Universal Address Book makes it easy to house all of your contacts and calendars—from your e-mail accounts, computer, and cell phone—in one convienient [sic] spot. Straightforward, simple to use and accessible from just about anywhere, this is the only address book you'll ever need.[91]

With this convenience comes significant risk. A centralized address book consolidates professional and personal addresses for the user's social network. In addition, the Comcast service allows a user to send birthday announcements (revealing birthdays of acquaintances) and send electronic cards, which informs the online provider of special events and the strength of links in the user's social graph. In addition, the tool encourages users to house all their e-mail accounts, including those on both their personal computer and their cell phone, in one "convenient" spot, creating a high-payoff target for those with legal or illegal access. Because the service is accessible from "just about anywhere," an opportunity for remote attack exists. Related advertising states that the universal address book is "the only address book you'll ever need—for life!" This encourages the user to use, and rely upon, the service for many years; if compromised, the service would reveal, not just the user's current social network, but his or her evolving network over long periods of time. Finally, the service advertises that users will never lose their information because the contacts are backed up online. This implies historical archives that could be subpoenaed or that an attacker could potentially compromise. In 2007, Gmail's contact listed proved vulnerable to disclosure to malicious web sites.[92]

WARNING

Many users inadvertently type the user ID and password of another online service as they attempt to log on to their e-mail. Your only protection is the faith you have in the company not to exploit the disclosure.

EMERGENT SOCIAL NETWORKS

Contrasted with web-based activities such as search or mapping, communications via e-mail, text, voice, and video are more easily tied to individual users. Each message requires addressing information in order to be delivered—addresses that are often unique to users, such as e-mail addresses and phone numbers. Phone numbers imply billing records that can be tracked back to users' real-world identities. E-mail addresses are typically used by individuals, not shared among groups of users. Many online e-mail services include the X-Originating-IP field in each e-mail's header information, which allows the e-mail to be directly tied to the IP address of the browser used to create and send the e-mail.[93] Such uniqueness enables anyone who can capture communications to quickly construct a graph of a user's social network. Knowledge of social networks is valuable because, along with user profiles, online companies exploit social networks to generate advertising revenue.

Social networks can emerge even with no interaction on your part. Even the simple act of receiving an e-mail creates a link between the sender and receiver, something beyond your ability to control. Even e-mails filtered by the online company still create the link. This might sound a little melodramatic, but every time an old friend contacts you from a webmail account, a little piece of your privacy dies.

WARNING

Monitoring and analysis of social networks allows communication providers to deduce social phenomena on a global scale.

An entity such as an ISP or free e-mail provider that has access to all or some of a user's messages can readily build a map of each communicating party. In some cases, such as with forwarded e-mails, each message contains multiple messages (and addressing information) that can be used to more rapidly develop the communication network. Also, in the case of forwarded e-mails, the originator might have little knowledge of the eventual destination of the communication. When you consider that millions of e-mail messages, phone calls, and text messages pass through a relatively small number of service providers, analysis on a global scale is possible with current technology and is likely occurring now. Both Google and Yahoo! have active plans to turn their e-mail systems into social networks, based on how often a user exchanges e-mail and text messages with other users. Brad Garlinghouse, Senior Vice President of Communications and Communities at Yahoo!, provides useful insight:

> The inbox you have today is what people send you, not what you want to see. We can say, 'Here are the messages from the people you care about most.' The exciting part is that a lot of this information already exists on our network, but it's dormant.[94]

Exciting indeed, and fraught with risk. The fact that online companies can build and analyze your social network from your messages, as well as determine "the people you care about most," is concerning on many levels. I see no reason such companies cannot also determine the same insights at the corporate or even nation-state levels.

COMPUTER ANALYSIS OF COMMUNICATIONS

Computers can easily analyze digital communications, contrasted with older analog technologies such as those found in most wired telephone networks and broadcast radio. Traditionally, humans who understood the target language analyzed communications. This approach doesn't scale well to the millions of messages being passed on the Internet. However, machine processing can now handle much of the load. The three main types of electronic human-to-human communications, in order of processing difficulty, are text, audio, and video. Text is in a format that computers easily can process via simple keyword matching and advanced natural language processing. Ironically, when users label their messages, perhaps using Gmail, to assist in their search, prioritization, and filtering of e-mail, they are adding important semantic information that makes machine processing easier. Such markup by individual users is the heart of the web, in the form of HTML, and a key reason search engines work so well.

WARNING

Advances in artificial intelligence raise another security concern. Computers are increasingly able to imitate humans communicating via online chat and encourage disclosure of sensitive information. Some bots even realistically "flirt" in online dating forums and capture personal information.[95]

Audio represents a more complex issue for machine analysis. Audio communications must typically be translated into text before processing, but this problem is largely solved. Tools such as Dragon Naturally Speaking claim up to 99% accuracy and even include optimized medical and legal variants.[96] However, speech-recognition software is processor intensive and cannot handle analysis of thousands or millions of concurrent communications, short of nation-state level resources. Eventually, large-scale voice processing will be possible as processor speed increases and algorithms improve.

Video contains visual information that is difficult to extract by machines, but there have been successful approaches in machine-processing of images. That being said, complete analysis of an image[97] lies beyond the reach of today's technology. The Completely Automated Public Turing Test to Tell Computers and Humans Apart (CAPTCHA) illustrates the problem. Invented by Carnegie Mellon University's Luis von Ahn, CAPTCHAs are specially constructed images that usually contain text. They are designed to be easily understood by humans, but be very difficult for machines to understand. CAPTCHAs are frequently used by online services such as Ticketmaster (www.ticketmaster.com) and Gmail, to prevent automated ticket purchasing and e-mail account signup. In other words, CAPTCHAs are designed to protect something of value from automated exploitation. Because CAPTCHAs serve in this gatekeeper role, they are under constant attack and serve as a catalyst for image-processing technology. Over time, attackers develop successful attacks, as they did in 2008 against the Gmail CAPTCHA.[98]

Computer analysis of communications is occurring now, powered by machine learning and natural language-processing technologies. A great example is Google's Gmail, which, according to Google displays "text ads and related links you might find useful and interesting."[99] But other examples include the analysis of e-mails for spam filtering, language translation, and antivirus protection. Note that these are the publicly acknowledged uses of machine processing of communications. It is a safe bet that many other uses will never be discussed overtly. Note that these services also create a disturbing paradigm, that computer analysis of communications is not a search, a dangerous legal precedent.[100]

SUMMARY

Previous chapters discussed the risks of search and the trail we leave behind that can be used to uniquely identify us. This chapter introduced the risks associated with the primary forms of online communication: e-mail, text messaging, instant messaging, voice, and video, all domains in which Google plays a leading role. Communications tell the online companies who we interact with, what we look like, what we sound like, who we are linked to socially and professionally, as well as the actual contents of the messages themselves, both mundane and extremely sensitive. Because online communications require unique characteristics, such as phone numbers, registered user accounts and e-mail addresses, all of these facets can be aggregated and combined with both our search activity and data collected from the myriad other tools available online.

ENDNOTES

1. Although earlier mail-like applications such as MAILBOX and SNDMSG date back to the mid-1960s, these tools were designed to send messages on a large shared computer, not across a network. For more information, see www.nethistory.info/History%20of%20the%20Internet/e-mail.html.

2. Peter Lyman and Hal R. Varian, "How Much Information?" School of Information Management and Systems. University of California at Berkeley, 2003. www.sims.berkeley.edu/how-much-info-2003, last accessed 29 February 2008.

3. Don Evett, "Spam Statistics 2006," *TopTenReviews*. http://spam-filter-review. toptenreviews.com/spam-statistics.html, last accessed 29 February 2008.

4. Tim Wilson, "Spam Reaching Record Volumes, Researchers Say," *Dark Reading*, 13 December 2007. www.darkreading.com/document.asp?doc_id=141350&WT.svl= news1_3, last accessed 1 March 2008.

5. "GCs to Employees: Think Before You Send," In-House Counsel, Law.com, 9 November 2007. www.law.com/jsp/ihc/PubArticleIHC.jsp?id=1194516243458, last accessed 12 March 2008.

6. Google is actively researching social network analysis; see http://code.google.com/ apis/socialgraph/ for one example.

7. Tom N. Jagatic, Nathaniel A. Johnson, Markus Jakobsson, and Filippo Menczer, "Social Phishing," *Communications of the ACM* 50, no. 10 (October 2007): 94–100. A prerelease version is available at www.indiana.edu/~phishing/social-network-experiment/phishing-preprint.pdf, last accessed 1 March 2008.

8. For an interesting look at the Phishing Underground, see www.net-security.org/ article.php?id=1110.

9. Yahoo! and Hotmail have about 250 million and 228 million, respectively.

10. "Welcome to Gmail," Google, 2008. www.google.com/accounts/ServiceLogin? service=mail&passive=true&rm=false&continue=https%3A%2F%2Fmail.google. com%2Fmail%2F%3Fnsr%3D1%26ui%3Dhtml%26zy%3Dl&ltmpl= default&ltmplcache=2, last accessed 29 February 2008.

11. "10 Reasons to Use Gmail," Google, 2008. http://mail.google.com/mail/help/intl/en/about.html, last accessed 29 February 2008.

12. Jeff Atwood, "A Question of Programming Ethics," Coding Horror Blog, 7 March 2008. www.codinghorror.com/blog/archives/001072.html, last accessed 12 March 2008.

13. See Privacy International's "Complaint: Google Inc.—Gmail E-mail Service," White paper for related interesting analysis, www.privacyinternational.org/issues/internet/gmail-complaint.pdf.

14. "More on Gmail and Privacy," Google, January 2007. https://mail.google.com/mail/help/about_privacy.html, last accessed 29 February 2008.

15. *Ibid.*

16. "Google Privacy Policy," Google, 14 October 2005. www.google.com/privacypolicy.html, last accessed 13 March 2008.

17. In 2007, Google offered a similar service for ISPs; see http://googleblog.blogspot.com/2007/05/google-apps-partner-edition.html.

18. "Colleges Outsourcing E-mail to MS Live, Google," Slashdot, 27 November 2007. http://it.slashdot.org/article.pl?no_d2=1&sid=07/11/27/2320230, last accessed 13 March 2008.

19. The extent to which Google mines e-mails is a matter of speculation.

20. It is also important to note that large e-mail companies receive thousands or more "out of office" e-mails from third-party addresses.

21. Don't forget that the files themselves can contain sensitive and personal metadata.

22. See www.boingboing.net/2006/02/18/miller-hunts-down-pe.html for an interesting story on disposable e-mail addresses.

23. Aaron Mannes and Jennifer Goldbeck, "Ontology Building: A Terrorism Specialist's Perspective," IEEE Aerospace Conference, 3–10 March 2007.

24. For one interesting approach, see the DidTheyReadIt service (www.didtheyreadit.com/), which lets a sender know whether the e-mail was sent, how many times it was read, whether it was forwarded, and the geographic region of the reader.

25. Dawn Kawamoto, "Worm Wriggles Through Yahoo! Mail Flaw," ZDNetAsia, 13 June 2006. www.zdnetasia.com/news/security/0,39044215,39367249,00.htm, last accessed 13 March 2008.

26. Liam Tung, "Gmail Cookie Vulnerability Exposes a User's Privacy," CNET News, 27 September 2007. http://news.cnet.com/2100-1002_3-6210353.html, last accessed 13 June 2008.

27. Robert Vamosi, "Researcher: Web 2.0 Vulnerable to Cookie Theft," NewsBlog, 2 August 2007. www.news.com/8301-10784_3-9754204-7.html, last accessed 13 March 2008.

28. Mark Rasch, "E-mail Privacy to Disappear," *Security Focus,* 2 November 2007. www.securityfocus.com/columnists/456, last accessed 11 March 2008.

29. Garett Rogers, "GMail Virus Scanning on the Way," Googling Google Blog, 30 November 2005. http://blogs.zdnet.com/Google/?p=44, last accessed 11 March 2008.

30. StankDawg, "MitM Domain Typo Attacks," DigitalDawgPound Blog, 26 October 2007. www.digitaldawgpound.org/stankdawg/post=245, last accessed 13 August 2008.

31. "E-mail Typosquatting Poses Leakage Threat," *SecurityFocus,* 21 February 2008. www.securityfocus.com/brief/685, last accessed 12 March 2008.

32. Note that this system also works with internal corporate employee image databases, which can eliminate the external information-disclosure risk.

33. Eric Lieberman and Robert C. Miller. "Face-mail: Showing Faces of Recipients to Prevent Misdirected E-mail." Symposium on Usable Privacy and Security, 2007. http://cups.cs.cmu.edu/soups/2007/proceedings/p122_lieberman.pdf, last accessed 12 March 2008.

34. Gmail also allows users to upload a picture of themselves and the people in their contact lists, filling in a missing detail of your social network. See http://mail.google.com/support/bin/answer.py?answer=38354&hl=en.

35. "Gmail: Google's Approach to E-mail," Google, 2008. http://mail.google.com/mail/help/intl/en/about_whatsnew.html, last accessed 13 March 2008.

36. Allowing spam e-mails to pass through e-mail filters, for a fee, may prove to be a future business model for free e-mail services. See http://slashdot.org/article.pl?sid=07/07/11/150225 for an excellent discussion.

37. The rapid pace of this change is proving unsettling for governments and telecommunications providers worldwide. For one example, see http://economictimes.indiatimes.com/articleshow/726843.cms.

38. "About Chat," Gmail Help Center, Google, 2008. http://mail.google.com/support/bin/answer.py?answer=33781&topic=13292&hl=en, last accessed 18 March 2008.

39. "It's Good to Chat," Google, 10 March 2008. http://mail.google.com/mail/help/chat.html, last accessed 18 March 2008.

40. Philipp Lenssen, "Google Talk Chatback Widget," Google Blogoscoped, 26 February 2008. http://blogoscoped.com/archive/2008-02-26-n90.html, last accessed 18 March 2008.

41. For online e-mail services such as Gmail.

42. "Instant Messaging Security Center," Akonix, 2008. www.akonix.com/im-security-center/, last accessed 18 March 2008.

43. For one interesting approach to securing instant messaging, see "Protecting IM from Big Brother," at http://it.slashdot.org/it/07/11/23/1324201.shtml.

44. Google Talk Guide, "Can My GTalk Discussion Be Tracked?" Google Talk, Google Groups, 21 November 2006. http://groups.google.com/group/Calls-Chats-and-Voicemail/browse_thread/thread/431d561bf7d6f7d6/e49343f783a06a1e?lnk=gst&q=encryption&rnum=1#e49343f783a06a1e, last accessed 15 June 2008.

45. Many of these services required the installation of closed-source, third-party applications, opening up the risk of running untrusted code on users' machines. More recently, open protocols such as Jabber (www.jabber.org/) and Extensible Messaging and Presence Protocol (XMPP) has fostered development of open source clients and servers.

46. Nate Mook, "Google Talk Opens to Other IM Services," *BetaNews,* 17 January 2006. www.betanews.com/article/Google_Talk_Opens_to_Other_IM_Services/1137530175, last accessed 19 March 2008.

47. "Google Talk for Developers: Open Communications," Google, 2008. http://code.google.com/apis/talk/open_communications.html#service, last accessed 19 March 2008.

48. "Google Talk Privacy Notice," Google, 7 February 2006. www.google.com/talk/privacy.html, last accessed 18 March 2008.

49. "Google Talk Privacy Notice," Google, 14 October 2005. www.google.com/talk/privacy_redline.html, last accessed 18 March 2008.

50. Of course, the user could send video, voice, and sound files as attachments to e-mail, but with these real-time communication systems, similar disclosures are inherent in the communication channel.

51. "Too Busy for Chat? Set Your Online Status in Google Talk As Idle," *Digital Inspiration,* 20 February 2008. www.labnol.org/software/tutorials/busy-chat-google-talk-online-status-hide-friends-idle/2327/m, last accessed 17 March 2008.

52. "Set Your Google Talk Status as Idle When You're Too Busy," *LifeHacker,* 22 February 2008. http://lifehacker.com/359789/set-your-google-talk-status-as-idle-when-youre-too-busy, last accessed 17 March 2008.

53. This shortcoming has led to a third-party application, gAlwaysIdle (www.galwaysidle.com/), that allows more fine-grained control.

54. Villu Arak, "U.S. and European PSP Slim & Lite Owners, Rejoice." Skype, 30 January 2008. http://share.skype.com/sites/en/2008/01/european_psp_slim_lite_ owners.html, last accessed 18 March 2008.

55. "Google Acquires Usenet Discussion Service and Significant Assets from Deja.com," Google, press release, 12 February 2001. www.google.com/press/pressrel/ pressrelease48.html, last accessed 8 March 2008.

56. "20 Year Usenet Timeline," Google, 2008. www.google.com/googlegroups/archive_ announce_20.html, last accessed 8 March 2008.

57. You don't reuse your passwords do you?

58. Saima: "My friend had ovarian cancer; now it spread to surrounding tissues." alt.support.cancer, 29 February 2008. http://groups.google.com/group/alt.support. cancer/browse_thread/thread/887aa311d764a1d1/c6795a11be487b2a#c6795a11be48 7b2a, last accessed 7 March 2008.

59. "Google Groups Privacy Notice." Google, July 2006. http://groups.google.com/intl/ en/googlegroups/privacy3.html, last accessed 8 March 2008.

60. "Google Groups Tour," Google, 2008. http://groups.google.com/intl/en/ googlegroups/tour3/index.html, last accessed 9 March 2008.

61. There is unconfirmed speculation that Google and Dell are planning an iPhone rival. See http://mobile.slashdot.org/article.pl?sid=08/01/30/1611204.

62. Search engine and browser companies are actively courting cell phone manufacturers to include their tools. For example, Motorola (the world's second-largest cell phone manufacturer) entered into an agreement to give its customers easy access to Google via cell phones distributed globally. See http://park.newsvine.com/_news/ 2006/01/06/50834-motorola-to-add-google-to-cell-phones.

63. "Global Cell Phone Penetration Reaches 50 Percent," Reuters, U.K., 29 November 2007. http://investing.reuters.co.uk/news/articleinvesting.aspx?type= media&storyID=nL29172095, last accessed 5 March 2008.

64. Wesley Chan. *All Aboard.* The Official Google Blog, 2 July 2007. http://googleblog. blogspot.com/2007/07/all-aboard.html, last accessed 14 June 2008.

65. "Grand Central Overview," GrandCentral from Google, 2008. www.grandcentral. com/support/howitworks/, last accessed 14 June 2008.

66. "GrandCentral Privacy Policy," GrandCentral from Google, 2 July 2007. www. grandcentral.com/legal/privacypolicy, last accessed 14 June 2008.

67. Other services include stock quotes, residential listings, product prices (based on ISBN or UPC), word definitions, language translation, and currency conversions.

68. Erin Fors, "Review Guide: Google Short Message Service (SMS)," Google, September 2006. www.google.com/press/guides/sms_overview.pdf, last accessed 5 March 2008.

69. "SMS (Beta) Privacy Policy," Google, 2008. www.google.com/mobile/sms/privacy.html, last accessed 5 March 2008.

70. The usage of logging an "encrypted version" of the incoming phone number is a bit vague. It could also mean that the number is stored as a one-way hash.

71. Note that Google's prototype location-based search located at http://labs.google.com/location now redirects to Google Maps at http://local.google.com/.

72. Modern cell phones, such as those produced by Motorola and BlackBerry, are often GPS-enabled. A number of applications provide GPS data to Google. For an example, see http://sourceforge.net/projects/gpsmapper/.

73. "Google Mobile Privacy Policy," Google, 9 November 2007. www.google.com/mobile/privacy.html, last accessed 17 February 2008.

74. Voice samples are likely collected when using voice recognition capabilities, but it is a common business practice to record voice communications "for your protection."

75. "Mobile World Congress 2008: Google and Nokia Team Up on Search." Official Google Mobile Blog, 12 February 2008. http://googleblog.blogspot.com/2008/02/google-search-on-nokia-phones.html, last accessed 17 February 2008.

76. Economists call this a transaction cost.

77. "Local Number Portability," Consumer and Governmental Affairs Bureau, Federal Communications Commission, 13 February 2008. www.fcc.gov/cgb/NumberPortability/, last accessed 19 March 2008.

78. "Google Threatens to End E-mail Service in Germany," Spiegel Online International, 25 June 2007. www.spiegel.de/international/germany/0,1518,490492,00.html, last accessed 19 March 2008.

79. "Google Talk Privacy Notice," Google, 7 February 2006. www.google.com/talk/privacy.html, last accessed 3 March 2008.

80. "Gmail Privacy Notice," Google, 14 October 2005. http://mail.google.com/mail/help/privacy.html, last accessed 3 March 2008.

81. The law surrounding the privacy of e-mail is constantly evolving. For one example, see http://yro.slashdot.org/article.pl?sid=07/06/21/0427227&from=rss.

82. Todd Bishop, "Microsoft Execs on Vista Problems," Todd Bishop's Microsoft Blog, 27 February 2008. http://blog.seattlepi.nwsource.com/microsoft/archives/132891.asp, last accessed 3 March 2008.

83. "Exclusive: The Sexually Explicit Internet Messages That Led to Fla. Rep. Foley's Resignation." ABC News, The Blotter, 29 September 2006. http://blogs. abcnews.com/theblotter/2006/09/exclusive_the_s.html, last accessed 3 March 2008.

84. Or not filtered, as in the case of advertisers paying to bypass spam filters.

85. Alma Whitten and J. D. Tygar, "Why Johnny Can't Encrypt: A Usability Evaluation of PGP 5.0. USENIX Security Symposium," 23 August 1999. Available online at www.cs.berkeley.edu/~tygar/papers/Why_Johnny_Cant_Encrypt/OReilly.pdf, last accessed 19 March 2008.

86. Carl Ellison and Bruce Schneier, "Ten Risks of PKI: What You're not Being Told About Public Key Infrastructure." *Computer Security Journal* 16, no. 1 (2000): 1–7. Available online at www.schneier.com/paper-pki.html, last accessed 19 March 2008.

87. Jeremy Kirk, "PayPal Asking E-mail Services to Block Messages," *Network World,* 27 March 2007. www.networkworld.com/news/2007/032707-paypal-asking-e-mail-services-to.html, last accessed 18 March 2008.

88. "How Pervasive Is ISP Outbound E-mail Filtering?" Slashdot, 31 January 2008. http://ask.slashdot.org/article.pl?sid=08/01/31/2130251, last accessed 18 March 2008.

89. T.V. Raman, "Google Translation + Gmail Help People Communicate," The Official Google Blog, 8 February 2008. http://googleblog.blogspot.com/2008/02/ google-translation-gmail-help-people.html, last accessed 27 February 2008.

90. Jonas Lindberg, "Merry Christmas, God Jul and 圣诞快乐." Google Talkabout Blog, 18 December 2007. http://googletalk.blogspot.com/2007/12/merry-christmas-god-jul-and.html, last accessed 27 February 2007.

91. "Comcast Universal Address Book," Comcast, 2008. http://universaladdressbook. comcast.net/universaladdressbook/, last accessed 27 February 2008.

92. Alex Bailey, "Gmail Vulnerable to Contact List Hijacking," *Tech Reads,* 1 January 2007. www.cyber-knowledge.net/blog/2007/01/01/gmail-vulnerable-to-contact-list-hijacking/, last accessed 1 March 2008.

93. Future, highly interactive Web 2.0 communication applications will assuredly provide additional ways to fingerprint users. One possible way is via their unique typing characteristics.

94. For a good example of social network analysis based on e-mail, visit www.xobni. com/ and consider what the Xobni tool can do based on locally stored e-mail messages.

95. Ina Fried. "Warning Sounded over 'Flirting Robots.'" News.com, 7 December 2007. http://news.cnet.com/8301-13860_3-9831133-56.html, last accessed 4 September 2008.

96. "Dragon Naturally Speaking," Nuance Communications, Inc., 2008. www.nuance.com/naturallyspeaking/business/, last accessed 28 February 2008.

97. This also includes the analysis of a single frame of video, which is essentially a still image.

98. "Google's CAPTCHA Busted in Recent Spammer Tactics," Websense Security Labs Threat Blog: 22 February 2008. www.websense.com/securitylabs/blog/blog.php?BlogID=174, last accessed 19 March 2008.

99. "Gmail: Google's Approach to E-mail," Google 2008. http://mail.google.com/mail/help/about.html#ads, last accessed 28 February 2008.

100. Mark Rasch, "Google's Gmail: Spook Heaven?" The Register, 15 June 2004. www.theregister.co.uk/2004/06/15/gmail_spook_heaven/, last accessed 19 March 2008.

Mapping, Directions, and Imagery

Before the dawn of online mapping and imagery services, we were forced to use printed books, such as the *National Geographic Atlas of the World,* to view the world, and the *Rand McNally Road Atlas,* to navigate unfamiliar locations. We shared directions to our homes via verbal instructions over the phone or written notes. Businesses distributed directions and small maps in paper brochures via the postal system and in brochure racks. High-resolution satellite imagery was available to a select few governments and largely unavailable to the masses. As a result, your interest in parts of the world, places you wanted to visit, and how you got there was largely a personal matter. Have times changed.

Free online mapping services include offerings by Google, AOL, Yahoo!, and many more. Each of these services allows you to view maps overlaid upon satellite[1] imagery and is tightly integrated with tools that give precise directions to desired locations. Wildly popular, AOL's MapQuest currently enjoys the largest share, with 53.9 million users per month, followed by Yahoo! Maps with 29.6 million and Google Maps with 28.9 million.[2] Over time, hundreds of millions of users utilize these services to find directions to points of interest, including homes of friends, businesses, and travel destinations.

These mapping tools have enriched lives by helping people navigate from place to place and explore the planet. Unanticipated uses have shown that these services have the power to do great good, including raising awareness of the crisis in the Darfur region of the Sudan[3, 4], assisting rescue efforts and damage assessment following Hurricane Katrina,[5] and monitoring the impact of Appalachian coal mining on nearby ecosystems[6] (see Figure 6-1). Google admirably encourages the use of its Google Earth tool to help build support for such worthy causes.[7] The future holds great potential in utilizing these tools to help build communities and facilitate citizen journalism.

So what is the harm in using these services? Well, it turns out, a lot. You face significant risks from both your use of these services and the content they contain. This chapter analyzes the information you disclose when using mapping and imagery services, including how your use of these tools discloses locations of your home, employer, family and friends, travel plans, and strategic intentions, and discusses how data mining can easily link seemingly disparate groups of people based on their interest in common locations. It also covers the risks inherent in the content itself, including camera-equipped cars capturing continuous streams of high-quality street-level photographs, collaborative analysis of satellite imagery, and your inability to trust the veracity of the images themselves.

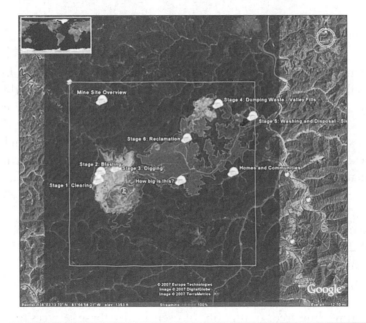

Figure 6-1   Use of Google imagery to highlight damage caused by Appalachian Region mining[8]

INFORMATION DISCLOSURE

Location, location, location. This is most important information you disclose when you use online mapping and imagery services. Ask yourself the following questions the next time you consider using Google Maps or Google Earth:

- Have you ever viewed your current location?
- Have you ever looked at the homes of family and friends?
- Have you shopped for a new home using mapping and imagery tools?
- Have you viewed locations that are strategically important to your employer?
- Has law enforcement used these tools to work on active cases?

Beyond simple locations, you are revealing a great deal of additional information through your interactions, including the following:

- The frequency of your interest
- How closely you zoomed in on the images
- How much time you spent at each zoom level
- Whether you used search to help find specific locations, businesses, and so on
- Whether you printed, saved, or shared specific images

As mentioned in Chapter 3, "Footprints, Fingerprints, and Connections," it is possible to use your IP address to identify the probable location of your computer. So when using mapping and imagery tools, not only are you disclosing areas of personal interest, but this information also can be paired with your actual location based on IP geolocation.

BASIC INTERACTION REVELATIONS

The primary way of interacting with the mapping interface involves dragging the image with the mouse and using the zoom slider. Even these simple interactions reveal a lot. Imagine all the points you've zoomed in on using Google Maps (see Figure 6-2). The sum total would be enlightening indeed. The set probably includes your hometown, previous homes, family members' homes, travel destinations, and your employer. If you revisit the same locations frequently, you are helping to identify their value to you.

Figure 6-2   The default Google Maps interface

Consider a real estate shopping example. Figure 6-3 depicts housing subdivisions in Las Vegas, Nevada. For this example, let's assume that you viewed the homes in the squares (at maximum zoom) every few days. At the same time, you conducted a large number of searches on "Las Vegas Real Estate." After two weeks of such activity, you zoom in on the home in the topmost square and click the Google Maps Link to This Page command. After e-mailing this link to your friends and family, they all click the link and view the home you intend to purchase.

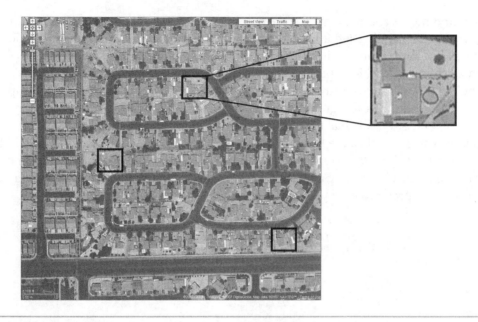

Figure 6-3 Shopping for a new home in a Las Vegas subdivision. By viewing the homes differing numbers of times and e-mailing a link to your friends and family, you are disclosing your priorities and your social network.

In actuality, your use of online mapping and imagery services is far more complex than this simple real estate example. You create a constantly lengthening trail of interaction data, including zoom level, size of the map, time and date, mapping location, and your IP address each time your browser requests updated information from the server. The following are examples of interaction data I collected while panning and zooming during a short Google Maps session. During the course of several minutes, my computer made more than 600 similar requests. Each URL resolves to a small graphical tile of the map.

http://mt1.google.com/mt?n=404&v=w2t.75&hl=en&x=9467&s=&y=12151&zoom=2&s=
http://mt0.google.com/mt?n=404&v=w2.75&hl=en&x=1180&y=1518&zoom=5&s=Ga
http://mt2.google.com/mt?n=404&v=w2.75&hl=en&x=1180&y=1517&zoom=5&s=G

Note that online mapping and imagery services are complex applications that will evolve over time and process data differently. In this case, my browser made a significant number of mapping data requests as I interacted with the system, but the size, resolutions, and frequency of interaction disclosures will vary from system to system. In other words, some systems will make frequent small requests for additional map data as the user zooms and moves about the map, while others will make less frequent but larger requests. In some cases, mapping and imagery systems will prefetch information in anticipation of a user's upcoming actions, without any direct interaction on the user's part.

In addition, by clicking options such as Print, E-mail, Link To This Page, or Save, you are helping to identify your intentions and importance of the given map. For example, when you create a link to a given location and share it with others, you create a connection between each individual the moment they open the e-mail and click the link. Similarly, when you click the Print command (see Figure 6-4), you create a strong indicator that you value the current map state enough to print a copy. From these combined streams of data, data-mining applications could detect and classify many types of activity you would prefer to keep private.

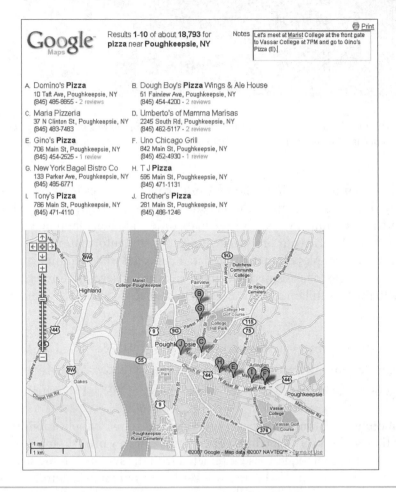

Figure 6-4   By clicking the Print link, you disclose that you significantly value the current map.

ALL THE RISKS OF SEARCH, NOW WITH LOCATIONS, TOO

Using Google Maps involves more than simply interacting with the display to locate areas of interest, or even printing, saving, or sharing maps. You can also search the map and jump immediately to addresses, zip codes, businesses, and cities of interest. Figure 6-5 shows a Google Maps search for "pizza in Poughkeepsie," the sample entry suggested on the Google Maps web page.

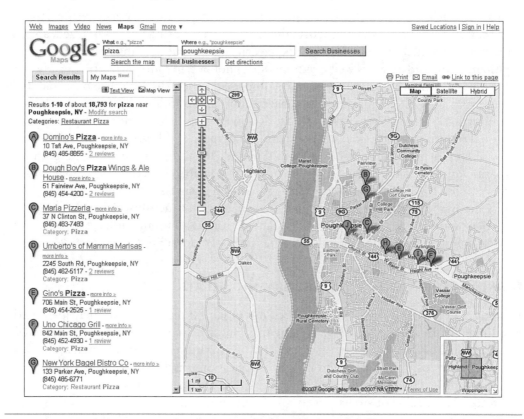

Figure 6-5   Using Google Maps to find pizza restaurants in Poughkeepsie

So what are the risks of combining search and mapping? Well, by doing so, you are combining the disclosure risks of search, as described in Chapter 4, "Search," with specific geographic locations and the interaction revelations described in the previous section. For example, by clicking one of the results in the search pane on the left side of the display, you can bring up specific details about one of the locations marked on the map. However, you are also disclosing—and, hence, strengthening—the link between the search you performed and what you deemed as important in the results. Say you were searching on a specific person and returned a number of results. By clicking on the link corresponding to the specific individual you were interested in, you've yielded a clue to the most relevant result.

PRIVACY-DEGRADING PERSONALIZATION

Enticed by such slogans as "Make Google Maps your maps," many users have personalized their maps. Google Maps supports the creation and sharing of personalized, annotated maps. Annotation includes marking favorite places and drawing lines and shapes to highlight paths and areas, as well as adding text, photos, and videos.[9] Unfortunately, the more you personalize your maps, the more information you disclose. The potential disclosure risks are quite significant. Users have almost an unlimited ability to share sensitive information and tie it to specific locations on the map. Some users will likely add personal or sensitive locations, such as their friends' home addresses or facilities at their place of employment. Such disclosure could provide the information required to link disparate profiles contained in an online company's databases. Recall that Google possesses extensive address databases for individuals and business, which enables them to create many additional linkages. In short, personalization functions, almost by definition, help compromise your anonymity. Many personalization functions in Google Maps require you to log in using a Google account, uniquely identifying your activity.

LINKING USER CLASSES VIA GEOGRAPHIC RELATIONSHIPS

Chapter 3 discussed various ways you and your organization can be uniquely identified and linked with other groups. When using mapping and imagery services, you provide another vehicle to tie together individuals and organizations. As I mentioned at the start of this chapter, using mapping and imagery applications discloses locations you are interested in, but now consider that you can be linked with other people who are also interested in the same or similar locations. A great example is that of your parent's home. Chances are, you have looked at it using Google Maps. I'll bet your siblings have done the same. Now ask yourself how many other people have zoomed in to that exact same location. My guess is, not many. Bingo, a unique characteristic shared by you and your family.

Now consider your company. Let's say that it has 1,200 employees located at 10 locations, some not publicly known. Imagine mapping activity from the IP address ranges used by your corporate headquarters, as well as the other locations, all seeking directions from Ministro Pistarini International Airport in Buenos Aires to the street address of a meeting site at the outskirts of the city. Because this activity is out of the norm, you've just created a unique set of characteristics that ties together your various company offices with a potentially sensitive meeting. You've also disclosed, with a high probability, the travel plans of the meeting participants, as well as given a clue to the strategic importance of Argentina to your company's planning.

ALL ROADS LEAD TO ROME

Using online services that provide directions reveals sensitive information. Typically, you enter a starting point and a destination, often using precise street addresses. As discussed in the preceding section, these addresses provide a very powerful means to tie together disparate individuals. The more specific and rarely used the addresses, the higher the possibility of creating a useful link between the two. Using direction-giving services (see Figure 6-6), you are also giving away your probable route of travel.[10] By clicking the Print option, you indicate that you will probably be traveling the route in the near future. Similarly, if you used the e-mail or Link To This Page options, you've then linked yourself with a group of individuals who will likely be traveling over the same route after they click the link.

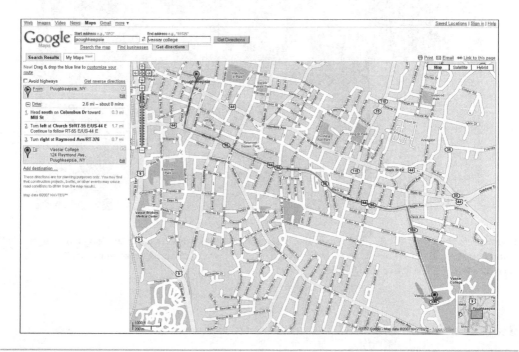

Figure 6-6 By using the Get Directions tab, you disclose two locations of interest and a probable path of travel between them.

Now imagine *all* the directions that your employees have generated using your company headquarters as a starting location and leading to destinations throughout the surrounding area (see Figure 6-7). You may be giving away the commuting routes of your employees, the locations of their homes, their lunch meeting venues, and perhaps even your company's strategic intentions. Similar searches could identify the home IP addresses of these employees, as well as many visitors to your company. Finally, if cookies were enabled on these machines, all of their online activities with a company such as Google could be tied together despite movement around the world. This is a security risk indeed.

Figure 6-7   Mock-up of a Google Map showing six notional directions requests to Google headquarters. If you consider all such requests to your corporate headquarters, such tools represent a significant disclosure threat, particularly over long periods of time.

TRACKING YOUR MOVEMENTS VIA MASHUPS

At the time of this writing, there are 50,000 Google mashups.[11] *Mashups* are a powerful innovation that enables users to plot virtually any sort of information with a geographic component on top of Google Maps.[12] As one blogger elegantly put it, "Now information on the web does not need to bind to just *what* and *how*. Your piece of information can also represent *where*."[13] Google Maps mashups have exploded in popularity and have been used for everything from locating street light cameras and inexpensive gas to identifying where UFOs have been sited (see Figure 6-8).[14] However, mashups combine the general sensitivity of using mapping services with two other important disclosures. The first is your interest in a given subject, such as evading red light cameras. Second, mashups identify your visit to a given web site. Typically, an online company knows if you visit only one of its web sites. By embedding a map inside a third-party web page, Google can track your activity as you hop around such sites.

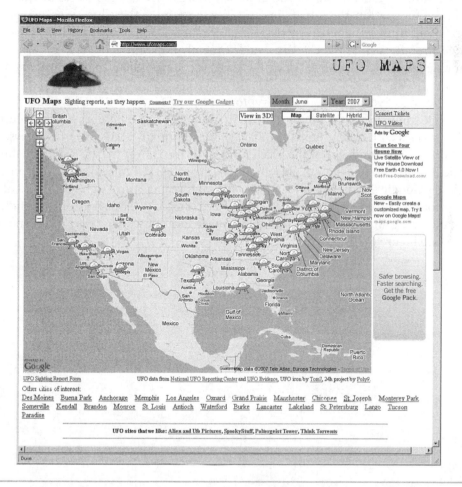

Figure 6-8 By embedding content in third-party web sites, such as in this Google mashup of UFO sightings, Google can track your activity as you move about the web.

CONTENT IS A THREAT, TOO

High-resolution satellite imagery was once the sole domain of intelligence agencies, but now high-quality imagery is available for free (think of the tools provided by Google, AOL, and Yahoo!). We've just looked at how our *interactions* with these services disclose sensitive information, but it is important to consider the *content* of these services, even if you never use them yourself. This class of threat is somewhat different, in that the content itself might be sensitive to those in the images, both from overhead and at street-level views. The advent of high-resolution overhead imagery being placed in the hands of the masses has dramatically changed the idea of physical security. Historically, national borders, fences, guards, and other safeguards have limited access to sensitive locations. Only nation-states had the capability to examine these locations, using, among other things, the relatively risk-free access provided by satellites and high-altitude aircraft, such as the U2. You couldn't merely hop onto Google Maps and zoom in for a detailed look. This level of easy access has changed the idea of security and privacy.

John Young's Eyeballing Series at Cryptome.org (see Figure 6-9) and Eyeball-series.org demonstrates the power these tools give us. Young combines high-resolution satellite images with other publicly available information to create powerful analyses of such things as the residence of the Vice President of the United States, India's Bhabha Atomic Research Center, and the National Security Agency. Similarly, Alex and James Turnbull's Google Sightseeing site (www.googlesightseeing.com) highlights areas of interest found in Google imagery data. They have categorized images from around the Earth, including aircraft, bridges, buildings, movie locations, spacecraft, and even naked people (see Figure 6-10).[15]

Figure 6-9 John Young's Cryptome.org and its companion site, Eyeball-series.org, contain excellent examples of sensitive overhead imagery. These sites also demonstrate the power of combining imagery with other publicly available information.

Figure 6-10   Googlesightseeing.com is a high-quality compendium of interesting and sensitive images found in Google imagery. Here it displays an article on the "Top 10 Naked People on Google Earth."

Whereas Google Sightseeing depends on tips from Google sightseers around the world to find interesting spots, Wikimapia takes a different approach. Wikimapia allows web users to directly annotate Google imagery. These annotations, some 4.5 million, are then visible to the world.[16] The concept is simple, cool, and useful, but the security risks are profound. *Any* user can annotate the maps, based on inside information, that would otherwise be impossible to detect via imagery alone. Figure 6-11 illustrates one such example. As you examine the figure, it is very unlikely that you could identify the structures at the center of the two large circles. Well, one Wikimapia kindly labeled these as

"Jump Towers." With a little research, you will find that these towers are used to train paratroopers at the U.S. Army's Airborne School.[17] The important lesson here is that it takes only one knucklehead to disclose something you or your company would have preferred to keep secret; with Wikimapia, or a similar tool, they can share it with the world.

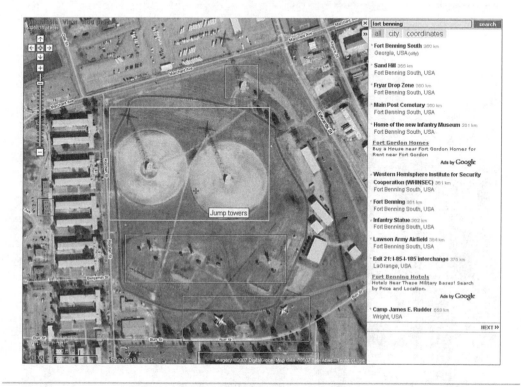

Figure 6-11   Web sites such as Wikimapia.com allow users to collaboratively analyze and annotate satellite imagery, such as this paratrooper training facility.

Today imagery is gathered via satellites, manned aircraft, unmanned aircraft, and even cars instrumented with cameras (see the section "Street-Level View"). In the future, we will see imagery gathered from virtually any platform you can imagine, and you can expect the resolution of the images to increase significantly as sensor technology improves. It seems as if we are living in an ever-increasing surveillance grid. Virtually every modern cell phone has a built-in camera, and many phones also have embedded GPS. The combination of the two has led to the rise of *geotagging,* which is the embedding of geographic information in various forms of media.[18] Sites such as flickr.com now allow easy publishing of geotagged images.[19, 20] (See Figure 6-12.) We also are seeing a significant increase in the number of government and commercially run surveillance

cameras, such as the British traffic wardens who were issued head-mounted video cameras[21] and the plans for creating a security veil of license plate readers and more than
3,000 public and private video cameras covering downtown New York City.[22]

Figure 6-12   In the future, we will see the rise of geotagged media, such as seen on Flickr. This image
depicts two sets of geotagged images of a well-known security researcher.

BASIC IMAGERY ANALYSIS

Imagery analysis[23] is the art of analyzing images to extract useful information. Overhead
imagery analysis has been practiced since 1858, when the first aerial image (of Paris) was

taken by Gaspar Felix Tournachon from a balloon. Images were later captured from cameras carried by pigeons (1903), kites (1906), and compressed air rockets (1906). Wilbur Wright took the first photograph from an airplane in 1909 of Centrocelli, Italy.[24] The intelligence value of overhead imagery did not go unnoticed by the military. Overhead images were collected during the U.S. Civil War, World War I, and World War II, but this increased in significance with the advent of satellite imagery. Corona was the United States' first photo reconnaissance system. It operated from August 1960 to May 1972 and was declassified in February 1995. During the 12-year program, it flew more than 100 missions and captured more than 800,000 images.[25] The satellites in the Corona program were given the KH (KeyHole) designator from KH-1 to KH-6, with a maximum ground resolution (that is, for the smallest discernible object) of 6 feet.[26]

Today Google Earth and Google Maps users enjoy significantly greater resolution with images collected using satellites and aircraft, opening up the art of imagery analysis to anyone with access to the Internet. These images, along with other information freely available on the World Wide Web, have magnified the sensitivity of the content of these online services. In the past, nations risked the lives of spies and service members to acquire what you now can simply download from your living room or office. Full coverage of the risk associated with overhead imagery is beyond the scope of this book; however, it is important to realize that although an untrained eye can detect sensitive information, an experienced imagery analyst can extract significantly more insight. Let's consider a few simple examples.

The first example is that of a humble parking lot. Google Maps has plentiful imagery of many cities with resolution capable of detecting relatively small objects, such as automobiles. Figure 6-13 shows an example of a shopping mall from Google Maps. Note that something as innocuous as a parking lot can reveal a great deal of information, such as the number of employees a company might have or whether the image was taken on a weekend or weekday.

If you've ever played a city building game, such as SimCity, you've carefully built a city by adding commercial, industrial, and residential zones, as well as transportation and public utilities. Similarly, you can analyze a city by deconstructing it layer by layer. See Table 6-1, which I've based on the menus of SimCity and other sources,[27] for more detailed examples. A profound security risk arises from skilled analysis, and we can do little to protect against it, unless we want to install camouflage netting over our homes and businesses.

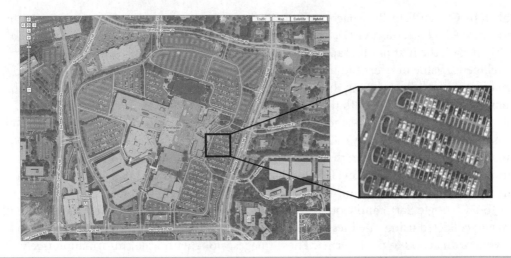

Figure 6-13   A shopping center from Google Maps with a high-resolution detail of individual cars

Table 6-1   Reverse-Engineering a City by Using City-Building Games to Provide an Analytic Structure

Category	Examples
Commercial	Businesses, shopping malls, parking lots
Communication	Telephone switching centers, cell towers, satellite downlinks, microwave and other antennas
Education	Colleges, schools, libraries
Industry	Mines, factories, warehouses, quarries
Law enforcement and other emergency services	Hospitals, prisons, ambulance, police and fire stations
Recreation	Zoos, parks, colleges, libraries, stadiums
Residential	Subdivisions, individual homes
Transportation	Railroads, roads, seaports, subways, tunnels, bridges
Utilities	Water supplies, power plants, power grid, power substations, water and sewage treatment facilities, recycling centers, garbage disposal facilities

IF SOMETHING IS SENSITIVE, JUST OBSCURE IT

The power of Google Maps in the hands of the masses has not gone unnoticed by world leaders. Leaders, including officials from Thailand, South Korea, and India, have raised concerns over the system's power to show sensitive facilities.[28] As a result, Google has received a number of requests (sometimes demands) to limit access.[29] A popular technique to appease such requests is obscuring the "sensitive" location. See Figure 6-14, which depicts the famous Sing Sing Prison in Ossining, New York. Notice that the prison itself (left side of image) is heavily obscured and the right side of the image is still crisp. Figure 6-15 shows another example. The image is a close-up view of the Indian Point Nuclear Power Plant, which supplies power to New York City. Again, it is heavily obscured. In both cases, officials clearly thought that these sites were too sensitive to display to the general public.[30] However, merely the act of obscuring the sensitive location might draw additional attention to it. Obscuring sensitive locations works reasonably well when you assume a lone analyst, but it is significantly less effective when confronted by a large group of like-minded viewers bent on identifying censored locations. The approach is even less secure when you assume that Google presumably received the original unaltered images and censored the images itself. They would have not only the original unaltered image, perhaps in even higher resolution than what is available on the web, but most likely also a master list of all sensitive sites. I'd like to have that list.[31]

Figure 6-14 Sing Sing Prison in Ossining, New York. Notice that the prison on the left side of the screen is heavily blurred, while the right side of the screen is crisp.

Figure 6-15   Maximum closeup of the Indian Point Nuclear Power Plant, Buchanan, New York. The entire plant is significantly obscured.

ACCURACY AND DECEIT

When using services such as Google Maps, the question arises regarding the accuracy of the results. Ask any taxi driver what he thinks about Google Maps or MapQuest directions. The results can, of course, be accidentally wrong or out-of-date. However, it is also prudent to consider that the results could be deliberately misleading. In addition, if you assume the possibility of a malicious ISP or Internet backbone provider, the images you receive might not be truthful, even if the source is providing accurate imagery, because it is possible to swap them en route.

STREET-LEVEL VIEW

Where overhead imagery found on mapping sites has enough resolution to view cars and, in a few major cities, people, Google Street View (http://maps.google.com/help/

maps/streetview/) significantly increases the risk to privacy. In StreetView you can very clearly view individuals. If you live in a location that has been imaged by StreetView, chances are, you, your home, your car, or someone you known is in the system.[32] It is important to note that, in response to privacy concerns, Google has begun testing face-blurring technology in mid-2008, as this book was going to press.

The street-level view depends on imagery gathered by vehicles instrumented with cameras. These vehicles are driven through the streets with cameras rolling (see Figure 6-16). Manpower intensive, not many areas have been covered, but those that have been are quite detailed and raise a number of concerns; visitors to domestic violence shelters, sunbathers, and patrons of adult bookstores have all been recorded. An interesting case that illustrates privacy concerns is that of EFF staff attorney Kevin Bankston, who was photographed both by Google's cameras[33] and by Amazon's A9 System, both of which generated significant negative press.[34] The learning point here is that if you are creating a system with privacy implications, you shouldn't include images of leading privacy advocates.

Figure 6-16 Google's StreetView coverage of San Francisco. Imaged streets are highlighted in blue.

RELATED MAPPING AND IMAGERY TOOLS AND SERVICES

Google Maps and Google Earth aren't the only popular mapping and imagery services available on the web. The following is a list of these and other popular tools.

- Google Earth (http://earth.google.com/)
- Google Maps (http://maps.google.com/)
- MapPoint (www.microsoft.com/mappoint/)
- Mapsonus (www.mapsonus.com/)
- MapQuest (www.mapquest.com/)
- Mobile GMaps (www.mgmaps.com/)
- TerraServer (www.terraserver.com/)
- TerraServer-USA (http://terraserver.microsoft.com/)
- TopoZone (www.topozone.com/)
- United States Geologic Survey (http://nmviewogc.cr.usgs.gov/)
- Windows Live Search (http://maps.live.com/)
- Yahoo! Maps (http://maps.yahoo.com/)

SUMMARY

We face two major threats regarding online mapping and imagery: the sensitive information we disclose through our interactions with these services and the content itself. Our interactions reveal locations of interest and the time we were interested in them. We might reveal travel plans, confidential facilities, our homes, or other sensitive locations. Direction-providing services indicate specific destinations as well as the probable routes you will take. Social networks emerge as we share these locations via hyperlinks with our friends, families, coworkers, and readers of our blogs. Even apparently unrelated people can be linked because they examine or seek directions to similar locations. Table 6-2 summarizes the actions you might take when using mapping and imagery services and the types of information you can disclose.

Table 6-2 Summary of Common Actions You Might Take When Visiting Mapping and Imagery Sites, Along with the Types of Information You Would Disclose

Action	Sample Disclosure
Simply visiting the site	IP address, type of browser, previously visited web site (via referer field), possible location (via IP geolocation), size of monitor, speed of Internet connection, possible processor speed.
Zooming, panning of display	Locations of interest, travel plans, possible location.
Viewing traffic	Your probable routes to and from your employer.
Using StreetView	Extremely precise locations of interest. Possible friends, family, and coworkers.
Customizing maps	Specific markers indicating places of interest.
Getting directions	Start points and endpoints of interest. Possible route you will take. Zip codes.
E-mailing a link	Social network, such as friends, family, and coworkers. Possible gatherings of these individuals and probable location of event.
Printing	Maps you want to share or use.
Searching the map	Specific street addresses and businesses of interest.
Logging in	Your unique account identity.
Saving locations	High-priority locations.
Using help	Your familiarity with the service.
Adding or editing your business	Direct association between you and a business.
Advertising on a mapping service	Direct association between you and a business.
Embedding a map in your web site	Direct association between you and a web site. Possible home or work address using WHOIS lookup.
Using 1-800-GOOG-411	The sound of your voice. Your telephone number.
Repeated use of service	Frequency and timing of interest. Comprehensive set of many disclosures. Cookies stored from previous visits.

The content itself also raises important security concerns. Your home, car, place of employment, perhaps even you, all probably exist in the terabytes of imagery data comprising Google Earth, Google Maps, StreetView, and similar services. In the future, we can safely assume that the number of sensors gathering information will increase. Beyond static images, we will see video, perhaps combined with data from terrestrial sound sensors. We see early approaches now. The California-based company Wild Sanctuary has more than 3,500 hours of "soundscapes" and software that can layer relevant recorded sounds in Google Earth.[35] AstroVision recently announced its plans to delive the "first live, continuous, true color image stream of Earth from space."[36]

We see only relatively sanitized data in publicly available systems. However, although it is likely occurring today, in the future it is easy to imagine multinational corporations sponsoring corporate overflights of locations of importance. Today we see powerful collaborative analysis of imagery through sites such as Google Sightseeing and Wikimapia, but in the future we can expect to see powerful automated processing augment these human-centric approaches. Advances in facial recognition,[37] machine vision, data mining, and even automated lip-reading[38] could one day be applied to global scale sensor data. Of more concern is that a future advance could be applied to *all* historical data. Even though a data-mining system cannot currently identify every face in Google's StreetView, a future system might well have this capability.[39]

At their heart, mapping, directions, and imagery sites are about combining sensor data with other semantic information, such as highway traffic data, into a seamless, easy-to-use tool. I would like to suggest simple-to-implement countermeasures to help protect your privacy from surveillance sensors. Unfortunately, this genie is out of the bottle; unless we see major changes in privacy legislation, we need to seek new approaches to privacy and learn how to live in this environment. Currently, nation-states can use such extreme measures as anti-satellite missiles[40] and armies can use battlefield deception and camouflage in an attempt to limit successful surveillance.[41] Both of these are unrealistic to us average citizens. As one friend aptly put it, "I don't want to live in a place where I need to wear a ski mask to my local mall to protect my privacy."

ENDNOTES

1. Actually, "satellite" imagery is a bit of a misnomer. In actuality, you will likely encounter imagery from aircraft as well.
2. Michael Liedtke, "Google to Unite Mapping Mashups," *USA Today,* www.usatoday. com/tech/products/services/2007-07-11-google-unite-maps_N.htm.
3. Tom Spring, "A Closer Look: Google Earth Darfu Awareness," PC World Blogs. 11 April 2007. http://blogs.pcworld.com/staffblog/archives/004070.html, last accessed 12 August 2007.

4. Robin Mejia, "The Satellite Images Document an Atrocity," WashingtonPost.com, 10 June 2007. www.washingtonpost.com/wp-dyn/content/article/2007/06/05/AR2007060501701.html?hpid=topnews, last accessed 12 August 2007.

5. Hurricane Katrina imagery, Google Earth web site. http://earth.google.com/katrina.html, last accessed 12 August 2007.

6. BetaNews Staff, "Google Earth Highlights Destruction," *Beta News,* 12 March 2007. www.betanews.com/article/Google_Earth_Highlights_Destruction/1173718101, last accessed 12 August 2007.

7. "What Is Google Earth Outreach?" Google Earth web site. www.google.com/earth/outreach/index.html, last accessed 12 August 2007.

8. "Google Earth with a Cause," CNET News, 7 June 2007. http://news.com.com/2300-1038_3-6189481.html?tag=ne.gall.latest, last accessed 12 August 2007.

9. Google Maps login. www.google.com/accounts/ServiceLogin?service=local&hl=en&nui=1&continue=http://maps.google.com/%3Fmid%3D1187481579, last accessed 18 August 2007.

10. Note also that crimes have been committed by looking up addresses of victims to find out where they live and work.

11. "Google to Unite Mapping Mashups," Slashdot.org, 11 July 2007. http://slashdot.org/articles/07/07/11/1236248.shtml, last accessed 12 July 2007.

12. Note that the term *mashup* can also mean the combinations of web resources in general and doesn't necessarily include Google Maps or location based data.

13. "Essential Resources for Google Maps," Lifehack.org, 19 November 2005. www.lifehack.org/articles/lifehack/essential-resources-for-google-maps.html, last accessed 22 August 2007.

14. "59 Things to Do with Google Maps Mashups," Google Maps Mania, 28 December 2006. http://googlemapsmania.blogspot.com/2006/12/50-things-to-do-with-google-maps.html, last accessed 22 August 2007.

15. Google Sightseeing, "Top 10 Naked People on Google Earth." http://googlesightseeing.com/2006/11/28/top-10-naked-people-on-google-earth/, last accessed 13 August 2007.

16. "Wikimapia—Let's Describe the World." www.wikimapia.org/, last accessed 21 August 2007.

17. U.S. Army Infantry home page, "1st Battalion, 507th Parachute Infantry Regiment Basic Airborne Course." www.infantry.army.mil/airborne/airborne/, last accessed 14 August 2007.

18. "Geotagging," Wikipedia. http://en.wikipedia.org/wiki/Geotagging, last accessed 21 August 2007.

19. "Flickr: Explore Everyone's Geotagged Photos on a Map." http://www.flickr.com/map, last accessed 21 August 2007.

20. Researchers at the University of Southern California are developing an interesting technology, entitled Viewfinder, that allows seamless integration of geotagged digital photos into 3D maps; see http://interactive.usc.edu/viewfinder/ and http://bits.blogs.nytimes.com/2008/04/03/a-3-d-viewfinder-for-a-shoebox-of-digital-photos/ for more information.

21. "British Traffic Wardens Issued CCTV Head Cameras," Slashdot.org. 23 May 2007. http://yro.slashdot.org/yro/07/05/24/027230.shtml, last accessed 21 August 2007.

22. "New York Plans Surveillance Veil for Downtown," Slashdot.org. 9 July 2007. http://it.slashdot.org/article.pl?sid=07/07/09/1738252, last accessed 21 August 2007.

23. Imagery analysis should not be confused with the related field of remote sensing, which is the acquisition from a distance of information from a wide variety of sensor types, including but not limited to imagery sensors.

24. "History of Aerial Photography," Aerial Arts—A Gallery of Fine Art Aerial Photography. www.aerialarts.com/History/history.htm, last accessed 14 August 2007.

25. "Corona," National Reconnaissance Office. www.nro.gov/corona/facts.html, last accessed 14 August 2007.

26. "Corona," Mission and Spacecraft Library, Jet Propulsion Laboratory—California Institute of Technology. http://samadhi.jpl.nasa.gov/msl/Programs/corona.html, last accessed 14 August 2007.

27. Joseph Mirabeau, "City-Building Games." www.slideshare.net/wuzziwug/city-building-games, last accessed 18 August 2007.

28. Katie Hafner and Saritha Rai, "Governments Tremble at Google's Bird's-Eye View." *The New York Times, OnlineEdition,* www.nytimes.com. 20 December 2005. www.globalsecurity.org/org/news/2005/051220-bird-view.htm as of 25 July 2007.

29. However, I'll bet a government has far more leverage to demand removal than you or I. Also, sometimes governments attempt to buy up all imagery taken of sensitive facilities or operations, a strategy nicknamed "checkbook shutter control."

30. In many cases, the resultant image looks as the censor applied a Photoshop-like filter. Similar filters have been shown to be reversible (see www.boingboing.net/2007/10/08/untwirling-photo-of.html), although, in the case of Google Maps, I would be surprised if this were the case.

31. It is just a matter of time until someone creates a web site that focuses on locations of censored sites.

32. The popularity of StreetView has spawned a number of interesting variants that are concerning from the security and privacy perspective. For a great example, see EveryScape (www.everyscape.com/aboutUs.aspx), which lets businesses build photo-realistic, interactive cities, streets, and sidewalks.

33. Kevin Poulsen, "EFF Privacy Advocate Sighted in Google Street View," Wired Blog Network, 11 June 2007. http://blog.wired.com/27bstroke6/2007/06/eff_privacy_adv.html, last accessed 22 August 2007.

34. A9 Maps, http://maps.a9.com/, last accessed 26 July 2007.

35. "Sounds Bring Google Earth to Life," BBC News, 10 May 2007. http://news.bbc.co.uk/2/hi/technology/6639977.stm, last accessed 13 August 2007.

36. AstroVision. www.astrovision.com/ourbus.html, last accessed 13 August 2007.

37. Declan McCullagh, "Call IT SuperBowl Face Scan I," Wired Online, 2 February 2001. www.wired.com/politics/law/news/2001/02/41571, last accessed 21 August 2007.

38. Steve Watson, "Lip Reading Surveillance Cameras to Stop Terror," Infowars.net, 27 April 2007. www.infowars.net/articles/april2007/270407lip_reading.htm, last accessed 21 August 2007.

39. As this book was going to press, Google announced that it would bow to privacy concerns and blur all faces in Street View; see http://blogs.pcworld.com/staffblog/archives/006970.html. That being said, Google will likely possess the raw unblurred images in its internal databases.

40. "2007 Chinese Anti-satellite Missile Test," Wikipedia. http://en.wikipedia.org/wiki/2007_Chinese_anti-satellite_missile_test, last accessed 13 August 2007.

41. Department of the Army. "FM 90-2: Battlefield Deception," Washington, DC, 3 October 1988. Available at http://fas.org/irp/doddir/army/fm90-2/toc.htm, last accessed 13 August 2007.

Advertising and Embedded Content

[My web history is] mine—you can't have it. If you want to use it for something, then you have to negotiate with me. I have to agree, I have to understand what I'm getting in return.[1]
—Sir Tim Berners-Lee

Publishing information is the backbone of web content, and bloggers and webmasters frequently rely on embedded content from companies such as Google to enhance the quality of their sites. Unfortunately, embedding third-party content is the equivalent of planting a web bug in web pages,[2] alerting the source of the embedded content to a user's presence on a given site and facilitating logging, profiling, and fingerprinting. More important, the source of the third-party content can aggregate these single instances and track users as they browse the web. This notion deserves restating: The simple act of web browsing across many disparate sites has the potential to generate a continuous stream of information back to the providers of third-party content. The more popular a given third-party service is, the more sites will deploy their content, and the greater the window of visibility on users' web surfing activity becomes. In the case of advertising networks such as Google/DoubleClick and web-analytics services such as Google Analytics, the risk is large indeed.

This chapter explores the risks associated with embedded content by focusing on Google's advertising network and Google Analytics, but it also provides an overview of other forms of embedded content that present related risks, such as embedded YouTube videos, maps, and Google's Chat Back Service.

CROSS-SITE TRACKING

As mentioned in Chapter 3, "Footprints, Fingerprints, and Connections," many web sites embed third-party content in their sites. Third-party content can take the form of legitimate images and video clips, among other forms of content, but it can also be used to track users as they surf the web. Advertisers and web-analytic services give webmasters enticing analysis tools and advertising profit, simply requiring that, in exchange, webmasters add small snippets of HTML and JavaScript to their pages. Unfortunately, such third-party content is a severe privacy and web-based information-disclosure risk because the user's web browser automatically visits these third-party servers,[3] where their visit is presumably logged and their browser tagged with cookies. More important, the larger the advertising network is, the larger the window a given company has on a user's online activity. For example, if a user visits 100 different web sites, each containing advertisements from a single advertising service, that service can observe the user as he or she visits each site. Figure 7-1 depicts cross-site tracking via an advertising network. In this figure, a user visits six distinct web sites, each hosting content from a single advertiser. In turn, the user's visits create one set of log entries on each of the six legitimate servers. However, because each visit contained an advertisement from a single advertising network, the advertiser is able to log all six visits.

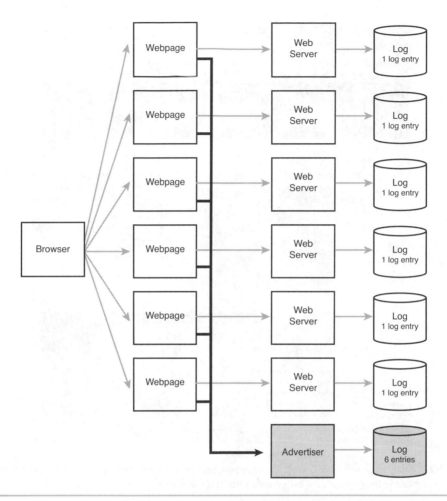

Figure 7-1 Example of cross-site tracking by an advertising network. When the user visits six distinct sites, he or she generates one set of log entries at each site. However, if each site contains advertisements from a single advertising network, the advertiser is able to record all six visits.

Let's look at a real-world example by visiting a popular web site, MSNBC (see Figure 7-2). As it turns out, the MSNBC web site is laden with third-party content.

Figure 7-2   Analyzing the MSNBC web site demonstrates that it contains a great deal of third-party content. The problem is rampant among other web sites, large and small.

In a world without third-party content, the user should simply receive content from MSNBC's domain, msnbc.msn.com. In the real world, however, the user visits 16 additional domains from 10 different companies. Two of these domains, DoubleClick and GoogleAnalytics, are owned by Google. The web browser provides the user with little assistance in detecting third-party content. The user simply sees the browser's status bar rapidly flicker as the browser contacts each new site. To provide a clearer picture, I captured the raw network activity using the Wireshark protocol-analysis tool and created Table 7-1 to detail each of the third party domains visited.

Table 7-1   Third-Party Sites Visited When Browsing the MSNBC Web Site

Domain	Notes
a365.ms.akamai.net a509.cd.akamai.net	Domain owned by Akamai.com, a mirroring service for media content
ad.3ad.doubleclick.net	Digital marketing service, acquired by Google
amch.questionmarket.com	Hosting web site where online surveys are posted
c.live.com.nsatc.net c.msn.com.nsatc.net rad.msn.com.nsatc.net	Registered to Savvis Communications, a networking and hosting provider
context3.kanoodle.com	Search-targeted sponsored links service
global.msads.net.c.footprint.net hm.sc.msn.com.c.footprint.net	Registered to Level 3 Communications, a large network provider
msnbcom.112.2o7.net	Registered to Omniture, a web analytics and online business optimization provider
prpx.service.mirror-image.net wrpx.service.mirror-image.net	Registered to Mirror Image Internet, a content delivery, streaming media, and web computing service
switch.atdmt.com view.atdmt.com	Registered to aQuantive, parent company to a family of digital marketing companies
www-google-analytics.l.google.com	Traffic measurement and interactive reporting service offered by Google

Think about it. Simply visiting a single web page from a popular news service informs *16* third-party servers of the visit, a 16-fold magnification of logging. This is not a manu-factured example, but it is representative of a common practice. Embedding third-party content in web sites is ubiquitous, and so is the problem. The end result is that web surfers are frequently tracked by companies they've never even heard of. It is also worth considering that information sharing via embedded content doesn't occur only with "third parties"—sharing can also occur between ostensibly separate entities that are actually owned by the same parent company. For example, the A9 search engine (an Amazon.com company) inserts search term–related Amazon book advertisements adja-cent to search results. These advertisements allow Amazon to track what A9 users search for, click through, and possibly buy online. If the user does make a purchase on Amazon.com, Amazon knows that user's real-world identity, including billing and ship-ping information. In the case of A9, Amazon makes clear on the A9 site that A9 is an Amazon.com company, but the important idea is that corporate ownership—and, hence, implicit information sharing—might not be obvious as users browse the web.

ADVERTISING

A famous New Yorker cartoon from 1993 showed two dogs at a computer, with one saying to the other, "On the Internet, nobody knows you're a dog." That may no longer be true.[4]
—Louise Story

Advertising is the fuel behind virtually all free online tools. Advertising is also the means for tracking your web surfing across the Internet. Anytime you visit sites that serve advertisements from a common advertising network, your activities can be logged. These logs can then be used to create precise profiles, facilitating tailored advertising. Importantly, log analysis isn't a static process. For example, advertising companies are actively developing technologies to anticipate people's next steps.[5] Based on the popularity of the largest web companies, the amount of information they can collect is staggering (see Figure 7-3).

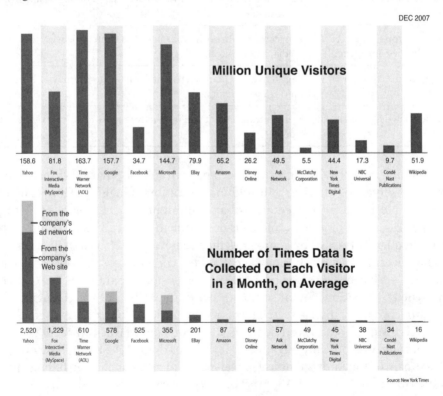

Figure 7-3   *New York Times* analysis of the data collection conducted by some of the largest online companies.

Web advertisements are big business, and some of the largest services are offerings by Google, including AdSense, AdWords, and DoubleClick. However, advertisements are appearing in many other forms. Microsoft is quietly offering an ad-funded version of its Works office suite.[6] Pudding Media, a San Jose–based startup, is offering advertisement-supported phone service.[7]

Google understands the growth potential of advertising. In 2007, the company announced that it would pay $3.1 billion to acquire DoubleClick, a leading online advertiser, whose current estimated revenues at the time were $150 million.[8] A year ago, Yahoo! made a similar, smaller-scale move by acquiring the online global ad network BlueLithium for approximately $300 million.[9] At the time of this writing Yahoo! was reportedly considering an agreement to carry search advertisements from Google, amid a potential hostile takeover attempt by Microsoft.[10] Although it is impossible to know for sure at this time, such an allegiance carries the very real potential of allowing Google to gather search terms, issue cookies, and conduct other activities based on Yahoo!'s extremely large user base. Make no mistake, a key component of such acquisitions and alliances is access to user data and the power it provides.

NOTE

Online advertising is a growth industry that is eating into traditional media markets. For example, the media-analysis company Simmons found that Internet video advertisements are 47% more engaging—and, hence, more effective—than traditional television advertisements.[11]

Chapter 3 should have convinced you that users scatter significant, and often personally identifiable, information behind as they surf the web. When *New York Times* reporter Louise Story decided to determine how personally identifiable the information maintained by large web companies is, she asked four large online companies a single question: "Can you show me an advertisement with my name in it?" Story provided the following summary of the responses.[12]

Microsoft says it could use only a person's first name. AOL and Yahoo! could use a full name, but only on their sites, not the other sites on which they place ads. Google isn't sure—it probably could, but it doesn't know the names of most of its users.

Although these results are telling in their own right, keep in mind that these are official responses provided to a *New York Times* reporter. In other words, these are legal opinions on the subject, as opposed to technical capability. What the four companies have the *capability* to do is an entirely different matter. Advertising networks are the net that allows large online companies to gather this precise information and use it for user profiling, data mining, and targeted advertising. Because of this capability to aggregate and analyze user information, advertising campaigns can follow users as they switch from independent sites. You might have encountered this technique when shopping online. For example, if you were searching for flat panel monitors on site X, when you hopped over to visit site Y, low and behold, there were advertisements for flat panel monitors.

Microsoft is openly touting an "Engagement Mapping" approach that seeks to move beyond the "outdated 'last ad clicked'" model by understanding "how each ad exposure—whether display, rich media or search, seen multiple times on multiple sites and across many channels—influenced an eventual purchase."[13] The article also states that Microsoft intends to use data on user behavior *before* clicking an ad to be able to say that an unclicked ad still made an impression. If the article is to be believed, Microsoft intends to collate that information with search queries and sites visited within the period of a day or a couple of days. Two questions immediately arise. Where does that other data come from (and is it a mere coincidence that Microsoft is seeking to acquire Yahoo! and other search companies)? Now that we are talking about keeping tabs of long-term user behavior, and hypothesizing why a user did this or that, what other kinds of data mining will this floodgate open? They are essentially saying, "We are going to dedicate a lot of resources to watching where you go and what you see on the web." The fact that Microsoft Windows is the most popular operating system on Earth[14] just magnifies the concern. The law surrounding online advertising and the collection of user data is still immature, so advertisers have a very wide lane in which to operate. For example, a U.S. Federal Court ruled that ads displayed by search engines are protected as free speech when deciding what advertisements to display.[15]

ADSENSE

Google AdSense[16], sometimes called Google Syndication, is an advertising service Google provides that allows webmasters to earn advertising revenue by hosting AdSense ads (see Figure 7-4). These revenues aren't trivial, commonly ranging from a few hundred dollars a month to $50,000 or more per year, making the service extremely popular.[17] AdSense advertisements are context-sensitive ads served by Google based on the hosting site's content. Unfortunately, merely visiting a web site hosting these advertisements informs Google of the user's IP address and gives Google the opportunity to log the user's visit and tag the user's browser with a cookie.

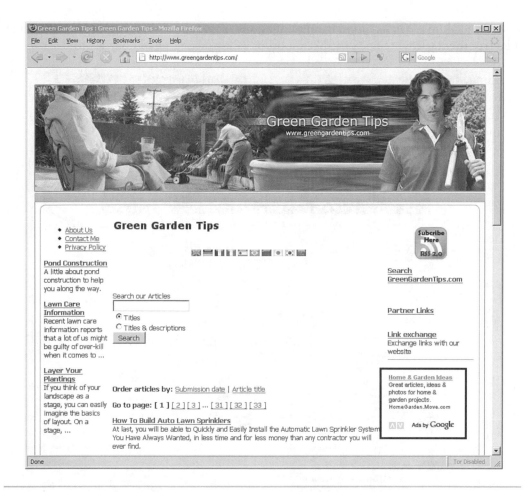

Figure 7-4 Screenshot of Google AdSense. Notice the (debatably) unobtrusive advertisement in the bottom-right corner. Embedded advertisements such as these alert the advertising network of your presence on a site.

AdSense isn't limited to textual ads on traditional web pages. Google is experimenting with AdSense for other forms of content, including RSS Feeds,[18] web site search boxes,[19] mobile content,[20] video, and Cost Per Action AdSense.[21, 22] Nor are AdSense and similar services limited to minor sites. Major online retailers also participate. For example, eBay signed deals to run ads from Google and Yahoo!.[23] Figure 7-5 shows an example with eBay and Yahoo!. When searching for an item on eBay, Yahoo! servers provide contextual advertisements, leaving open the likelihood of Yahoo!'s logging of eBay visitors.[24]

Figure 7-5   Screenshot of Yahoo! advertisements embedded in an eBay web page. Because these ads are pulled directly from Yahoo! servers, user information such as cookies and IP addresses is disclosed directly to Yahoo!.

> **WARNING**
>
> It is also important to consider the identity-disclosure risks from the perspective of the webmaster, who must use the user's registered Google account to log on to the service and use the web interface to administer his or her accounts.[25]

The future of AdSense is difficult to determine. Some analysts believe that Google is acquiring sites that will provide traffic itself instead of paying adverting fees to third-party sites.[26]

ADWORDS

AdWords is a fundamental part of Google's business model. According to the BBC, every time a user conducts a search on Google, the company makes 12¢ in revenue.[27] When you consider that Google receives more than 60 billion searches per year in the United States alone, you can see that the program generates huge profit. Google believes that AdWords "is the largest program of its kind."[28] Using AdWords, would-be advertisers bid on search terms that are displayed as part of the user's search results; the better the placement, the higher the cost. AdWords are relatively unobtrusive, but quite effective, advertisements (see the right side of Figure 7-6).[29]

AdWords poses both information-disclosure risk and other security risks. Attackers have used AdWords and similar services to misdirect users to malicious sites; see the "Malicious Ad Serving" section later in the chapter.[30] However, Google's AdWord Partners are a significant information-disclosure risk because searches from these sites can be sent to Google. According to Google those who have already joined their "growing advertising network" include AOL, Ask.com, Ask Jeeves, AT&T Worldnet, CompuServe, EarthLink, Excite, and Netscape.[31] Even third-party search engines that delete their logs locally are still at risk. Take, for example, Ask.com, who took an industry-leading position by offering AskEraser, a function that deletes search activity from Ask.com servers.[32] However, Google delivers the bulk of Ask's advertisements, so user information, including the search query and IP address, are passed back to Google each time a page is served to a visitor.[33]

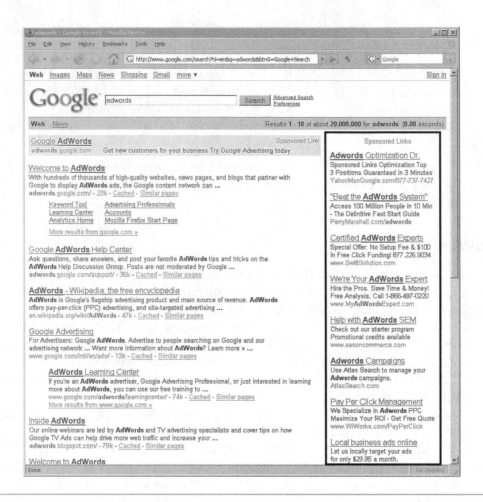

Figure 7-6   Screenshot of Google AdWords. Notice the advertisements on the right side of the image.

GOOGLE DOUBLECLICK

DoubleClick is a major online advertising service, long criticized for using cookies and IP addresses to track users as they surf the web.[34] DoubleClick is an extremely popular advertising service and counts a large number of Fortune 500 companies as clients. In 2007, Google announced a definitive agreement with DoubleClick for $3.1 billion in cash to acquire the company. The acquisition drew the attention of the U.S. Federal Trade Commission and European Regulators, who investigated antitrust and privacy implications but eventually acquiesced.[35, 36, 37, 38] Google closed the acquisition of DoubleClick shortly thereafter.[39]

WARNING

DoubleClick allows users to opt out of its ad-serving and search products by issuing a special cookie. This is an elegant solution from the perspective of DoubleClick because users concerned enough to opt out might delete this cookie by accident as they remove other traditional tracking cookies. One possible solution is a browser plug-in that allows easy-to-use and fine-grained cookie control, although this approach still assumes that companies employing opt-out cookies will honor the request and not log user activity anyway.[40, 41]

The implications of a combined Google–DoubleClick dreadnaught are significant. Google excels in search advertising (AdWords) and simple textual advertisements (AdSense). On the other hand, DoubleClick excels in "display advertising," such as flashy banner ads and video advertisements, which reach between 80% and 85% of the web population.[42, 43] The end result is a broad net that permits Google to track a user's web searches and web site visits, with the potential to impact the privacy interests of more than 1.1 billion Internet users worldwide.[44] This acquisition underscores the fact that mergers and acquisitions are about data, including both existing data stockpiles and access to continued data streams.

NOTE

Google's acquisition of DoubleClick places significant competitive pressure on Microsoft.[45] As a response, Microsoft actively sought to acquire Yahoo! to increase its advertising reach.[46]

ADVERTISING RISKS

Advertising poses more risks than those already discussed regarding AdWords, AdSense, and DoubleClick. Attackers can exploit advertising networks to compromise end-user machines, unethical interface techniques can trick users into disclosing sensitive information, and historically unbiased network providers can insert advertisements as the web pages make their way to the user's browser.

MALICIOUS AD SERVING

Advertising networks are more than just information-disclosure risks. They also serve as a malware attack vector. Advertising services pay web site owners for publishing advertisements on their web sites. A very common technique is the banner ad we've all seen at the top of web pages. Such ads usually take the form of animated GIF files, but they now include many image and video formats. Individuals and organizations that want to advertise using such a service create a media file and pay an advertiser a fee, and the advertiser serves the image to thousands of visitors of sites that belong to its advertising network. The risks here are twofold. Attackers have created misleading advertisements as a means to draw traffic to a malware serving or other malicious web site.[47] The users' trust of the advertisement company and the hosting web site increases their trust of the advertisements, leaving web surfers more vulnerable to such an attack. Virus writers have used the Google Adwords service to serve text ads that appeared to link to legitimate destination sites, but silently infected vulnerable web surfers by routing users through an intermediate, malicious site. Attackers also have used a vulnerability in Internet Explorer to compromise visitors as they passed through the intermediate site, before ultimately arriving at the legitimate site.[48]

The ads themselves have also been used to attack the web user directly. Malformed graphical images are one common technique. For example, a banner advertisement displayed on MySpace served spyware to more than one million visitors. In this case, attackers exploited a flaw in the way Windows processed Windows Meta File (WMF) images to install a Trojan horse.[49] Because the attack occurs when the browser displays the image, the user needn't click the advertisement to be infected. Another attack, served by DoubleClick, used rich media advertisements created in Adobe Flash to exploit a similar vulnerability, with the malicious advertisements appearing on extremely popular sites, including those of *The Economist* and Major League Baseball.[50] Rich media advertisements are highly interactive and are becoming increasingly popular. Even the seemingly simple task of securing browsers against malicious images is proving difficult, and complex, rich media tools such as Flash are proving to be an even greater challenge.[51] Other complex environments, such as ads embedded in Adobe PDF files, are now being explored as ways to reach potential customers, and I expect that similar issues will arise.[52]

> **NOTE**
>
> Google has taken an active role in countering malicious advertisements and web sites. For example, Google warns users of potentially malicious sites by clearly labeling suspect sites in their search result listings. As another example, Google's I'm Feeling Lucky search button no longer automatically redirects a user to a suspicious site; instead, the user is presented with a list of search results instead.[53]

MALICIOUS INTERFACES

Beyond malicious ad serving, advertisers employ another concerning strategy that I call *malicious interfaces.* In the idealistic world of interface design theory, interface designers always operate in the best interests of their users. Designers carefully study user tasks and painstakingly craft interfaces and applications to help users accomplish them. However, in the world of online advertising, the exact opposite is true. Designers frequently violate design best practices to coerce or mislead users into viewing advertising. Examples abound on the web: fake hyperlinks that pop up advertisements, giant advertisements that cover the text of articles, distracting advertising videos that begin playing the moment a page is viewed, banner ads with fake buttons that appear to be a part of the interface, advertisements embedded in video clips ... the list goes on. Malicious interface designers are creative; new "innovations" are coming out regularly. The only constraining factor appears to be the tolerance of the user. The invasiveness of advertisements is getting worse. You may have heard the term "banner blindness." Users quickly learned that banner ads are of little value and ignore the advertisements, to the point that they barely perceive banner ads anymore. This defense mechanism has forced advertisers to become more aggressive in capturing user attention.[54, 55]Although, I don't claim that Google employs malicious interface design, the trend is concerning; it seems that malicious interface designers are carefully seeking the sweet spot between making advertising profit and annoying the user so much that they abandon a given site altogether.

WARNING

In many cases the link displayed by an embedded advertisement is not the actual link. Nor will hovering over the link display the destination URL in the user's browser status bar. The actual link goes first to the ad server so the click can be logged. The user's browser is then redirected to the page chosen by the advertiser.

HOSTILE NETWORKS

As carriers of key components of network infrastructure, ISPs and web hosting services are flexing their muscle to place advertisements in front of users. For example, domain registrar and web hosting provider Network Solutions hijacked customers' unused subdomains to resort to ad-laden "parking" pages.[56] As another example, bloggers Lauren Weinstein and Sarah Lai Stirland reported Canadian ISP Rogers modification of web pages en route (see Figure 7-7).

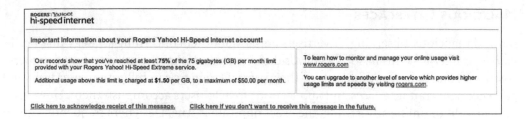

Figure 7-7   Screenshot of an ISP altering a Google web page

Inserting advertisements into web pages as they transit an ISP is potentially very big business. ISPs already have access to a tremendous amount of personal information about users' online activity. This data is a veritable gold mine if used to target online advertising. Some ISPs are reportedly selling significant amounts of user data to online marketers.[57] In the United Kingdom, three major ISPs have announced plans to use user clickstream data to insert relevant advertisements as they surf, through a new startup called Phorm.[58] ISP data contains some of the most sensitive information disclosures made by online users. If this advertising technique becomes widespread, virtually every web surfer's activities will be passed on to advertisers in some form. Fighting the issue will be difficult, and users might find that they are faced with little alternative than to accept this new status quo.

AFFILIATE SERVICES

Affiliate advertising isn't just confined to Google via its AdSense and DoubleClick programs. It is a popular marketing practice in which, in its common form, web authors embed advertisements that contain unique tracking data to identify the correct affiliate to compensate. Such advertisements can be static—that is, the advertisement exists entirely on the server of the web author. In this case, the user must click the advertisement before the advertiser is aware of the user. However, many affiliate services provide dynamic content that is pulled directly from the online company without any action by the user, immediately linking the user to the visited web site (see Figure 7-8 for an example). In addition, the online company might tag the user with a cookie or retrieve an existing cookie, opening the possibility of identifying the user by name, billing address, and shipping address.

Figure 7-8 Example of Amazon affiliate network dynamic advertisements. Some affiliate networks, such as Amazon, encourage web authors to embed these advertisements into their web content, allowing the user to be logged, tagged with a cookie, and perhaps identified by name, merely by visiting the web page containing the advertisement.[59]

FACEBOOK BEACON

Facebook's Beacon illustrates both the detailed insight that large online companies have into the activities of their user populations and the lengths some companies will go to increase profit. Facebook's Beacon service allows Facebook users to share their purchases from affiliated online companies, such as books, movies, and gifts, with their Facebook friends.[60] However, when the service was first offered, participation was "opt out." The end result is that many users were infuriated and the civil action group MoveOn.org initiated a very effective online petition that rapidly gained more than 50,000 supporters.[61] MoveOn even blamed Facebook for "ruining Christmas" because the Beacon advertising system allowed users to see holiday present purchases made by friends and family.[62]

Shortly thereafter, Facebook changed the service to "opt in" by requiring explicit user permission before publishing purchases to the user's Facebook friends.

OTHER CROSS-SITE RISKS

The preceding sections illustrated the risks associated with AdWords, AdSense, and DoubleClick, but cross-site information-disclosure risks do not end with advertising. The web functions thanks to hyperlinks and embedded content. Through these vectors, Google and other large companies can gather tremendous amounts of user information and help link clusters of information to individual users, companies, and other organizations. The following examples share one common characteristic: Each relies upon third-party web masters to embed tracking (or trackable) content into their web sites. Most web masters would not add such content arbitrarily; instead, they are enticed by at least a nominal incentive for cooperation.

> **WARNING**
>
> Embedding Google or other third-party content into a web page isn't the only concern. Posting your own content on a Google-hosted service, such as Blogger, YouTube, or Orkut, allows Google to track all users to the site. In addition, you become dependent on Google and its ideas about censorship, privacy, and quality of service.

GOOGLE ANALYTICS

Google Analytics is a free tool for webmasters that provides a powerful and intuitive interface for analyzing web log data (see Figure 7-9).[63] Google Analytics is part of a class of applications that provide statistical and graphical analyses of web visitor activity based on web server log data and (optionally) on data gained via cookies placed on users' computers, web bugs, and JavaScript code. Such tools display site visitor reports (for example, geographic locations of visitors, most active visitors, and browsers used), page view reports (for example, entry/exit pages, most popular time of day, and number of requests for each page), server reports (for example, amount of bandwidth consumed and which files were requested), and referer reports (for example, search queries and referring URLs). Other popular web analytics software includes Webalizer (www.mrunix.net/webalizer/) and WebTrends (www.webtrends.com/).

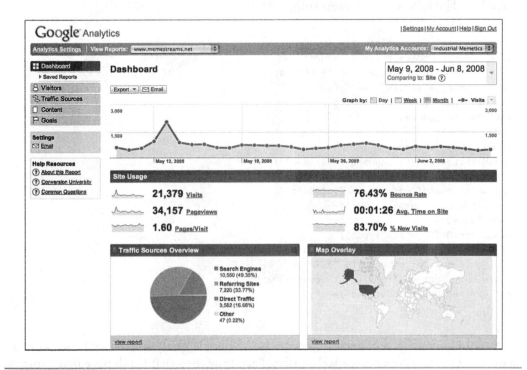

Figure 7-9 Google Analytics gives Google the capability to track users as they visit any Google Analytics member site.

Google Analytics is easy to install. Webmasters need only paste code similar to the following into web pages they want the service to track.

```
<script src="http://www.google-analytics.com/urchin.js"
type="text/javascript">
</script>

<script type="text/javascript">
_uacct = "UA-994065-1";
urchinTracker();
</script>
```

This code is straightforward JavaScript. It serves as a hook in each web page to contact Google whenever a page is loaded and download a JavaScript file called urchin.js. The _uacct variable stories a unique tracking code assigned to the webmaster. The script then launches the urchinTracker() function in the newly downloaded urchin.js file. Unfortunately, the code within urchin.js is far more complex and apparently obfuscated.[64, 65] The following is a short snippet:[66]

```
function urchinTracker(page) {
 if (_udl.protocol=="file:") return;
 if (_uff && (!page || page=="")) return;
 var a,b,c,xx,v,z,k,x="",s="",f=0;
 var nx=" expires="+_uNx()+";";
 var dc=_ubd.cookie;
 _udh=_uDomain();
 if (!_uVG()) return;
 _uu=Math.round(Math.random()*2147483647);
 _udt=new Date();
 _ust=Math.round(_udt.getTime()/1000);
 a=dc.indexOf("__utma="+_udh);
 b=dc.indexOf("__utmb="+_udh);
 c=dc.indexOf("__utmc="+_udh);
 if (_udn && _udn!="") { _udo=" domain="+_udn+";"; }
 if (_utimeout && _utimeout!="") {
 x=new Date(_udt.getTime()+(_utimeout*1000));
 x=" expires="+x.toGMTString()+";";
 }
```

Although many webmasters sing the praise of Google Analytics, the tool also poses a significant privacy concern for web surfers. Each time they visit a web page that contains the request to download urchin.js, the user's web browser contacts a Google server and downloads and then executes the script, leaving behind all the typical web-browsing footprints described in Chapter 3. The urchin.js script presumably discloses additional information, but Google does not provide specific details. The primary risk of Google Analytics is that it gives Google the capability to track users as they browse from web site to web site, including the use of cookies.[67] There is no official count of the number of participating web sites, but several years ago, an analyst estimated the number to be about 237,000.[68] The number now is presumably far greater. Some of the most popular sites on the web employ Google Analytics, such as Slashdot.org, which downloads Google's newer ga.js script, an equally difficult script to interpret. You can see a snippet in Figure 7-10.

```
var _gat=new Object({c:"length",p:"cookie",b:undefined,bb:function(d,a){this.wb=d;this.Hb=a},o:"__utma=",
O;h--){o=d.charCodeAt(h);a=(a<<6&268435455)+o+(o<<14);c=a&266338304;a=c!=0?a^c>>21:a})return a},B:functio
c(d)){escape(d)},z:function(d,a){var c=decodeURIComponent,h;d=d.split("+").join(" ");if(c instanceof Func
v:function(d,a){return d.indexOf(a)},D:function(d,a,c){c=_gat.b==c?d[_gat.c]:c;return d.substring(a,c)},m
c("alltheweb","q"),c("gigablast","q"),c("voila","rdata"),c("virgilio","qs"),c("live","q"),c("baidu","wd")
"/";d.ha=100;d.Da="/__utm.gif";d.ta=1;d.ua=1;d.F="|";d.sa=1;d.qa=1;d.nb=1;d.f="auto";d.C=1;d.Ga=1000;d.Mc
i[s][0]+b,e)}}.Eb=function(){return n.b==g||g==f.t()};f.Ba=function(){return m?m:"-"};f.Qb=function(k){m
for(var b=0;b<j[y];b++)if(b<4&&!n.Ea(j[b])){j[b]="-";f.tc=function(){return p};f.Ic=function(k){p=k};f.ic
b){var e=f.U,i=B.1,s;f.Ha(k);B.1=b;for(s=0;s<e[y];s++)if(!t(e[s][1]())})e[s][3]();B.1=i};f.Yb=function(){1
new Image(1,1);u.src=h.Da+r;u.onload=function(){j()}}}if(1==B||2==B){var x=new Image(1,1);x.src={"https:"=
m}p.g(j.ca,new p.h.ab(r,d,a,c,h,o)};else{m.Xb=r;m.Oa=d;m.K=a;m.qb=c;m.Jb=h;m.Kb=o});_gat.h.$.prototype.Bb
n){n=new f.h.$(d,a,c,h,o,j,m,r);f.g(p.la,n)}else{n.mb=a;n.Wb=c;n.Vb=h;n.Sb=o;n.sb=j;n.Ub=m;n.vb=r}return
new ActiveXObject(n+".6");p="WIN 6,0,21,0";f.AllowScriptAccess="always";p=f.GetVariable(t)}catch(B){}if(!
a.n&&a.n.javaEnabled(){}?1:0;a.yb=o?j();c;a.rb=h.d(a.a.characterSet?a.a.characterSet:{a.a.charset?a.a.chars
v[z];if(f(q,t(1.wb))){x=y(x,"?").join("&");if(f(x,"&"+1.Hb+"")){u=y(x,"&"+1.Hb+"=")[1];if(f(u,"&")}u=y(u.
q=y(q,"/")[0]}if(0==m.v(q,"www.")}q=m.D(q,4);return new m.k.q{p,q,p,"(referral)","referral",p,u)};j.kc=fu
"";x=j.kc(j.a.location);if(j.r.H&&q.Eb()){z=q.Ca();if(!r(z)&&!f(z,";")}(q.Ra();return"")}z=n(e,m.X+1,";")
F21:F;q.Rb([i,j.ja,F,k,1.ka()].join(".")};q.Ra()}return"&utmcn=1")else return"&utmcr=1"}};_gat.k.q=functi
a(d.ra)});_gat.k.q.prototype.zb=function(d){var a=this,c=_gat,h=function(o){return c.z(c.B(d,o,"|")}}};a.u
l[j][b]};if(a.b!=e){if(k)v+=j[b];v+=x(e);k=false}else k=true)return v}function x(1){var v=[],k,b;for(b=0;b
[1.M()],k;for(k in c)if(a.b!=c[k]&&!1.yc(k)}a.g(v,k.toString()+u(c[k]))}return v.join("")};d._setKey=func
o)}};_gat.cc=function(d,a){var c=this;c.Wc=a;c.Dc=d;c._trackEvent=function(h,o,j){return a._trackEvent(c.
i){if(o(b)||o(e)||o(i))return"-";var s=r(b,c.o+a.e,e),w;if(!o(s)){w=f(s,".");w[5]=w[5]?w[5]*1+1:1;w[3]=w[
""==g.f||"none"==g.f){g.f="";return 1}q();if(g.nb)return c.t(g.f);else return 1};a.lc=function(b,e){if(o(
return b};a.Oc=function(b){if(a.P()){var e="";if(a.j!=h&&a.j.M().length>0)e+="&utme="+c.d(a.j.M());e+=a.I
a.a.createElement("script");b.type="text/javascript";b.id="_gasojs";b.src="https://www.google.com/analyti
o(i.za())){E=x(G,"&",e};a.L=true}else{C=f(i.I(),".");s=C[0]}else if(F)if(!I||!J){E=x(b,";",e};a.L=true}el
function(){var b;if(!B){a.zc();a.e=a.rc();a.s=new c.Y(a,g)}if(z()}a.xc();if(!B){if(z()){a.va=a.lc(a.a.r
r(b,"gaso=","&";r(a.a[c.p],c.Sa,";";if(a[c.t]>=10){a.A=e;if(a.V.addEventListener}a.V.addEventListener("lo
if(g.J&&g.J[t]>0}a.Jc();a.Oc(b);a.L=false}};a._trackTrans=function(){var b=a.e,e=[],i,s,w,A;a._initData()
1[w[e]};i=f[w[e],g.f};for(s=0;s<i[t];s++)i[s]=1(i[s]);if("T"==1[0]}a._addTrans(i[1],i[2],i[3],i[4],i[5],i
a.G,a,a,e)}};a._link=function(b,e){if(g.H&&b){a._initData();a.a[n].href=a._getLinkerUrl(b,e)}};a._linkB
function(){a._initData();return new c.Z};a._sendXEvent=function(b){var e="";a._initData();if(a.P()){e+="&
false;return w};a._trackOutboundUrl=function(b){a._initData();if(a.P()){var e=new c.Z;e._setKey(6,1,b);y.
b)};a._clearIgnoredRef=function(){g.ga=[]};a.Tc=function(){return g.ga};a._setAllowHash=function(b){g.nb=
function(){return g.ta};a._setLocalGifPath=function(b){g.Da=b};a._getLocalGifPath=function(){return g.Da}
a._setCampContentKey=function(b){g.db=b};a._setCampIdKey=function(b){g.eb=b};a._setCampMediumKey=function
```

Figure 7-10 Screenshot of the Google Analytics script `ga.js` downloaded from Google when users visit Slashdot.org

The risk of being tracked across 250,000 or more web sites is concerning enough, but the true risk of Google Analytics is that the user data can be combined with web sites participating in Google's AdSense and AdWords programs, enabling the company to track users across a broad swath of the most popular portions of the web. Users see only a brief flicker in their browser's status bar as their browser contacts Google's servers. The potential of "free" web-analytics software is not lost on Google's competitors; both Yahoo! and Microsoft recently released free web-analytics tools.[69, 70]

CHAT BACK

Google's Chatback service enables web authors to embed a status indicator, a "badge," directly into their web pages. When the page is loaded, the badge (see Figure 7-11) indicates whether the user is available for communication via Google Talk. Merely visiting the page causes the user's browser to pull the Chatback badge from Google's servers, leaving behind footprints in their logs. Clicking the link can start an online conversation, leaving open the eavesdropping and logging risks discussed in Chapter 5, "Communications." Although this is a text-based service, similar risks exist via VoIP "call-me buttons" offered by companies such as Jajah, Jangle, Jaxtr, Tringme, and Grand Central.[71, 72]

Figure 7-11   Sample Google Chatback badge. Web authors place small snippets of Google-provided code in their web pages, and visitors to the page can see whether the author is available to chat via Google Talk.

YOU TUBE VIDEOS

Embedding YouTube videos is an extremely popular practice by web authors (see Figure 7-12). When doing so, authors place code similar to the following in their web pages.[73]

```
<object height="350" width="425">
<param name="movie" value="http://www.youtube.com/v/KJukKpQDVLQ">
<param name="wmode" value="transparent">
<embed src="http://www.youtube.com/v/KJukKpQDVLQ"
 type="application/x-shockwave-flash" wmode="transparent"
 height="350" width="425">
</embed>
</object>
```

Notice that the code embeds a movie object pulled from Google's servers. Again, users need only visit a page containing an embedded YouTube video to leave themselves open to tracking by Google, even if the page is run by a third party and there are no DoubleClick or AdSense advertisements.

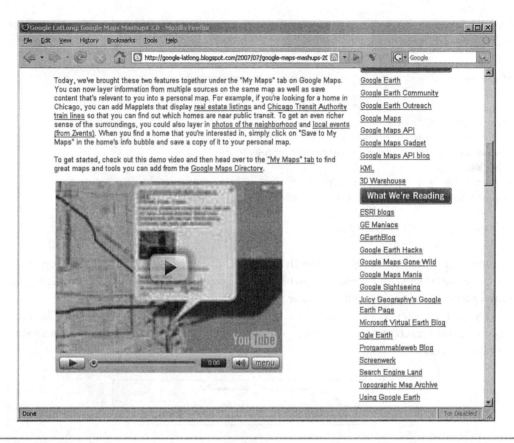

Figure 7-12 Example of a YouTube video embedded in a web page. When the image is merely displayed in the user's browser, that user can be immediately logged by YouTube.

SEARCH ON YOUR WEB PAGE

Another common practice is for web authors to include a Google Search box on their site (see Figure 7-13). Although some visitors find this useful, it also facilitates the disclosure of search queries, as well as the user's IP address and the site he or she is visiting, to

Google. In some implementations, the disclosure takes places only when the user clicks Submit, as in the following code:[74]

```
<form method="get" action="http://www.google.com/search">

<input type="text" name="q" size="31"
 maxlength="255" value="" />
<input type="submit" value="Google Search" />
<input type="radio" name="sitesearch" value="" />
 The Web
<input type="radio" name="sitesearch"
 value="askdavetaylor.com" checked /> Ask Dave Taylor<br />

</form>
```

However, note the Google logo in the image. If the webmaster includes the logo on the page, he or she can choose to download the image directly from Google; this immediately informs Google when someone visits a given site.

Google also offers AdSense for search, which helps webmasters earn revenue by creating a custom search engine for a site.[75] Along with customized search results, users see targeted advertisements.

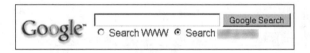

Figure 7-13 Many web sites include a Google search field, which encourages users to disclose search terms and the site they are visiting.

FRIEND CONNECT

Friend Connect is a new service offered by Google that enables web authors to add social networking facets to their sites by embedding small snippets of code. Google Friends Connect "offers a core set of social gadgets such as member management, message board, reviews, and picture sharing."[76] Figure 7-14 shows a sample site provided by Google and illustrates several concerns with Friends Connect. Visitors to the site are offered the opportunity to sign in using their existing credentials, which uniquely identifies them to Google or one of several other participating services, including Yahoo! and AOL. The sites' members, photos, and comments can be disclosed. In addition, because this site includes an embedded YouTube video and two Friend Connect widgets, the user can be logged three times by Google's servers by merely visiting the site. Friend Connect is an interesting service that will likely be very popular. Therein lies the risk: Friends Connect and future generations of social networking applications will amplify user disclosure and facilitate uniquely identifying users.

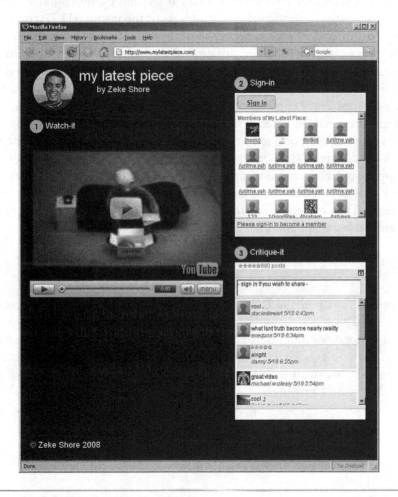

Figure 7-14 Google's new Friends Connect service enables web authors to add social networking functions to their sites.

EMBEDDED MAPS

Another common practice, and subsequent cross-site disclosure risk, is embedding maps within web pages. From hotels to tourist attractions, to business and social events, web authors rely upon third-party mapping services such as Google Maps and MapQuest to provide easy-to-use, interactive maps for their site's visitors. Unfortunately, the practice also informs the mapping service of the IP address of the visitor, HTTP cookies, the site the user came from, and a location he or she is interested in. For example, in Figure 7-15, a web author for an academic conference directly embedded a Google map into the conference web site.[77] Thus, every potential conference attendee who browses the conference's directions page immediately informs Google, and possibly Yahoo! and MapQuest, of his or her interest in the conference and probable attendance. With thousands, perhaps millions, of embedded maps in sites across the web, this practice greatly extends the cross-site visibility of large online companies such as Google and Yahoo!. The future of information-disclosure risks associated with embedded mapping is likely to worsen. Simple mapping is giving way to *mapplets* (or *mashups*), which combine mapping with virtually any type of location-based data (think homes for sale, local coffee shops, or driving ranges). The end result is a growth in the type and quantity of information disclosed via embedded maps and their progeny.

> **NOTE**
>
> The term *mashup* applies to far more than just mapping. Mashups are a core Web 2.0 tenet and apply to web applications that combine more than one data source into single integrated tools. Beyond mapping, examples include combinations of images, videos, news, search, and shopping data.[78] Mashups increase information-disclosure risks because their use can share user information with many disparate mashup data source providers.

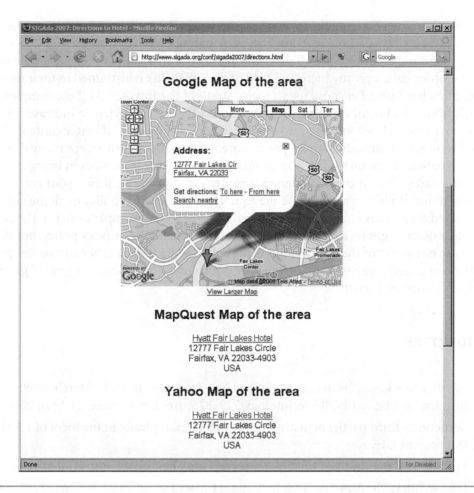

Figure 7-15 Embedded maps in web pages immediately inform the mapping service of the user's visit to a given web page, as well as that user's interest in a specific area, as is the case for this academic conference.

SUMMARY

Web browsing isn't a one-to-one conversation with a single web site. Instead, embedded content such as maps, images, videos, advertisements, web-analytics code, and social networking widgets immediately disclose each user's visit to a third party when that user merely views a page in his or her web browser. Web authors and webmasters gain a great deal of value by embedding these "small snippets of code" in their web sites, such as gaining access to advertising revenue, free web-analytics reports, improved customer contact, and richer, more compelling web content. The true benefit is to the online companies, which gain a greatly increased field of view that isn't constrained to their own properties, but instead encompasses a major swath of the Internet. As these companies innovate and field compelling new services, expect their field of view to increase further, as webmasters and web authors across the Internet embed new and better content. A key conclusion is that embedded third-party content forces the user to accept many different privacy policies from many different companies, most likely without even being aware of it. This creates a lowest common denominator effect of privacy policies; your real privacy in terms of visiting a web site is the equivalent of the worst policy of all the sites embedded there. This is a huge issue. Consider the MSNBC example earlier in the chapter. Most users might be aware that they fall under the MSNBC privacy policy, but they likely are not aware of the information being collected by the ten other companies providing embedded content, let alone the finer points of each of these companies' privacy policies, if they even exist.

ENDNOTES

1. Rory Cellan-Jones, "Web Creator Rejects Net Tracking," BBC, 17 March 2008. http://news.bbc.co.uk/2/hi/technology/7299875.stm, last accessed 21 April 2008.

2. Sometimes third parties actually employ web bugs, typically in the form of a 1×1 transparent GIF.

3. For advertisements, these third-party servers are often called *central ad servers*.

4. Louise Story, "To Aim Ads, Web Is Keeping Closer Eye on You," *The New York Times*, 10 March 2008. www.nytimes.com/2008/03/10/technology/10privacy.html?_r=1&oref=slogin, last accessed 2 May 2008.

5. *Ibid.*

6. Ina Fried, "Microsoft Quietly Offering Ad-Funded Works," CNET, 18 April 2008. www.news.com/8301-13860_3-9922750-56.html?tag=nefd.top, last accessed 10 May 2008.

7. Louise Story, "Company Will Monitor Phone Calls to Tailor Ads," *The New York Times*, 24 September 2007. www.nytimes.com/2007/09/24/business/media/24adcol.html?_r=3&ei=5065&en=5822f6a12e575488&ex=1191297600&partner=MYWAY&pagewanted=print&oref=slogin&oref=slogin&oref=slogin, last accessed 10 May 2008.

8. Catherine Holahan, "Google's DoubleClick Strategic Move," *BusinessWeek,* 14 April 2007. www.businessweek.com/technology/content/apr2007/tc20070414_ 675511.htm, last accessed 2 May 2008.

9. Mark Hendrickson, "Yahoo! Acquires Ad Network Blue Lithium," *TechCrunch,* 4 September 2007. www.techcrunch.com/2007/09/04/yahoo-acquires-ad-network-bluelithium/, last accessed 10 May 2008.

10. Kevin Delaney, "Yahoo!–Google Pact May Be Close," *The Wall Street Journal,* 2 May 2008. http://online.wsj.com/article/SB120968562237161201.html?mod=rss_ whats_news_technology, last accessed 2 May 2008.

11. Nate Anderson, "Study: Ads in Online Shows Work Better Than Ads on TV," Ars Technica, 26 December 2007. http://arstechnica.com/news.ars/post/20071226-study-ads-in-online-video-work-better-than-ads-on-tv.html, last accessed 17 May 2008.

12. Louise Story, "Where Every Ad Knows Your Name," *The New York Times* Bits Blog, 10 March 2008. http://bits.blogs.nytimes.com/2008/03/10/where-every-ad-knows-your-name/?hp, last accessed 10 May 2008.

13. "Microsoft to Test New Measure of Web Ads," Reuters, 25 February 2008. http:// www.reuters.com/article/internetNews/idUSWNAS219120080225?feedType=RSS&f eedName=internetNews&pageNumber=1&virtualBrandChannel=0, last accessed 11 May 2008.

14. David Legard, "IDC: Consolidation to Windows Won't Happen," *LinuxWorld,* 27 April 2004. www.linuxworld.com.au/index.php/id;940707233;fp;2;fpid;1, last accessed 2 July 2008.

15. "Google Ads Are a Free Speech Issue," Slashdot, 28 February 2007. http://yro. slashdot.org/yro/07/02/28/0139222.shtml, last accessed 10 May 2008.

16. This section focuses on information disclosure risks and does not cover Click Fraud, the illegitimate clicking of advertisements to generate revenue or charge an advertiser. See www.businessweek.com/magazine/content/06_40/b4003001.htm for more information.

17. Jeffrey Graham, "Google's AdSense a Bonanza for Some Web Sites," *USA Today,* 10 March 2008. www.usatoday.com/tech/news/2005-03-10-google-ads-usat_x.htm, last accessed 5 May 2008.

18. "What Is AdSense for Feeds?" Google AdSense Help Center. www.google.com/ adsense/support/bin/answer.py?hl=en&answer=20012, last accessed 5 May 2008.

19. "Google AdSense for Search," Google AdSense, 2008. www.google.com/adsense/ static/en_US/WsOverview.html?hl=en_US, last accessed 5 May 2008.

20. "AdSense for Mobile Content," GoogleAdSense, 2008. www.google.com/adsense/www/en_US/mobile/, last accessed 5 May 2008.

21. Shamim Samadi, "AdSense for Video Now in Beta," Google Blog, 21 February 2008. http://googleblog.blogspot.com/2008/02/adsense-for-video-now-in-beta.html, last accessed 5 May 2008.

22. "Google Testing AdSense Cost Per Action (CPA)," Search Engine Roundtable, 21 June 2006. www.seroundtable.com/archives/003988.html, last accessed 17 May 2008.

23. Juan Carlos Perez, "Merchants Say eBay Ad Programs Drive Buyers Away," *ITWorld*, 8 October 2007. www.itworld.com/Tech/2403/071008ebayads/, last accessed 11 May 2008.

24. eBay also has its own contextual advertising network; see http://slashdot.org/article.pl?sid=06/06/11/013216.

25. Google AdSense sign-in page, Google AdSense, 2008. www.google.com/adsense/login/en_US/?gsessionid=JjtK8kJKBuw, last accessed 5 May 2008.

26. Mitch Ratcliffe, "How Google Falls: Unprofitable in 2009," ZDNet, Rational Rants Blog, 15 February 2007. http://blogs.zdnet.com/Ratcliffe/?p=265, last accessed 10 May 2008.

27. Mark Ward, "Searching for the Net's Big Thing," BBC News, 13 March 2006. http://news.bbc.co.uk/1/hi/technology/4780648.stm, last accessed 6 May 2008.

28. "Company Overview," Corporate Information, Google, 2008. www.google.com/intl/en/corporate/index.html, last accessed 6 May 2008.

29. Google is also experimenting with video ads on search result pages; see http://bits.blogs.nytimes.com/2008/02/14/google-tests-video-ads-on-search-results-pages/.

30. For an insightful overview of AdWords attacks, see StankDawg's Defcon 13 talk, available at www.defcon.org/html/links/defcon-media-archives.html#dc_13.

31. "Google Partners Put You in Front of More Potential Customers," Google, 2008. https://adwords.google.com/select/partner.html, last accessed 6 May 2008.

32. "About AskEraser," Ask.com, 2008. http://sp.ask.com/en/docs/about/askeraser.shtml, last accessed 5 May 2008.

33. Thomas Claburn, "Google Keeps What Ask.com Erases," *Information Week*, 13 December 2007. www.informationweek.com/news/internet/ebusiness/showArticle.jhtml;jsessionid=BQP3K401V1M1QQSNDLRSKH0CJUNN2JVN?articleID=204802233&_requestid=54316, last accessed 5 May 2008.

34. Gwendolyn Mariano, "DoubleClick Able to Settle Privacy Suits," CNET News, 21 May 2002. www.news.com/DoubleClick-able-to-settle-privacy-suits/2100-1023_3-919895.html, last accessed 16 May 2008.

35. Steve Lohr, "Google Deal Said to Bring U.S. Scrutiny," *The New York Times,* 29 May 2007. www.nytimes.com/2007/05/29/technology/29antitrust.html?_r=2&ref=business&oref=slogin&oref=slogin, last accessed 16 May 2008.

36. "E.U. Lobby Says Google, DoubleClick Merger Hurts Privacy," Reuters, 20 December 2007. www.reuters.com/article/internetNews/idUSL2051059120071220, last accessed 16 May 2008.

37. Grant Gross, "FTC Approves Google/DoubleClick Deal," *Macworld,* 20 December 2007. www.macworld.com/article/131204/2007/12/doubleclick.html, last accessed 16 May 2008.

38. "European Regulators Approve Google–DoubleClick Deal," CBC News, 11 March 2008. www.cbc.ca/technology/story/2008/03/11/tech-google-doubleclick.html, last accessed 16 May 2008.

39. "Google Closes Acquisition of DoubleClick," Google Press Release, 11 March 2008. www.google.com/intl/en/press/pressrel/20080311_doubleclick.html, last accessed 15 May 2008.

40. "DART Ad-Serving and Search Cookie Opt-Out," DoubleClick, 2008. www.doubleclick.com/privacy/dart_adserving.aspx, last accessed 16 May 2008.

41. Note that DoubleClick's opt-out cookie does not prevent ad targeting based on the user's operating system, Windows version, local time, or IP address.

42. Louise Story and Miguel Helft, "Google Buys an Online Ad Firm for $3.1 Billion," *The New York Times,* 14 April 2007. www.nytimes.com/2007/04/14/technology/14deal.html, last accessed 16 May 2008.

43. Stefanie Olsen, "Privacy Concerns Dog Google–DoubleClick Deal," CNET News, 17 April 2007. www.news.com/Privacy-concerns-dog-Google-DoubleClick-deal/2100-1024_3-6177029.html, last accessed 16 May 2008.

44. Electronic Privacy Information Center Complaint with the Federal Trade Commission, 20 April 2007. http://epic.org/privacy/ftc/google/epic_complaint.pdf, last accessed 16 May 2008.

45. Clint Boulton, "Meet Google: Search Giant, Monopolist Extraordinaire," Google Watch Blog, Eweek.com, 24 December 2007. http://googlewatch.eweek.com/content/google_vs_microsoft/meet_google_search_giant_monopolist_extraordinaire.html, last accessed 16 May 2008.

46. Frank Rose, "Microsoft's Bid for Yahoo! Is All About Big-Budget Brand Advertising," *Wired Magazine,* 24 March 2008. www.wired.com/techbiz/it/magazine/16-04/bz_microsoft_yahoo, last accessed 15 May 2008.

47. StankDawg, "Hacking Google AdWords," Defcon 13, 2005. www.defcon.org/images/defcon-13/dc13-presentations/DC_13-Stankdawg.pdf, last accessed 2 July 2008.

48. Brian Krebs, "Virus Writers Taint Google Ad Links," Security Fix Blog, WashingtonPost.com, 25 April 2007. http://blog.washingtonpost.com/securityfix/2007/04/virus_writers_taint_google_ad.html, last accessed 4 May 2008.

49. Brian Krebs, "Hacked Ad Seen on MySpace Served Spyware to a Million," Security Fix Blog, WashingtonPost.com, 19 July 2006.

50. Betsy Schiffman, "Hackers Use Banner Ads on Major Sites to Hijack Your PC," Wired.com, 15 November 2007. http://www.wired.com/techbiz/media/news/2007/11/doubleclick, last accessed 4 May 2008.

51. Nonmalicious Flash applets hosted on web pages have also been shown to be vulnerable to attack. See Dan Goodin's "Serious Flash Vulns Menace at Least 10,000 Websites," www.theregister.co.uk/2007/12/21/flash_vulnerability_menace/

52. Eric Auchard, "Adobe, Yahoo! test running ads inside PDF documents." Reuters, 28 November 2007. www.reuters.com/article/marketsNews/idUKN2754715120071129?rpc=44&sp=true, last accessed 4 May 2008.

53. Robert Freeman, "I'm Feeling Lucky," Frequency X Blog, IBM Internet Security Systems, 29 April 2008. http://blogs.iss.net/archive/FeelingLucky.html, last accessed 17 May 2008.

54. Jakob Nielsen, "Banner Blindness: Old and New Findings," Alertbox blog, 20 August 2007. www.useit.com/alertbox/banner-blindness.html, last accessed 7 May 2008.

55. An interesting exception is NCSoft's game *City of Heroes,* which makes viewing in-game advertisements optional; see http://yro.slashdot.org/article.pl?sid=08/04/06/0554230.

56. Cade Metz, "Network Solutions Hijacks Customer Subdomains for Ad Fest," *The Register,* 11 April 2008. www.theregister.co.uk/2008/04/11/network_solutions_sub_domain_parking/, last accessed 8 May 2008.

57. Henry Blodget, "Compete CEO: ISPs Sell Clickstreams for $5 a Month," Seeking Alpha, 13 March 2007. http://seekingalpha.com/article/29449-compete-ceo-isps-sell-clickstreams-for-5-a-month, last accessed 8 May 2008.

58. "U.K. ISPs to Start Tracking to Serve You Ads," *TechDirt,* 18 February 2008. http://techdirt.com/articles/20080218/024203278.shtml, last accessed 8 May 2008.

59. For example, an Amazon cookie disclosed by the user's browser might have been associated with previous Amazon purchases and, hence, tied to shipping and billing information.

60. "Facebook Beacon," Facebook Business Solutions, 2008. www.facebook.com/business/?beacon, last accessed 18 May 2008.

61. Henry Blodget, "Facebook's 'Beacon' Infuriate Users, MoveOn," Silicon Alley Insider, 21 November 2007. www.alleyinsider.com/2007/11/facebooks-beaco.html, last accessed 18 May 2008.

62. Josh Catone, "Is Facebook Really Ruining Christmas?" ReadWriteWeb, 21 November 2007. www.readwriteweb.com/archives/facebook_moveon_beacon_privacy.php, last accessed 2 July 2008.

63. Kristen Nicole, "Google Analytics Gets a Beautiful New Interface," Mashable.com, 8 May 2007. http://mashable.com/2007/05/08/google-analytics/, last accessed 15 May 2008.

64. The density of the code could also be seen as an attempt to decrease the size of the file, to improve response time.

65. Blogger Garett Rogers provides an introductory analysis to the operation of urchin.js at http://blogs.zdnet.com/Google/?p=39.

66. The full script is more 13 pages long. You can view it at www.google-analytics.com/urchin.js

67. For additional information on Google Analytics cookies, see www.customizegoogle.com/block-google-analytics-cookies.html.

68. Garett Rogers, "How Do I Know the Number of Google Analytics Accounts?" Googling Google ZDNet Blog, 28 November 2005. http://blogs.zdnet.com/Google/?p=42, last accessed 15 May 2008.

69. "Microsoft adCenter Analytics Registration," Microsoft Digital Advertising Solutions, 2008. http://advertising.microsoft.com/advertising/adcenter-analytics-registration, last accessed 15 May 2008.

70. Aurelie Pols, "Yahoo! Buys Indextools: 80% of the Functionality of Omniture for Free!" OX2 Web Analytics Blog, 8 April 2008. http://webanalytics.ox2.eu/2008/04/15/yahoo-buys-indextools-80-of-the-functionality-of-omniture-for-free/, last accessed 15 May 2008.

71. Nick Gonzalez, "TringMe: Phone Free Click to Call," *Tech Crunch*, 2 October 2007. www.techcrunch.com/2007/10/02/tringme-phone-free-click-to-call/, last accessed 17 May 2008.

72. Erik Schonfeld, "Google Talk Adds a Chatback Widget," *TechCrunch*, 26 February 2008. www.techcrunch.com/2008/02/26/google-talk-adds-a-chatback-widget/, last accessed 17 May 2008.

73. Thai Tran, "Google Maps Mashups 2.0," Google Lat Long Blog, 11 July 2007. http://google-latlong.blogspot.com/2007/07/google-maps-mashups-20.html, last accessed 17 May 2008.

74. Dave Taylor, "How Can I Add a Google Search Box to My Web Site?" Ask Dave Taylor, 10 December 2004. www.askdavetaylor.com/how_can_i_add_a_google_ search_box_to_my_web_site.html, last accessed 19 May 2008.

75. "The Power of Google Search on Your Site," Google AdSense, 2008. www.google. com/adsense/www/en_US/afs/index.html, last accessed 19 May 2008.

76. "More Info About Google Friend Connect," Google Friend Connect BETA, 2008. www.google.com/friendconnect/home/moreinfo, last accessed 18 May 2008.

77. SIGAda2007, Association for Computing Machinery Special Interest Group on Ada Conference web site, 10 October 2007. www.sigada.org/conf/sigada2007/ directions.html, last accessed 23 May 2008.

78. "Mashup (Web Application Hybrid)," Wikipedia, 2 July 2008. http://en. wikipedia.org/wiki/Mashup_(web_application_hybrid), last accessed 2 July 2008.

Googlebot

Webbots, sometimes called *web crawlers* or *web spiders,* are computer programs that gather information from the web. They interact with servers using common protocols such as HTTP and SMTP. In many ways, they gather the same information humans could gather, but only many times faster. Bots aren't magic; they operate in the same manner as a web browser or e-mail client, but without the requirement for constant human intervention. By taking humans out of the loop, webbots can relentlessly troll the web downloading pages, reading e-mails, and collecting information on behalf of their master. Webbots raise an interesting point about the lifespan of information: Whatever information is posted on the web should be considered disclosed forever. One just need visit the Internet Wayback Machine, which archives more than 85 billion web page snapshots collected since 1996.[1]

Google's automated crawler script, *Googlebot,* is a key component of Google's high-quality search results. By routinely visiting millions of web pages, Google can determine their contents and any changes that have occurred. Googlebot will almost certainly visit most anything that is posted to the public Internet.

Earlier chapters focused on information that users provide as they use Google's tools and services. Googlebot is different; it collects only information posted to the publicly accessible web. That being said, this stockpile of information is unprecedented in the history of mankind. Using the web, people are constantly revealing sensitive information about themselves, their friends, their enemies, and their employers. In geek circles, it isn't uncommon to hear someone remark about inappropriate postings they made on the Usenet discussion system many years ago, and their continued existence in online archives. For today's generation, I hear the same comments about YouTube, MySpace, and Facebook postings. Companies face the same battle; it seems as if every week another story emerges about a company posting confidential documents to the web. Unfortunately, when these disclosures are made publicly, they are available for all to see; it is safe to assume that they have been recorded in some form. Just ask AOL about its search dataset; Broward County, Florida, about its county records; or any Google hacker about the security vulnerabilities found online.[2,3]

Whether each page is obviously sensitive or merely innocuous appearing, the web provides a rich complement to the one-on-one disclosures covered earlier in the book. Because of its constantly changing nature, determining the size of the publicly available web is tricky, but it contains more than 19 billion individual web pages, 1.6 billion images, and 50 million audio and video files.[4] Googlebot collects these items, feeding the results back to Google for processing, data mining, and further analysis. These public disclosures can then be linked to profiles created from web-based information disclosures gathered from other online tools, such as search and e-mail. I think of Googlebot as the ultimate reconnaissance tool, thanks to its ubiquitous presence, speed, and relative invisibility. Webmasters *expect* Googlebot to visit and download information from their site.

This chapter covers how Googlebot works and examines the tracks it leaves behind in web server logs. Perhaps more important, the chapter covers the risks associated with Googlebot and other similar webbots, including the types of information they can find, how they can deeply spider large web sites, how they can be misused or spoofed, and how information they gather can be linked to other forms of online activity.

How Googlebot Works

The inner workings of Googlebot are proprietary and, hence, not publicly available. However, the basic operation of Googlebot can be gleaned from Google's few published documents on the subject[5], as well as webmaster and search engine optimization forums. Googlebot speaks HTTP; requests web pages, images, and documents; and feeds the data to back-end processors and databases. In many instances, Google stores copies of these objects and makes their *cached,* locally maintained, copy available as part of the search results returned when a user makes a query (see Figure 8-1).[6] Similarly, Google makes some file types (such as .pdf) available in HTML format (see Figure 8-2).[7] HTML-formatted versions are maintained by Google and can be available online even if the original content is pulled down.

Google Help : Search Features
If you click on the "Cached" link, you will see the web page as it looked when we indexed it. The cached content is the content Google uses to judge whether ...
www.google.com/help/features.html - 68k - Cached - Similar pages

Figure 8-1 Some of the files Googlebot collects are made available as part of Google search results. Note the Cached link.

[PDF] **TOP SECRET**:
File Format: PDF/Adobe Acrobat - View as HTML
Top Secret: The Battle for the Pentagon Papers, by Geoffrey Cowan and ..... be a **secret document**. But it's not a **secret**, despite the Academy Award-winning ...
www.latw.org/acrobat/**secret**.pdf - Similar pages

Figure 8-2 For file formats such as PDF, Google makes available an HTML version. This version is maintained by Google and often exists even if the original content is pulled down. Note the View as HTML link.

Google uses links extracted from the web pages Googlebot collects to help determine the ranking of web pages in search results. This process is at the heart of Google's web page ranking algorithm. The key idea is that web pages that link to a given page are essentially "voting" that the destination page is worth visiting. The more "important" the linking page is, the stronger the vote. In other words, if *The New York Times* web site links to a page, it counts more than a link from Bob's personal page. Although this concept is simple enough, it has been a driving factor of Google's high-quality search results and subsequent success.

NOTE

The full workings of Google's web page ranking algorithm are a closely guarded secret, but you can read the seminal paper "The PageRank Citation Ranking: Bringing Order to the Web," which is available online.[8]

A great deal of speculation on webmaster forums surrounds Googlebot variants. Google doesn't provide an official answer, but informed observers believe there are at least two main types, Googlebot (aka Deepbot), which visits less frequently but more deeply, and Freshbot, which frequently visits sites with constantly changing content, such as a news web site.

NOTE

If you are interested in learning more about how webbots work, including how to write your own, see *Webbots, Spiders, and Screen Scrapers: A Guide to Developing Internet Agents with PHP/CURL,* by Michael Schrenk (No Starch Press, 2007).

GOOGLEBOT'S FOOTPRINTS

Googlebot's activity is evident in the logs of web servers it visits. The following is an example log entry from my rumint.org web server showing a Googlebot visit.

```
66.249.67.207 - - [02/Dec/2007:03:15:20 -0700]
"GET /robots.txt HTTP/1.1" 404 1695 "-" "Googlebot/2.1
(+http://www.google.com/bot.html)"
```

The first field is the IP address is the server running Googlebot (66.249.67.207). For now, I'm assuming that this address actually belongs to Google, but we will verify this assumption in the "Spoofing Googlebot" section later in the chapter. The next field is the date and time of the visit (02/Dec/2007:03:15:20 -0700).[9] Googlebot used the HTTP GET command to request a robots.txt file. My web server returned an HTTP error code (404) indicating the file wasn't available and returned an error page of 1695 bytes. The final field is the HTTP user agent field which is the name of the software agent that made the request. For traditional web browsers you'd see user agents such as "Mozilla/5.0 (Windows; U; Windows NT 5.1; de; rv:1.8.1.9) Gecko/20071025 Firefox/2.0.0.9," "Mozilla/5.0 (X11; U; Linux x86_64; en-US; rv:1.8.1.10) Gecko/20071126 Ubuntu/7.10 (gutsy) Firefox/2.0.0.10," and "Mozilla/4.0 (compatible; MSIE 6.0; Windows NT 5.1; SV1; .NET CLR 1.1.4322; .NET CLR 2.0.50727)." In this case the software agent is *Googlebot* version 2.1.[10] Note that the field also contains a link to information about the bot for interested webmasters, "http://www.google.com/bot.html." The user agent field is easily spoofed, I'll cover more on this in the "Spoofing Googlebot" section later in the chapter.

Table 8-1 lists all of rumint.org's Googlebot visits for that day. For brevity, I've removed all the fields that didn't change from entry to entry. During a 24-hour period, Googlebot checked 25 files (out of about 150 on the site).

Table 8-1   A Visit by Googlebot as Seen in Web Server Logs

Time	Requested Document	HTTP Status Code
03:15:20	"GET /robots.txt HTTP/1.1"	404 (Not Found)
03:15:20	"GET /gregconti/publications/ HTTP/1.1"	403 (Forbidden)
08:15:09	"GET /gregconti/publications/20040427_IAW_TIKE_Poster_Extended_Abstract.pdf HTTP/1.1"	304 (Not Modified)
08:16:07	"GET /gregconti/publications/wpes15-abdullah_v09.pdf HTTP/1.1"	200 (OK)
08:16:08	"GET /gregconti/publications/20060311_IZ_Google_web.ppt HTTP/1.1"	200 (OK)
08:21:26	"GET /gregconti/publications/IAW2001_Information_Warfare_Simulation.pdf HTTP/1.1"	304 (Not Modified)
08:21:31	"GET /gregconti/publications/20050813_VizSec_BinaryRainfall.pdf HTTP/1.1"	304 (Not Modified)
08:22:53	"GET /gregconti/publications/20050813_VizSec_IDS_Rainstorm.pdf HTTP/1.1"	200 (OK)
09:23:40	"GET /gregconti/publications/20060331_cga_info_overload.pdf HTTP/1.1"	304 (Not Modified)
09:27:50	"GET /gregconti/publications/20060311_IZ_Viz_web.ppt HTTP/1.1"	200 (OK)
19:10:51	"GET /robots.txt HTTP/1.1"	404 (Not Found)
19:10:52	"GET /gregconti/publications/20040428_CISSE_SIGSAC.pdf HTTP/1.1"	200 (OK)
19:13:35	"GET /gregconti/publications/WMC_2003_MAADNET.pdf HTTP/1.1"	200 (OK)
19:15:41	"GET /gregconti/publications/20050312_IZ4_Conti.ppt HTTP/1.1"	200 (OK)
22:41:08	"GET /gregconti/publications/20040731-DEFCON-12-Conti.ppt HTTP/1.1"	304 (Not Modified)
22:41:12	"GET /gregconti/publications/FIE_2002_Brief_Final.ppt HTTP/1.1"	304 (Not Modified)
22:44:20	"GET /gregconti/publications/WISE3_Conti.doc HTTP/1.1"	304 (Not Modified)
22:44:38	"GET /gregconti/publications/20060806_Defcon_Googling_Distro.pdf HTTP/1.1"	200 (OK)
22:44:56	"GET /gregconti/publications/200705_IEEE_SP_CostofFreeWebTools.pdf HTTP/1.1"	304 (Not Modified)

continues

Table 8-1   Continued

Time	Requested Document	HTTP Status Code
22:44:59	"GET /gregconti/publications/FIE_2002_Distributed_Development.doc HTTP/1.1"	304 (Not Modified)
22:45:00	"GET /gregconti/publications/cyber_corps.doc HTTP/1.1"	304 (Not Modified)
22:45:06	"GET /gregconti/publications/20050418_IA_Krasser(final).pdf HTTP/1.1"	200 (OK)
22:46:26	"GET /gregconti/publications/20050312_IZ4_Conti.ppt HTTP/1.1"	200 (OK)
23:07:50	"GET /gregconti/index.html HTTP/1.1"	200 (OK)
23:34:44	"GET /gregconti/publications/20060303_BH_Europe.pdf HTTP/1.1"	304 (Not Modified)

Googlebot first checked for the existence of a `robots.txt` file, the location where webmasters can leave instructions for visiting webbots. I don't use a `robots.txt` file, so my web server returned a 404 status code (file not found).[11] In the absence of any webmaster guidance, Googlebot proceeded to make 24 more requests. The next request was an attempt to gain a listing of all the files in the `/publications` directory. From the perspective of a search engine bot, getting the listing of all files in a directory makes a great deal of sense because it can then request every file without missing any. However, many webmasters, myself included, block these requests (hence the 403 [Forbidden] response) because such listings can provide a visitor with information you might prefer visitors didn't have.[12]

Next, Googlebot proceeds to request individual PDF (.pdf), Powerpoint (.ppt), and Microsoft (.doc) files. Puzzlingly, these requests have no apparent order, some were downloaded directly (those with a `200 (OK)` status code), and others were used with a conditional `GET`. In HTTP, a conditional `GET` is used to see if a file was changed (304 [Not Modified] status code). Presumably, Google already has a copy of these files. If the files had changed, Googlebot would have downloaded the current file. The use of a conditional `GET` helps prevent wasted processing and bandwidth, both on the web server and by the webbot, that comes with needlessly downloading files. Without inside information, Googlebot is a bit of an enigma. It visits at seemingly random times and downloads seemingly random files. (Two days after this example, Googlebot visited and downloaded the main HTML page (index.html) and two text [.txt] files, then left.) Googlebot's behavior is the subject of much debate by search engine optimizers and web masters. You may find SEO Chat Forums (http://forums.seochat.com/) a useful site to visit for the latest analysis and speculation.

ROBOTS.TXT

I've always found webmasters' use of the `robots.txt` files as a security mechanism a bit puzzling. Webmasters place the file in the root directory of their domain, such as www.domain.com/robots.txt, to give instructions to webbots. Well-behaved robots, such as Googlebot, check for the existence of the file and obey the instructions. Googlebot uses two basic rules, *User-Agent* and *Disallow.* User-Agent specifies the name of the robot, and Disallow specifies the files or directories the rule applies to. A possible use of a `robots.txt` file is to request that certain files not be added to the Google index. A simple example of this follows:

```
User-agent: Googlebot
Disallow: /
```

These are the rules that apply to Googlebot; the request is to block it from visiting the entire site. The / is used to specify the highest-level directory and all those below it. For `robots.txt` files to work, they must be readable by visitors. Consider a longer example containing excerpts from the www.whitehouse.gov site:

Disallow:	/history/africanamerican/text
Disallow:	/history/art/europeanworks/text
Disallow:	/history/eeobtour/images/text
Disallow:	/history/firstladies/photoessay/LadyBird/text
Disallow:	/history/grounds/garden/photoessays/spring/text
Disallow:	/history/grounds/kids/kidsgarden/text
Disallow:	/history/hispanicheritage/text
Disallow:	/history/life/text
Disallow:	/history/photoessays/diplomaticroom/text
Disallow:	/history/presidents/text
Disallow:	/history/quiz/valentines/text

Another popular way to give instructions to webbots is to use the HTML <META> tag. By including it in the header section of a web page, webmasters can specify whether the page should be indexed and whether the webbot should follow links contained within it.

The following is a web page fragment that instructs webbots to not follow links and not index the content.[13]

```
<html>
<head>
<title>Sample Page</title>
<META NAME="ROBOTS" CONTENT="NOINDEX, NOFOLLOW">
</head>
```

An interesting example of the use of webbot tags is the controversy surrounding the use of Wikipedia links to artificially boost Google search index placement. Individuals seeking to boost their search ranking would add spurious links from Wikipedia pages to their sites. Search bots would crawl these links, and because they were located in the popular Wikipedia site, the destination page would receive a rankings boost. In 2007, Wikipedia announced that all outbound links would include the nofollow tag, in an attempt to end the practice.[14]

The robots.txt file and HTML <META> tag are not access-control mechanisms—that is, you shouldn't rely upon them to prevent access to sensitive information. (The best way to do this is to never place the information on the web in the first place.) Nothing can prevent a webbot from ignoring these instructions altogether. In addition, because the robots.txt file is publicly readable, the listing of directories and files in the robots.txt file might even highlight sensitive areas to an attacker.

> **NOTE**
>
> I've always thought it would be interesting to create a search engine that indexes *only* off limits files and directories in robots.txt files and those with restrictive Robots <META> tags.

Both the robots.txt file and Robots <META> tag are relatively coarse-grained technologies. Driven by publishers of newspapers, magazines, online databases, books, and journals, there is a growing movement for more precise standards to better control access and use of their intellectual property.[15] The Automated Content Access Protocol (ACAP) (see www.the-acap.org/) is one such initiative.

POPULAR SEARCH WEBBOTS

Googlebot isn't the only searchbot on the Internet. Most search engine companies use webbots to continually troll the web and gather information, as do individual and academic researchers. The following is a list of some that webmasters commonly see, including major players (Ask Jeeves, Googlebot, and Microsoft's msnbot). Also included are Baiduspider from the Chinese search engine Baidu, twiceler from the "stealth" start-up Cuill, a very active bot from France's Exalead, and Yeti from the South Korean search engine Naver, among others.

- Ask Jeeves/Teoma, http://about.ask.com/en/docs/about/webmasters.shtml
- Baiduspider, http://www.baidu.com/search/spider_jp.html
- Cuill, http://www.cuill.com/twiceler/robot.html
- Discovery Engine, www.discoveryengine.com
- Exalead, www.exalead.com/about/document/53
- Googlebot, www.google.com/bot.html
- msnbot, http://search.msn.com/msnbot.htm
- Yeti, www.naver.com
- Webmon,[16] www.btinternet.com/~markwell/webmon/
- Speedy Spider, www.entireweb.com/about/search_tech/speedy_spider/
- Yahoo!, http://help.yahoo.com/help/us/ysearch/slurp

RISKS OF GOOGLEBOT AND ITS COUSINS

The primary risk of Googlebot and its ilk comes from placing sensitive information on the web, whether you do this personally, a coworker does it, or a third party does it. Although you might carefully consider what you personally post, it is beyond your control to prevent others from placing sensitive items on the web. When Googlebot copies a file, there's no opportunity to reverse the disclosure. Even if the file never appears in Google's search result listings,[17] you've given it to Google. Google's internal cache of documents likely far outstrips the fraction that the company makes publicly available.

On the publicly accessible web, trying to hide web content from search companies is a futile exercise. Even if a webmaster hasn't linked the content, someone or something else might have. Web servers can provide listings of entire directories, robots.txt files can be ignored, a link to the content might appear in a Gmail, a user might suggest a link to Google (www.google.com/addurl/), or someone could examine listings of newly created

Internet domains. In addition, there is also speculation that some web browsers and/or toolbars reveal links visited to third parties. In short, attempting to hide publicly accessible information from Googlebot and other bots is a bad idea.

SPOOFING GOOGLEBOT

Bots are prevalent on the web; in essence, they hide in plain sight. Webmasters expect to see numerous entries in their logs—in fact, they often design their sites to make visits more likely, to increase search engine placement. Most bots exhibit enigmatic behavior and arrive at seemingly random times, downloading seemingly random files. Their inner workings are closely held company secrets. At the same time, bots download a major portion of the web and can determine when files are updated, what pages link to other pages, and even whether servers (or individual services) are up or down. I can't think of a better reconnaissance technique. Making matters worse is that third parties can purport themselves as Googlebot. Without much work, an attacker could construct a bot that looks like Googlebot (the main field to spoof is the HTTP user agent field). You can try spoofing yourself. Smart IT Consulting (www.smart-it-consulting.com) has a page that will let you visit web pages purporting to be Googlebot or a number of other web bots (see Figure 8-3).

Under the guise of Googlebot, the attacker could collect information without raising any red flags.[18] The primary countermeasure to webbot spoofing is to verify the IP address of the bot. Some search engines publish the IP addresses of their bots, but Google does not[19] (official information on Googlebot is very sparse). However, as I mentioned in Chapter 3, "Footprints, Fingerprints, and Connections," finding the owner of an IP address is straightforward. In the web server logs earlier in the chapter, the visitor claiming to be Googlebot came from the 66.249.67.207 IP address. Using a reverse IP address lookup (www.arin.net/whois/), I can confirm that Google owns the address.

```
OrgName:    Google Inc.
OrgID:      GOGL
Address:    1600 Amphitheatre Parkway
City:       Mountain View
StateProv:  CA
PostalCode: 94043
Country:    US

NetRange:   66.249.64.0 - 66.249.95.255
CIDR:       66.249.64.0/19
NetName:    GOOGLE
NetHandle:  NET-66-249-64-0-1
Parent:     NET-66-0-0-0-0
NetType:    Direct Allocation
```

```
NameServer: NS1.GOOGLE.COM
NameServer: NS2.GOOGLE.COM
NameServer: NS3.GOOGLE.COM
NameServer: NS4.GOOGLE.COM
Comment:
RegDate:    2004-03-05
Updated:    2007-04-10


OrgTechHandle: ZG39-ARIN
OrgTechName:   Google Inc.
OrgTechPhone:  +1-650-318-0200
OrgTechEmail:  arin-contact@google.com
```

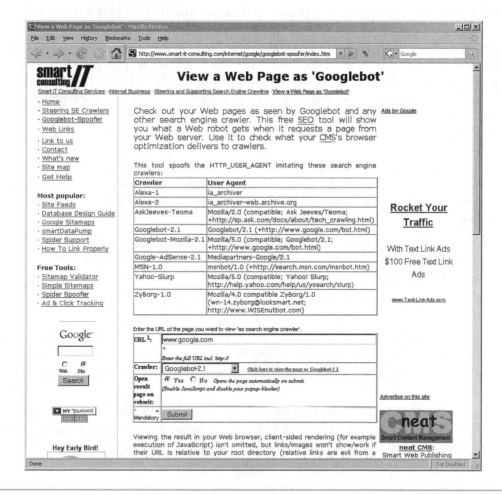

Figure 8-3   By changing the HTTP user agent field to match a common webbot, it is easy to masquerade as Googlebot or any other bot.

NOTE

To see lists of search engine spiders and user agent strings, including Alta Vista, Excite, Google, InfoSeek, Lycos, and Yahoo!, among others, visit www.iplists.com/.

PLACING SENSITIVE INFORMATION ON THE WEB

The core threat Googlebot poses is its role as a vacuum cleaner of virtually all publicly available information on the Internet. In many cases, individuals might not realize that the information they were storing was located on the "Internet" or that it could be accessed by the public. Multiple Googlebots spider page after page, collecting both innocuous and sensitive information that people have placed on the Internet. The term *spidering* means to download a web page and follow the links the page contains, repeating the process until a desired amount of information is collected. This is at the heart of how search webbots function. Individually, each page might contain rather innocuous information, but when the process is repeatedly executed, problems can arise. The sum of the information gathered can reveal a great deal. Consider the following:

- Dell posted a specification for future Dell laptops on publicly available servers. Googlebot visited the site and downloaded the documents, and Google made them available via its search engine. Even after Dell removed the documents from the web, they were still available via Google's cache function.[20]

- Drexel University College of Medicine placed a patient database of 5,500 records on the web. It contained addresses, telephone numbers, and detailed writeups of diseases and treatments.[21]

- Google has been pushing for states to open up their data and place it online, striking deals with Arizona, California, Utah, and Virginia.[22]

- Military bloggers have posted sensitive operational information online, prompting the U.S. Army to compel soldiers to stop blog posting without clearing the content with their superiors.[23] Milblogging.com currently tracks 1,864 military blogs in 34 countries.

- Facebook and MySpace users continually post sensitive information online.[24] Consider the bank intern who asked to miss work due to a "family emergency" and instead attended a party, posting pictures of the party to his Facebook page.[25] In another case, the owner of a consulting firm checked the Facebook page of a promising job applicant. She found that the candidate's page contained explicit photographs and commentary regarding the student's sexual escapes, drinking, and pot smoking, along with comments from friends.[26]

- European software firm SAP spidered competitor Oracle's customer service web site using customer logon credentials it acquired, and extracted thousands of proprietary, copyrighted materials Oracle had developed for its own support customers.[27] Oracle sued SAP in response.[28]

These examples demonstrate the type of sensitive information people will post online. After they do so, they lose control of the information, and it could easily end up indexed by Googlebot.

GOOGLE HACKING

The availability of sensitive information on the web gave rise to Google hacking, the process of using advanced Google queries to locate sensitive information on the web. An example follows:

```
"login: *" "password: *" filetype:xls
```

This queries Google for Excel spreadsheets (.xls files), potentially containing usernames and passwords.[29] It works, as do many of the other 1,422 queries in the Google Hacking Database, a repository of search queries known to provide sensitive information (http://johnny.ihackstuff.com/ghdb.php).[30] Table 8-2 summarizes the types of sensitive queries users have discovered and placed in the database.

Table 8-2 Sensitive Queries Available in the Google Hacking Database

Category	Number of Entries
Advisories and vulnerabilities	215
Error messages	68
Files containing juicy info	230
Files containing passwords	135
Files containing usernames	15
Footholds	21

continues

Table 8-2 Continued

Category	Number of Entries
Pages containing login portals	232
Pages containing network or vulnerability data	59
Sensitive directories	61
Sensitive online shopping info	9
Various online devices	201
Vulnerable files	57
Vulnerable servers	48
Web server detection	72

For more on Google hacking, read *Google Hacking for Penetration Testers,* Volume 2, by Johnny Long (Syngress, 2007).[31] When you think about the sensitive information that is available via Google's publicly available interface, you should also consider what information could be pulled by Google insiders with unrestricted access to the raw database and, presumably, the ability to precisely construct queries using powerful industry-standard tools such as the Structured Query Language (SQL) and regular expressions.[32] As we saw in Chapter 4, "Search," even Google's advanced user queries are still quite constrained, in comparison.

EVIL BOTS

At this point, it is worth asking, what could an evil bot akin to Googlebot do? I've already mentioned the value of Googlebot as a reconnaissance tool, but bots can achieve other, direct forms of mischief. A number of web crawlers working in concert could mount a distributed denial-of-service (DDoS) attack against web sites and other online services by repeatedly requesting documents, eventually overwhelming the servers. However, I don't see this as a realistic threat from a major online company such as Google, unless it suffered a massive (and unlikely) compromise of the machines that control Googlebot. The real threat of DDoS comes from a botnet, networks of compromised home and work computers.

Due to an unfortunate overlapping of terminology, note that a botnet is an entirely different animal than a webbot. Botnets arise when attackers have placed malicious software on a large number of compromised machines, effectively placing each machine under a single attacker's control, sometimes called a bot army. Botnets of up to one million machines exist and have been used in successful DDoS attacks, but not at the behest of large online companies.

That being said, interesting attacks are possible using webbots. Bots speak a number of protocols and could execute attacks against those services. Researchers discover new attacks each day, and the bots could be programmed to execute them against an individual server, class of servers, or even every server the bot encounters. Sound unlikely? Perhaps, particularly in the case of large online companies, but not impossible. Recall that webbots continually troll the web looking for links to follow, and that many web servers can be attacked via malformed links. Security researcher Michal Zalewski exploited both of these facts by placing sample malicious links on a web page frequented by webbots; see the following list.

```
http://somehost/cgi-bin/script.pl?p1=../../../../attack
http://somehost/cgi-bin/script.pl?p1=;attack
http://somehost/cgi-bin/script.pl?p1=|attack
http://somehost/cgi-bin/script.pl?p1=`attack`
http://somehost/cgi-bin/script.pl?p1=$(attack)
http://somehost:54321/attack?`id`
http://somehost/AAAAAAAAAAAAAAAAAAAAA...
```

A few days later, the webbots returned[33] and tried some of the tainted links against the target host. The key idea is that Zalewski was able to trick webbots of major online companies into executing attacks of his choosing against any machines he desired.[34] Zalewski's experiment points out an entirely new threat vector.

SUMMARY

Googlebot is the untiring front end of the Google data collection machine. Its concept is simple: Googlebot just automates the web browsing process and passes information back to Google's back-end servers. It augments the tremendous disclosures people provide via their use of online tools with information that people place on the publicly accessible web. With at least 19 billion constantly changing web pages and 50 million blogs,[35, 36] there is a vast sea of information to troll. In a world where it is very easy to post information, it takes only a small percentage of users to post sensitive information, deliberately or accidentally, and have it captured, cached, and made publicly available by Google. And web users have a marked propensity to post sensitive information. Even innocuous-appearing information will contain unique attributes (think e-mail and street addresses, phone numbers and names) that can link content to user profiles. Hard drives are getting cheaper by the day. So after such information is disclosed, it is safe to assume that it will exist forever. However, you shouldn't be concerned with just these files; the biggest threat could come from corporate archives of the entire web. Although some sites attempt to archive snapshots of the web,[37] a massive corporation such as Google could archive much of the web on a routine basis.

Googlebot is the ultimate reconnaissance engine for Google, but not end users. End users access the publicly available database built via Googlebot. Thus, our reconnaissance engine is the Google search interface and what Google deems to make publicly accessible. Visits from Googlebot are expected and welcomed. Most web masters construct their sites to make them Googlebot friendly, to gain higher search rankings. The future of webbots is off the charts; bot developers are constantly innovating. Current bots can read e-mail, send e-mail, follow links, fill in forms, monitor web sites, download files, and capture images. If the information is available on the Internet, sooner or later, it will be visited by a bot. One can only imagine what Google can gather from across the Internet after years and decades of collection.

ENDNOTES

1. Internet Archive, Wayback Machine. www.archive.org/web/web.php, last accessed 18 June 2008.

2. "Welcome to the Google Hacking Database." http://johnny.ihackstuff.com/ghdb.php, last accessed 4 December 2007.

3. Jaikumar Vijayan, "Data Exposure: Counties Across the U.S. Posting Sensitive Info Online," *ComputerWorld,* 12 April 2006. www.computerworld.com/securitytopics/security/privacy/story/0,10801,110453,00.html?from=story_package, last accessed 4 December 2006.

4. Tim Mayer, "Our Blog Is Growing Up and So Has Our Index," Yahoo! Search Blog, 8 August 2005. www.ysearchblog.com/archives/000172.html, last accessed 2 December 2007.

5. "How Google Crawls My Site," Google Webmaster Help Center. www.google.com/support/webmasters/bin/topic.py?topic=8843, last accessed 5 December 2007.

6. In 2006, a Nevada district court ruled that the Google cache did not violate copyright law; see www.eff.org/deeplinks/2006/01/google-cache-ruled-fair-use.

7. I have also heard reports that some engine bots actually parse the contents of zip archive files and make the results available in their search indexes.

8. Lawrence Page, Sergey Brin, Rajeev Motwani, and Terry Winograd, "The PageRank Citation Ranking: Bringing Order to the Web," The Stanford Digital Library Technologies Project, 1999.

9. I've skipped the two hyphen fields, which indicate the identity of the requester but are rarely used.

10. You can find a detailed explanation of web server logs here: http:/httpd.apache.org/docs/1.3/logs.html.

11. A full list of HTTP status codes is available at www.w3.org/Protocols/rfc2616/rfc2616-sec10.html.

12. Of course, this isn't a guarantee of security, but in most cases, blocking web server directory listings is a security best practice.

13. "About the Robots <META> Tag," The Web Robots Pages. www.robotstxt.org/meta.html, last accessed 7 December 2007.

14. Nik Cubrilovic, "Wikipedia: Special Treatment for Wikia and some Other Wikis." *TechCrunch,* 28 April 2007. www.techcrunch.com/2007/04/28/wikipedia-special-treatment-for-wikia-and-other-wikis/, last accessed 18 June 2008.

15. Anick Jesdanun, "Publishers Seeking Web Controls," WashingtonPost.com, 30 November 2007. www.washingtonpost.com/wp-dyn/content/article/2007/11/29/AR2007112902207.html, last accessed 7 December 2007.

16. Webmon isn't a search engine bot, per se, but it is interesting nonetheless. Webmon is a personal tool that enables web users to monitor web sites and informs them when a page changes.

17. Although the disclosure to Google did occur, you can make a request to Google to prevent it from showing in search results. See www.google.com/support/webmasters/bin/answer.py?answer=35301 and www.oreilly.com/pub/h/220 if you want to try putting the genie back in the bottle. Of course, by making the request, you are drawing attention to the sensitivity of the document.

18. Wget is a popular, high-quality tool that allows noninteractive downloads from the web (www.gnu.org/software/wget/manual/wget.html) and can be configured with any desired HTTP user agent field.

19. Matt Cutts, "How to Verify Googlebot," Google Webmaster Central Blog, 20 September 2006. http://googlewebmastercentral.blogspot.com/2006/09/how-to-verify-googlebot.html, last accessed 10 December 2007.

20. Elinor Mills, "Dell Gets Googled," WebWatch, 2 February 2006. http://networks. silicon.com/webwatch/0,39024667,39156123,00.htm, last accessed 10 December 2007.

21. Christopher Null, "Google: Net Hacker Tool du Jour." Wired.com, 4 March 2003. www.wired.com/techbiz/it/news/2003/03/57897, last accessed 11 December 2007.

22. "Google Pushes to Open Public Records," Slashdot.org, 30 April 2007. http://yro. slashdot.org/yro/07/04/30/2313211.shtml, last accessed 11 December 2007.

23. Noah Shachtman, "Army Squeezes Soldier Blogs, Maybe to Death." Wired.com, 2 May 2007. http://www.wired.com/politics/onlinerights/news/2007/05/army_ bloggers, last accessed 11 December 2007.

24. See Helen Popkin's article "Friends Don't Let Friends Join MySpace," www.msnbc. msn.com/id/18706138/.

25. "Bank Intern Busted by Facebook," *Valleywag,* 12 November 2007. http://valleywag. com/tech/your-privacy-is-an-illusion/bank-intern-busted-by-facebook-321802.php, last accessed 11 December 2007.

26. Alan Finder, "For Some, Online Persona Undermines a Resume," *The New York Times,* 11 June 2006. www.nytimes.com/2006/06/11/us/11recruit.html?ex= 1150171200&en=a7e75eac3e20cb38&ei=5087%0A, last accessed 11 December 2007.

27. Although Google was not involved in this instance, this case demonstrates how easy it is to acquire propriety materials after a user account is acquired.

28. "Oracle Sues SAP." Oracle.com, 3 July 2007. www.oracle.com/sapsuit/index.html, last accessed 10 December 2007.

29. Googler. "login: *" "password: *" filetype:xls. Google Hacking Database, 6 September 2006. Last accessed 11 December 2007.

30. Also see the article "Googling Up Passwords," by Scott Granneman, www. securityfocus.com/columnists/224.

31. You might also want to try out the wikto web server assessment tool, which auto- mates queries from the Google Hacking Database, www.sensepost.com/research/ wikto/.

32. See www.regular-expressions.info/ for more information on regular expressions.

33. Presumably "somehost" was a server under his control.

34. See Zalewski's *Phrack* magazine article (www.phrack.org/issues.html?issue= 57&id=10) and his book *Silence on the Wire* (No Starch Press, 2005) for more information.

35. As of this writing, blogging is ten years old and the number of blogs has been growing exponentially. See "Happy Blogiversary," by Tunku Varadarajan, http://online.wsj.com/article/SB118436667045766268.html.

36. David Sifry, "State of the Blogospher," Sifry's Alerts, 7 August 2006. www.sifry.com/alerts/archives/000436.html, 12 December 2007.

37. The best example is the nonprofit Internet Archive's Wayback Machine, www.archive.org/web/web.php.

Countermeasures

9

Web-based information disclosure is a battlefield. Programmers, lawyers, policy makers, informed web users, privacy advocates, and companies square off on all sides of the issue. Meanwhile, typical users carelessly provide sensitive information through their use of online tools, and unbeknownst to these users, their computers and web browsers churn out identifying information. This chapter covers techniques you and your employer can apply now to help increase your anonymity and privacy, and touches on promising areas that will likely assist in the future. This list isn't complete, nor is it intended to be. However, it is based on years of studying the problem. For security practitioners, some of what I propose might sound like common sense, but I believe these points are worth stating or restating. Regardless of your background, I believe you'll find some new ideas that you can apply.

Short of abstinence, no clear solution exists for protecting yourself and your company from web-based information disclosure. However, you can do a number of things to reduce the threat. Some are easy to do and some are harder, but each adds to your protection. Of course, each countermeasure comes with a cost. You must evaluate how much information you are giving away and consider the effectiveness and cost of the countermeasure, in terms of time, money, lost utility, and annoyance.

Unfortunately, no single clear solution exists. If you attempt to use all the techniques presented in this chapter, you will create a nearly intolerable web-browsing experience. Instead, you need to choose which techniques you apply. As Sun Tzu, the famous Chinese military strategist, said, "He will win who knows when to fight and when not to fight." Consider the severity, degree, and likelihood of the risk, and then choose countermeasures that help mitigate the risk to a level that you find acceptable, while still enabling you to use the web in an efficient and effective way. At the same time, we don't want countermeasures to be so detrimental to online companies that they threaten the tools and online innovation we value.

PATCHING USERS

In computer security, the concept of patching involves applying a small update to a piece of software to fix a vulnerability. For we humans, the best patch and biggest countermeasure you can apply to address the problem of web-based information disclosure is to become an informed user. Understand what you are giving away in terms of personal information, and know the long-term impact of your disclosures. Take a long-term view; consider not just a single online session, but the sum total of *all* your disclosures over the course of years and decades. This book should have opened your eyes to the threat, but you must assume personal responsibility. This includes informing your friends, coworkers, and management, as well as teaching your children, lest we fail to protect the next generation. Remember, the threat is not static: Appealing new tools, nefarious marketing strategies, and questionable technical innovations appear daily. You can't just remain idle—you must continually reevaluate the threat to maintain the privacy of your personal information.

RAISED AWARENESS

If becoming an informed user is the most effective countermeasure, what key points should you understand and how exactly do you raise awareness? The first step is to help people recognize that a problem exists. I've found that showing people queries from the AOL dataset is extremely effective. The easiest way to do this is to show or send people to one of the web front ends to the data: AOL Stalker (www.aolstalker.com), AOLSearchlogs.com (http://data.aolsearchlogs.com), or AOL Psycho (http://aolpsycho.com/) (see Figure 9-1). When people are confronted with the most sensitive hopes and dreams of other users, it is very hard to argue that a problem doesn't exist.

> **NOTE**
>
> For an approach to help people observe the magnitude of their own activities, see the "Self-Monitoring" section later in this chapter.

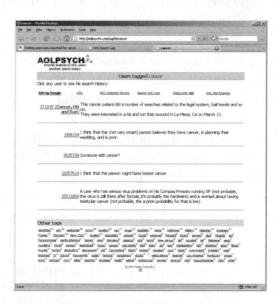

Figure 9-1 To convince people of the importance of the threat, send them to the AOL dataset in one of the web front ends, such as AOL Stalker (left), AOL SearchLogs (right), or AOL Psycho (bottom).

KNOW WHAT YOU ARE DISCLOSING

Now that you have people's attention, what do you tell them? They must understand these critical ideas:

- Consider each new tool carefully and understand the implications of the personal information that is disclosed through its use. Realize that no online company truly offers its tools and services for free.[1]
- How well do you trust the party you are sharing information with? Do you trust the governments and law enforcement agencies in which they operate?
- Consider how much of what you are sharing you would ever share with your parents, spouse, or coworkers.
- Read what privacy policies say directly *and* what they say between the lines. (I know, reading privacy policies is about as fun as ingesting a spoonful of cod liver oil, but informed users should be aware of what they are agreeing to.)
- Watch where you visit. When possible, spread activities around multiple online sites.
- Think in terms of years' or decades' worth of disclosures, not single instances or even days.
- Watch what you type when using online tools. The information, could be intercepted by your ISP and is surely logged by online companies.
- Set your browser to delete cookies at the end of each session and, if possible, to reject third-party cookies.
- Don't set the default home page to an online company. Doing so provides a heartbeat to the company every time you open the browser.[2, 3]
- Disclose the minimum information to accomplish a task.
- Remember that web surfing can be tracked across many sites via third-party advertising, such as that offered by Google/DoubleClick, as well as web traffic analysis software such as Google Analytics.

The purpose is to help make users appreciate the magnitude of their disclosures and make informed decisions. Unfortunately, comprehensive tools that support these decisions aren't available; that's where usable security can help.

> **NOTE**
>
> A little paranoia is a healthy thing when it comes to security.

USABLE SECURITY

Protection against web-based information disclosure demands usable security. Usable security seeks to help people remain secure by creating systems that are designed to be effective, efficient, understandable, and easy to use. Such systems don't waste users' time and attention; instead, they seek to disturb users only when they need to make a decision. Importantly, they don't just send the user a cryptic error message; they provide just the right information at just the right time. Often this means silently protecting the user with no interaction; security is invisible and just works. Chances are, you've seen many failures. The textbook example is SSL certificate mismatches. Normally, when you visit a web site that uses SSL encryption, your transactions are quietly protected behind the scenes (you simply see a padlock in the corner of your browser), but when a certificate doesn't match the domain name of the site you are visiting (or another similar error), you are presented with a cryptic error message[4] (see Figures 9-2 and 9-3). Such a mismatch might mean that an attacker is attempting to intercept your communications, but, more likely, a misconfigured web server is causing the error. Such errors are so frequent that most users just ignore the warning, defeating the purpose of the security check in the first place.

> **NOTE**
>
> It is important to note that as this book was going to press, Mozilla released Firefox 3.0, which includes a number of security and privacy enhancements. I encourage you to take a look.

For examples of interesting usable security studies, see Alma Whitten and J. D. Tygar's seminal paper "Why Johnny Can't Encrypt" (from the Proceedings of the 1999 USENIX Security Symposium), and Lorrie Cranor and Simson Garfinkel's *Security and Usability: Designing Secure Systems That People Can Use* (O'Reilly, 2005).

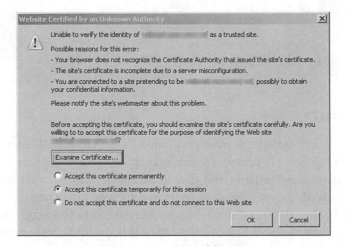

Figure 9-2   When you visit a web site with misconfigured SSL, you are presented with a cryptic error message. Most users ignore this warning altogether, defeating its purpose.

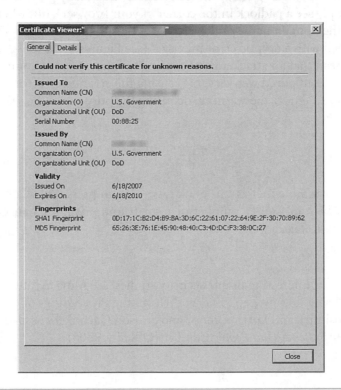

Figure 9-3   Clicking the Examine Certificate button in Figure 9-2 brings up an even more cryptic warning.

Usable security is an active research area; for the latest information, I recommend following the output of the Symposium on Usable Privacy and Security (SOUPS), held at Carnegie Mellon University. Chaired by Lorrie Cranor, SOUPS is a leading venue where researchers share their work on such things as field studies of security or privacy technology, new applications of existing models or technology, innovative security or privacy functionality and design, lessons learned from deploying and using usable privacy and security features, usability evaluations of security and privacy features, and security testing of usability features.[5] I also recommend the Usable Security Blog by Ka-Ping Yee (http://usablesecurity.com/) if you want to monitor developments on a more frequent basis.

To create usable systems that protect against web-based information disclosure, we must get into the minds of users and find out why they do what they do. This includes their assessment of trust of online companies, how they believe their personal information will be secured and used, and what type of cost-benefit analysis they make as they use online tools. One colleague suggested to me that perhaps today's users are faced with no other solution than to use free online tools. Similar to rats forced to endure electric shocks to receive food pellets, web users might have no other real option than to give up portions of their personal information to remain part of the wired world. For more on this idea, I suggest you study the concept of "learned helplessness."[6]

As we seek technical solutions to help individuals and organizations protect themselves, the systems must be designed so that they are usable. As I alluded to in the introduction to this chapter, a trade-off exists between usability and privacy using today's technology—each current approach comes at a cost. This doesn't have to be the case, but it appears to be the current situation. In the next section, I present some promising technical approaches and highlight their advantages and usability impact.

TECHNICAL PROTECTION

Although getting people to clearly understand the implications of web-based information is an important part of a complete solution, it isn't sufficient. Users and organizations need tools that provide the technical underpinnings to buttress their high-level desires. These technical solutions must degrade the semantic information that users provide and minimize the ways they can be fingerprinted, profiled, and linked to other users and groups. Comprehensive solutions should limit cookies, diffuse disclosures, encrypt appropriate activity, protect network addresses, avoid registered user accounts, and minimize sensitive data stored on users' computers, to guard privacy and help ensure anonymity. Many of these solutions center on the web browser. In this section, I focus on the popular Firefox browser because it is free, extensible, open source, and available for a large number of platforms. Firefox has a great many options and extensions designed to protect privacy.

CONTROLLING COOKIES

One of the easiest and most effective countermeasures is to reduce or eliminate the cookies that accumulate on your computer. Recall that cookies are small text files that are placed on your computer when you visit a site. Two types of cookies exist. One can exist for only a short time (session cookies); the other can exist for a very long time (persistent cookies). Initially, browsers provided only basic cookie-management capabilities: accept all, reject all, and ask. This approach didn't work very well. Accepting all cookies permitted web surfers to be tagged with many types of cookies. Rejecting all cookies wasn't a viable solution because many web sites required cookies to function properly. Asking users if they wanted to accept or reject cookies soon became an untenable annoyance. Fortunately, modern browsers provide more intelligent alternatives. Figure 9-4 shows the Options menu from the Firefox browser.

Figure 9-4 To help lock down your browser, configure it to delete cookies when the browser is closed, as shown here in the Firefox browser's options menu. However, this technique does not provide protection during extended web-browsing sessions.

As you examine the figure, note the cookie options it makes available. I recommend accepting cookies from web sites because they are necessary for many popular web sites to function, but notice that I've also chosen to keep cookies only until I close Firefox.[7] This ensures that whatever cookies I've picked up during a given online session are deleted when I close the browser. However, this isn't a perfect solution. Your typical web-browsing session might last hours. During this time, you will surely pick up tens or hundreds of cookies. Although cookies won't identify your browser from each web-browsing session, you can be identified during a session, both when you return to a web site and when you browse the web and visit sites with shared third-party content, such as Google/DoubleClick advertisements. To filter cookies from a specific web site, you can click the Exception button shown in Figure 9-4 and configure Firefox to block cookies from the doubleclick.net domain (see Figure 9-5). You might think that it would be best if you also had the option to block all third-party cookies. That functionality was previously possible in Firefox, but it was removed in Version 2.0, possibly due to legal concerns, but has reappeared in Version 3.0 as this book was going to press. I recommend blocking third-party cookies if your browser allows you to do so. To keep tabs on the latest tools and techniques, I recommend monitoring Firefox's Privacy and Security plugins at https://addons.mozilla.org/en-US/firefox/browse/type:1/cat:12. You can find the latest extensions to your browser, many of which are designed to augment Firefox's built-in privacy and security features.

NOTE

Your online activities can also be tracked using cache-based and visited link–based techniques. See www.safecache.com/ and www.safehistory.com/ for two popular Firefox add-on countermeasures.

However, blocking cookies has a downside. It's tedious to manually configure your browser (or browsers) to block many different suspect domains. In some cases, by deleting cookies, you lose preferences you've configured on a web site. You can't have it both ways. Either you appear as a new user each time you visit, or the web site recognizes you and customizes your experience appropriately. However, I believe the overall effort of cookie management is worth it. As you move among physical locations with a computer, your IP address will change, but unless you configure your browser to delete cookies, you will be instantly identified, even if you hop from your home to a hotel in Amsterdam.

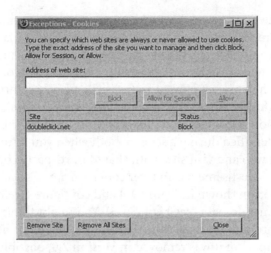

Figure 9-5 To block cookies from a specific domain, use Firefox's exceptions capability. In this example, I'm blocking cookies from doubleclick.net.

DIFFUSING OR ELIMINATING YOUR DISCLOSURES

As I mentioned earlier in the chapter, the best way to eliminate web-based information disclosure is to avoid revealing the information in the first place, whether this is your search queries, network address, or other online interactions. However, this option isn't always easy or practical. You can add three technical enhancements to your browser to help.

Content Filtering

As you saw in Chapter 7, "Advertising and Embedded Content," when you visit a popular web site, your browser is probably pulling in content from, and leaving behind footprints on, a number of third-party sites. You can prevent this by employing your own proxy. Privoxy (www.privoxy.org/) is one powerful free option (see Figure 9-6.) A proxy acts as an intermediary between your web browser and the destination web site. Proxies have the capability to change both your outgoing and incoming traffic. For example, Privoxy can block web bugs, banner ads, cookies, and referer values. Because Privoxy is under your direct control, you can use it to tweak your outgoing and incoming traffic to your heart's content. It enables an extreme level of customization, such as blocking advertisements and third-party content. Performance overhead is generally minimal, but the flexibility it provides requires intermediate to advanced technical expertise. Also, a local installation of Privoxy can't provide full anonymous surfing; your IP address is still revealed. To provide this additional level of protection, you need to pair Privoxy with an anonymizing proxy or an anonymization network, such as Tor. I cover this topic in more detail later in the chapter.

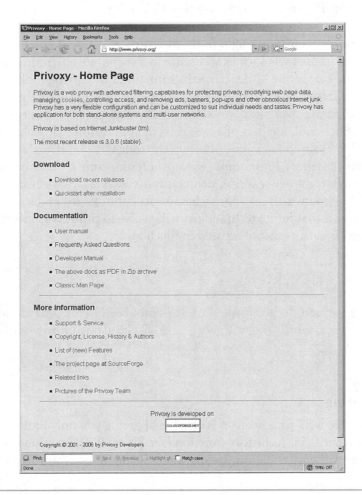

Figure 9-6   The Privoxy Web Proxy provides fine-grain control over your inbound and outbound web traffic. It can block third-party advertisements and cookies.

In addition to maintaining your own proxy, at the corporate level, you can use a tool such as Websense (www.websense.com/) to filter content and monitor data flows across the network. Websense is useful in preventing people from visiting web sites that corporate management doesn't condone. In my opinion, correct use of a tool such as Websense is tricky. At work, I've encountered problems with Websense when searching for information on the web and been denied access to web sites I've had a legitimate need to visit. (This is an artifact of my employer's configuration of the tool, not the tool itself.) However, if you are trying to reign in information-disclosure issues across a medium to large company, you might find a tool such as Websense useful.

My suggestion to use tools such as Websense in a corporate environment is done with some trepidation. Corporate IT departments sometimes use spying tools as a way to monitor their collective organizational disclosures, creating a privacy threat to their employees. Companies then must seek the difficult balance between corporate and individual privacy. Such tools are part of a new class of application that seeks Data Leak Prevention (DLP). Examples include offerings by Code Green Networks (www.codegreennetworks.com/), Proofpoint (www.proofpoint.com/), Reconnex (www.reconnex.net/), Vericept (www.vericept.com/), and Verdasys (www.verdasys.com/).[8] DLP is a nascent field—many current approaches use straightforward pattern-matching techniques, but I expect that future technologies will evolve to protect against the more subtle information-disclosure risks discussed in this book.

NOTE

You might also want to investigate the Greasemonkey Firefox plug-in, which enables you to customize the way a web page displays in your browser using small bits of JavaScript.[9]

Self-Monitoring

When you surf the web, your browser is capable of giving you only limited information on your past activities via its history function (see Figure 9-7). Imagine if you had the capability to track the information you disclosed during weeks, months, or years.

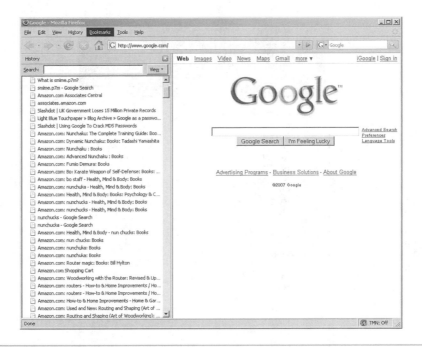

Figure 9-7 The Firefox browser's history function. Traditional browser history functions show you only web sites you've visited, not your disclosures.

With an improved history function—a browser history on steroids, if you will—you could monitor your exact disclosures over time. This is the approach security researcher Kulsoom Abdullah took when she created a prototype browser plug-in to monitor search queries over time (see Figure 9-8).[10]

Although Abdullah's plug-in is a prototype, I believe the approach has great promise. By creating tools that enable users to self-monitor their activities, you elevate user awareness. People can then understand the magnitude of their disclosures and self-regulate their activities as appropriate. The advantage of this approach is that you are not directly threatening the business model of online companies. Instead, you are simply providing users with a clear picture, and raising awareness, of their own activities. To extend Abdullah's work, I believe the best self-monitoring solution should include not just search queries, but also visualizations and summaries of most types of information disclosures, such as a social graph of e-mails touching Gmail accounts and maps showing directions requested.

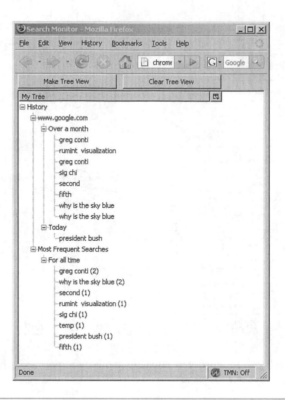

Figure 9-8 Search Term Monitor browser plug-in. Created by security researcher Kulsoom Abdullah, this prototype Firefox plug-in enables users to track their search queries over time.

Google does provide a Web History function (see Figure 9-9), but I believe a browser-based approach is best. A properly designed tool can show you disclosures across all the sites you visit, be integrated cleanly with the browser, protect your locally stored data, and avoid having to trust a third party such as Google. In contrast, the Google Web History tool works for only some of its services, and it requires you to create a registered user account and to install the Google toolbar for advanced functionality. More importantly, although Google Web History enables users to stop storing their activity and remove items, it deletes information only from the users' views. Google still maintains its own independent logging system, "as is a common practice in the industry." [11] Thus, logging might still occur despite a naïve user's beliefs to the contrary.

Ultimately, I'd like to see large online companies take the lead in providing individual users with empowering plug-ins that support self-monitoring and share the results as open-source projects. Such plug-ins would assist users with making informed information-disclosure decisions *before* they pass sensitive data to online companies.

Figure 9-9   Google's Web History service

Both of these approaches are single-user solutions. Organizations might also need to monitor their collective activities. A promising research area is to create an organizational-level tool that enables self-monitoring in an intuitive way. Such a system would raise an entirely new set of privacy concerns but, in some instances, would be warranted, such as a hospital seeking to ensure that sensitive information isn't leaking out to online companies as the result of the collective web activities of its personnel.[12]

Search Term Chaffing

The term *chaffing* comes from the military air-combat community: Aircraft eject chaff, small strips of metal, to throw off targeting radars and radar-guided missiles. This concept is very applicable in the context of web-based information disclosure. As you use online tools, you are providing a noise-free stream of information, such as search terms or mapping locations; by doing so, you are making it easy to identify legitimate activity. Chaffing seeks to include false or misleading activity in this stream, to conceal your real activity and intent.

Chaffing will certainly reduce the quality of information you provide to an online company, but the approach has several significant challenges. First, you are consuming unnecessary resources from online companies. Let's consider search. To process the steady stream of spurious search queries, search engines will work much harder. Each query must be looked up in a database to provide appropriate search results. By needlessly requesting information, you force the search engine to continually process useless requests. Each unneeded network connection consumes the company's valuable network bandwidth, processing power, RAM, and storage. The result is slower response times for other users. Although the impact might be inconsequential for a small number of users, if chaffing is widely adopted, it could cause a significant slowdown in service for many users. To maintain high-quality service, the search engine will need to add significantly more information-processing resources and increase network bandwidth to handle the strain, at a considerable cost. Chaffing might generate a large, easily detected footprint and online companies will likely deem it malicious. You would be polluting the information environment used to provide high-quality search results for other users, and undermining the business model of the search company. Online companies thus wouldn't tolerate such behavior for long and almost assuredly would deny access to users who behaved in such a way, claiming violations of terms of service, if the practice became widespread. You must decide the morality of using such a tool and determine whether you want to use it.

A chaffing system must be carefully designed to provide comprehensive protection. A real query must be indistinguishable from a fake query, to provide reliable protection. This is very difficult to do in practice. Any inconsistency provides a hook that enables filtering algorithms to identify your real queries, defeating your intent. Think about it. When you search the web, you aren't usually looking for a single piece of information; you often reformulate the query to provide a better result. Your chaffing application must hide your original query and any reformulations in a sea of noise—a difficult proposition. In most cases, you click on a link after you conduct a search. True, your chaffing tool could simulate clicking on links, but it will be very difficult to hide the fact that a machine is choosing from the results instead of a human. Any statistical deviation would provide a clue to your actual intent. The same applies to the timing of your queries. An obvious approach for machines is to randomly time queries to the search engine. To insert your real query into the stream of fake queries, you might need to wait until the time is right, delaying your access to information. To overcome these challenges, researchers are exploring applications of chaffing.

The best example is TrackMeNot by New York University's Daniel Howe and Helen Nissenbaum (see Figure 9-10).[13] TrackMeNot is a Firefox browser plug-in that attempts to address many of the technical issues surrounding search query chaffing. Most notably, it seeks to mimic human search queries by intelligently timing spurious queries and dynamically evolving queries to mirror real searches, instead of using a static word list.

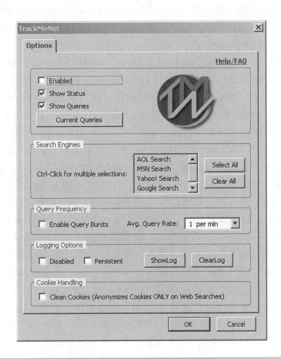

Figure 9-10 TrackMeNot is a Firefox browser plug-in that hides your real search queries amid a sea of fake ones.

ENCRYPTION

Cryptography, the practice and study of hiding information, and *encryption*, the process of transforming information to make it unreadable to anyone except those who possess special knowledge,[14] are frequently cited as cures for most security problems. Although encrypting information can help solve some problems involving web-based information disclosure, it isn't a panacea. Jon Callas, Chief Technology Officer of PGP Corporation, captured the essence of the challenge when he said, "Cryptography has to be usable, and usable by people who have real jobs. Cryptography is not magic pixie dust that you can sprinkle on a problem and make it secure."[15] I agree wholeheartedly. However, encryption can help in a number of ways.

Employing SSL, the underlying cryptographic protocol of secure HTTP (i.e., HTTPS), will frustrate eavesdropping by all but a well-resourced eavesdropper,[16] unless you're a browser contains specially crafted certificates.[17] Employers can create these certificates, incorporating them into standardized workstation images and giving the employer the ability to easily eavesdrop. Online companies can also use SSL to help protect against eavesdropping, often when logging in or when using web mail. I don't expect that SSL will be used to protect all forms of online activity, such as search, because the cryptographic algorithm will increase processing overhead, which, in turn, slows interactions and requires additional servers. Because SSL protects only the communication itself, the protocol doesn't protect you from the online companies you are communicating with; they are trusted partners in the communication.[18] In addition, SSL doesn't protect the source and destination IP address of your packets or other packet header information because this information is needed to route your packets across the Internet to the correct destination. Analyzing these unencrypted "message externals" is a well-studied field called traffic analysis, which can reveal such things as time and duration of communication, sites you've visited, and size of messages.[19] Even the simple act of using encrypted communications might appear incriminating and draw unwanted attention.[20]

The trend away from the desktop invites you to store information on the servers of online companies. You must trust that these companies are carefully protecting it. These companies can and should use encryption to protect their user data. Doing so deters the casual attacker or thrill-seeking employee and helps ensure that only authorized employees have access. Online companies must not overlook the security of backup tapes; they should be encrypted and the keys protected.

When your data is in someone else's possession, you are placing a great deal of trust in that person. However, you can take matters into your own hands by encrypting the data before you store it. I suggest encrypting files that you store with PGP (www.pgp.com/) or GPG (www.gnupg.org/). These tools aren't particularly easy to use, but if you are interested in high-grade encryption, they're a well-vetted approach. Don't rely on password protection offered by popular word processors and spreadsheets—these passwords will block only your little sister.

NOTE

Researchers are exploring ways to use cryptographic techniques to safely enable anonymous sharing of information. Much of this is based on the work of Dr. David Chaum. Visit www.chaum.com/ for an overview of his seminal work.

Despite its strength, cryptography suffers from many drawbacks. The foremost is a false sense of security. Encryption is only as good as the key. The threat of physical violence has a strange way of making people far more likely to share sensitive information such as passwords and encryption keys. In general, the mathematical underpinnings of popular encryption techniques are sound, but the individual implementations of these techniques are frequently flawed. Even worse are situations in which individuals attempt to create their own encryption techniques. I know enough about cryptography to know that only the experts, myself not included, should create cryptographic systems. These same experts will tell you that a given encryption technique should be considered ephemeral, at best. The relentless advance of processor speed guarantees that what was previously rigorously secure will be an open book at some point in the future. We've seen this happen many times throughout history. For example, when the East German secret police shredded documents in 1989, they probably didn't consider that computers would be reassembling the documents 18 years later.[21] When the United States adopted the Data Encryption Standard (DES) in 1976, they didn't expect that a research team in 1997 would crack a DES message in 96 days, or that another team in 1999 would crack a DES-encrypted message in approximately 22 hours.[22] A single advance, such as a breakthrough in quantum computing, could render today's best encryption technology obsolete overnight. Worse yet, all historical encrypted communications could likewise be compromised if some enterprising eavesdropper had the records on hand.

Finally, consider using full-disk encryption on your hard drive. Doing so dramatically reduces the risks of data disclosure if the drive is lost or stolen. With the highly visible security breaches occurring in government and industry, and the increasing number of laws compelling such organizations to inform consumers of lost data, more people are using full-disk encryption as a solution. On-the-fly, full-disk encryption is computationally intensive and will decrease performance, but it is a potent form of protection. A great place to start is by exploring TrueCrypt (www.truecrypt.org/), a popular, free, and open-source on-the-fly encryption utility.

PROTECT YOUR NETWORK ADDRESS

Along with cookies, your network IP address uniquely identifies you to online companies every time you visit. Your address might also be included in the header information of each e-mail you send. Blocks of IP addresses are allocated to ISPs, companies, organizations, and educational institutions.[23] In the time of modem communication, you were better protected because each time you dialed in, you were likely given a different IP address. This changed with broadband communication. ISPs and other providers often issue IP addresses to their broadband customers that change rarely. This doesn't have to be the case. The Dynamic Host Configuration Protocol (DHCP) is widely used to allocate IP addresses inside address blocks, such as on a corporate network, and you can configure it to frequently update IP addresses.[24] However, DHCP is constrained by the organization's pool of addresses, which might be small.

Because IP address allocations are publicly available, someone could easily trace back an address to the owner of the IP address block.[25] From there, tracing back to your specific account requires information maintained by the IP block owner. This doesn't mean you are safe; an attacker or law enforcement official could acquire these records and determine the exact user of a specific IP address at a given point in time. You must have an IP address to communicate on the Internet; however, you can hide, mask, or frequently update your true IP address to make such backtracking difficult or impossible.

Anonymizing Proxies

Perhaps the best hope for anonymous web browsing is the anonymizing proxy. Anonymizing proxies act as intermediaries between you and the destination web site. They make requests on your behalf, filter some identifying information (such as cookies, browser header fields, etc.), replace your IP address with theirs, and pass responses back to you (see Figure 9-11). Because of their sensitive role in masking your activities, anonymizing proxies should not log this activity, as logs might be stolen or subpoenaed. By using such a service, you are placing a great deal of trust in the administrator of the service. If you use only one anonymizing proxy, that single site will know your IP address, the site you visited, and most likely the content of your communications—information that could be exploited. I wouldn't be surprised if some people didn't set up anonymizing proxies solely to observe the traffic of people who want to remain anonymous, so tread carefully. Another important aspect of anonymizing proxies is scalability. Through their design, proxies introduce latency in online activities; chains of proxies add even more latency. Individual users might find these issues tolerable, but large-scale, corporate-grade anonymizing proxies are an open problem that requires more research to achieve scaleable solutions for large organizations.

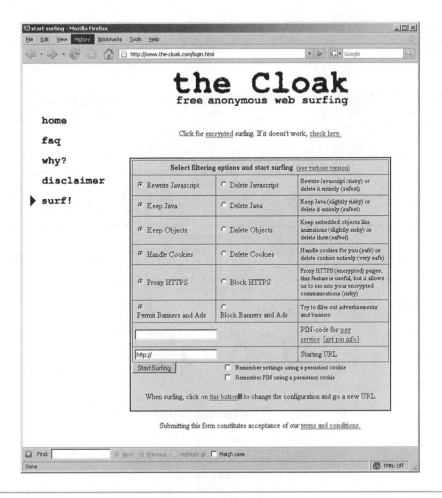

Figure 9-11 The Cloak anonymous web proxy. Anonymizing web proxies act as an intermediary between your browser and destination web site, mask your IP address, and can filter such things as cookies and browser header fields.

The best way to address this shortcoming is to chain proxies (see Figure 9-12). This entails going through a number of intermediate proxies (each causes a performance slowdown, but an increase in anonymity[26]) until you reach your desired level of protection. If you include proxies from foreign countries, you gain the advantage of delaying or preventing government or law enforcement attempts to trace back your activities. Although you can use a single proxy or a small number of proxies without undue latency, you can't chain proxies indefinitely. Additional proxies will eventually make web browsing intolerably slow. As you explore the use of proxies, you might want to investigate the SwitchProxy and FoxyProxy Firefox plug-ins, which help you manage multiple proxies.[27]

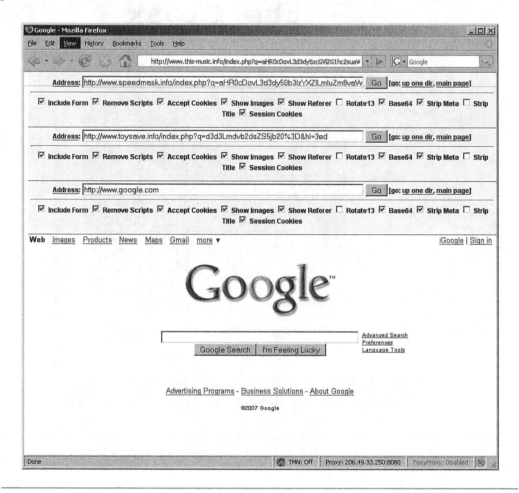

Figure 9-12 Chaining proxies. In this image, I'm going through two proxies, speedmask.info and toysave.info, before using Google. Chaining proxies helps mask your activities but will eventually bring your browser to a crawl.

Tor

No discussion of anonymous surfing would be complete with discussing Tor. Thousands of people use it for a wide variety of reasons, including to conceal online activities by bouncing communications around a network of relays run by volunteers around the world.[28] Tor is an anonymization network that resists traffic analysis because it randomly routes your communications between these relays via encrypted links. In doing so, Tor hides both the destination and the contents of users' traffic from the ISP and other adversaries watching their connections; Tor also hides users' IP addresses from the destination servers. In essence, Tor creates a virtual circuit between you and your desired destination in which each relay in this chain knows only the address of the preceding relay and the address of the next relay.

Initially, Tor was considered difficult to configure, but times have changed. The Tor Project bundles Tor with Privoxy, Vidalia, and Torbutton.[29] I've already discussed Privoxy, but Vidalia and Torbutton are worth describing. Vidalia (http://vidalia-project.net/) is a cross-platform controller GUI for Tor that makes configuration easy (see Figure 9-13). Torbutton (https://addons.mozilla.org/en-US/firefox/addon/2275) is a Firefox plug-in that enables you to easily enable or disable the browser's use of Tor (see Figure 9-14).[30] The end result of this bundle is you can get Tor up and running in approximately five minutes. Tor has even spawned specialized browsers that rely on the Tor network, such as Torpark, which evolved into the XeroBank browser (http://xerobank.com/xB_browser.html). Finally, to verify that Tor is enabled and to help fine-tune your browser, you might want to try a web-based Tor verification site, such as TorCheck (https://torcheck.xenobite.eu/) (see Figure 9-15).

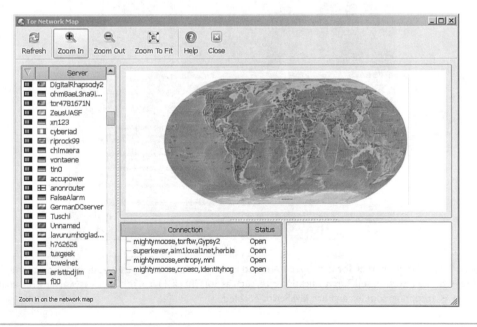

Figure 9-13 Vidalia is an easy-to-use graphical user interface for Tor. In this image, Vidalia displays a list of available Tor relays.

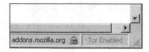

Figure 9-14 The Torbutton Firefox browser plug-in enables you to turn Tor on and off with a single mouse click.

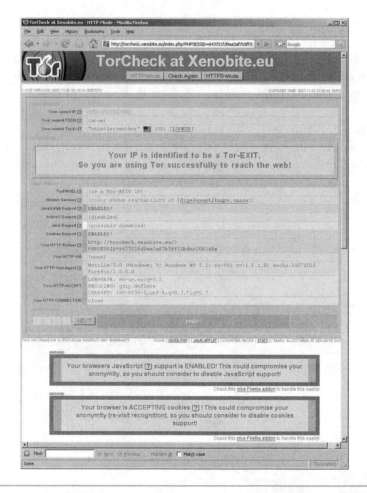

Figure 9-15 To verify that Tor is properly enabled and that you've configured your browser correctly, consider trying a web-based Tor verification site, such as TorCheck. Here, TorCheck is warning me that my browser is accepting cookies and has JavaScript enabled.

As with any anonymization technique that relies on a third party, you must trust that the technique is reliable and does not contain a hidden vulnerability that would defeat its purpose. This applies to Tor as well, but Tor is widely trusted because its source is freely available and researchers of all types, including the hacker community, academia, and industry, have heavily analyzed the theory and implementation.[31]

> **NOTE**
>
> For the technically minded reader, I suggest reading the excellent, seminal paper on web anonymity "Crowds: Anonymity for Web Transactions," by Michael Reiter and Avi Rubin, available at http://citeseer.ist.psu.edu/20850.html.

No solution is perfect, and Tor is no exception. Although the anonymization network Tor forms consists of encrypted links, traffic analysis is possible if an attacker can observe both the point of entry and the exit of the network.[32] Similarly, because Tor must eventually communicate with the outside world, eavesdroppers on the communications from the Tor exit node can observe the contents of the activity, such as e-mail addresses and passwords, even if they do not know the source IP address of the e-mail user.[33] Some Tor nodes are malicious, but it takes more than one node to connect the origin with the destination. However, a malicious exit node, the last node the user transits before leaving the Tor network, is particularly bad because it can see decrypted traffic even if it does not know the source. To avoid this drawback, the underlying communications themselves must be encrypted, with SSL being a likely choice. Domain name lookups, the protocol that translates domain names into IP addresses, are also a weakness because the requests might occur directly with DNS servers outside the Tor network, if the user hasn't properly configured a countermeasure such as Privoxy. Privoxy is often paired with Tor and used to filter cookies and route DNS traffic through the Tor network. Occasionally, other attacks are discovered.[34, 35] Tor isn't a cure-all; if you leave cookies turned on or type in personally identifying information, Tor can't protect you.

> **NOTE**
>
> Browser plug-ins such as Java, Flash, ActiveX, RealPlayer, Quicktime, and Adobe's PDF viewer can sometimes reveal your IP address. For more secure browsing, you need to uninstall your plug-ins or investigate tools that enable you to selectively block this content.[36] Try typing `about:plugins` into the address bar of Firefox to see a list.

Although you can get Tor up and running in five minutes, Tor is not fast. But development continues to address this point. In my opinion, the biggest usability drawback of Tor is speed. However, you can't blame Tor for this. If you are bouncing your browsing across a number of relays, some across different continents, *and* encrypting each link, it is reasonable to expect some slowdown. In addition, one of the biggest contributors to Tor network slowdown is congestion due to heavy usage users. As such, organizers of the Tor network are always interested in additional volunteers, to help increase the number of relay nodes and, hence, the performance of the Tor network. Note that Torbutton helps address the speed issue by allowing you to enable Tor when you desire anonymity and to disable it when you require speed.

To summarize, Tor is one of the most robust ways to anonymize your online activities, but it isn't bullet proof. Spend time learning how it works, configuring your browser, and carefully analyzing your online activity to make sure you use it correctly.

NOTE

Tor isn't the only high-grade mechanism for anonymizing your online activities. Also consider exploring the Java Anonymous Proxy (http://anon.inf.tu-dresden.de/index_en.html) to protect your web surfing, and Mixminion (http://mixminion.net/) and Mixmaster (http://mixmaster.sourceforge.net/) to use e-mail anonymously.[37]

Employ a NAT Firewall

Network Address Translation (NAT) firewalls aren't just an important measure to help hide your IP address; they are also an effective tool in protecting your network. The Internet Protocol (IP) was designed so that each computer on the Internet would have its own unique IP address. IPv4 is currently the most popular; it allocates 32 bits for IP addresses, which equates to roughly 4.3 billion addresses for the entire Internet. However, as the number of Internet users grew, available IP addresses became scarce and people sought means of conserving addresses. NAT is one solution. It uses a network device, usually a router, between an internal network and the public Internet. On outgoing communications, the router replaces internal IP addresses with an external IP address. For returning traffic, the router performs the reverse operation, replacing the external IP address with the internal address. In this way, a small network, such as a home network, or a large network can share a few public IP addresses, or even a single one.

From the privacy perspective, NAT helps hide your activity in a pool of other users. The degree of protection varies based on the size of the internal network. If you have just two computers on the internal network, you don't gain much privacy protection. But if you have a large corporate network of tens of thousands, you gain a lot of protection. Although your individual activity is masked by the activities of others, NAT doesn't provide complete protection. NAT is usually employed by people who share the same network, such as home networks and companies. So although your individual activity is masked, an online company can easily identify activities of the group as a whole. In addition, if individual users fail to block cookies, they can still be uniquely identified, despite the masked IP address. However, NAT is a widely available and well-vetted technology, and other than taking a small performance hit for the address translation performed on the router, it is seamless and easy to use. I recommend that you use it.

Alternate Surfing Locations

Other approaches to protecting network addresses include surfing from network hot spots, such as those found in coffee shops, hotel rooms, airports, and Internet cafés.[38] The advantage is that these locations break the connection between the network address at one's home or place of employment. The downside is that cookies, semantic disclosures, and registered user accounts can still provide the capability to identify the user if they're not carefully managed. Additionally, such public hotspots are known to be rife with malicious activity, including eavesdropping and network attacks.[39]

AVOID USING REGISTERED ACCOUNTS

This should be an obvious one, but it is worth stating. If you are concerned about being uniquely identified by a given online site, don't register a user account. It doesn't matter if you have no cookies on your computer and come from a new IP address every single time you visit; by logging in with your user ID and password, you've uniquely identified yourself—game over.

It is important to note that progress is being made in online identity management, sometimes called persona management. The key idea is that you can create a number of different online identities and easily and rapidly move between them. As these systems evolve, I expect that you will be able to present different appearances to different web sites. When dealing with online companies, you might decide to disclose as little information as possible to conduct a given transaction. In another situation, you might decide to reveal a great deal more to enable customization. A complete solution doesn't currently exist, but researchers are working on the problem. For one promising approach, see Xu, Zhang, Chen, and Wang's "Privacy-Enhancing Personalized Web Search" from the 2007 World Wide Web Conference.[40] I also suggest monitoring the research occurring at the annual Workshop on Privacy in the Electronic Society (WPES).

Minimizing Data Retention on Your Computer

So far, most of this chapter has focused on limiting web-based information disclosure, but it is worth mentioning that you should also consider limiting the data retained by your computer from your online activities. Your computer will likely contain a great deal of personal information, such as your word processing documents, spreadsheets, and tax returns. You shouldn't add to it all your browser cache, browsing history, saved form information (think credit cards), and saved passwords. These records exist in configuration files your browser uses to provide these services, making them a plump target for attackers.[41]

For basic protection, Firefox makes this easy by providing a number of choices on its Options menu. I say "basic protection" because even selecting the most rigorous options under Firefox might still leave traces behind. The classic example is that when you delete a file on your personal computer, it isn't really gone. The raw data still exists on the disk until is written over. You might want to explore additional software that rigorously removes the traces you leave behind on your PC.[42] If only it was this easy on the web.

Policy Protection

Technical solutions and an informed user population aren't the only ways to protect yourself and your organization against the security risks of web-based information disclosure. You can buttress these measures with informed policy and plans of action, implemented at the personal, organizational, and national levels. Policy solutions cover a wide spectrum of approaches, including do-not-track lists, informed usage policies, petitions to senior decision makers, support for privacy organizations, data anonymization, and limited data retention and generation.

> **Note**
>
> To help track the constantly evolving policy landscape, consider monitoring or attending the Computers, Freedom, and Privacy Conference (www.cfp.org/).

Do-Not-Track Lists

Mirrored after the use of do-not-call lists to deter telemarketers, some privacy groups are advocating the implementation of do-not-track lists for online consumers. The key idea is to enable online users to easily opt out of being tracked online. Under the plan, advertisers would be required to register web sites that perform tracking to a centralized Federal Trade Commission database so that consumers could opt out of such activity. The long-term efficacy of do-not-track lists remains to be seen, but the plan is a good example of using policy-making organizations, such as the Federal Trade Commission, to provide oversight of online companies.[43]

Individual and Organization Policies on Web-Based Information Disclosure

In the "Patching Users" section, I discussed many aspects of individual and organizational ways to teach people about the risks associated with web-based information disclosure; however, awareness is only part of the battle. The informal guidelines I suggested must be backed up with clear policies, perhaps with the appropriate punishments for noncompliance. Whether this means teaching your children never to disclose sensitive information on the web or teaching your employees to always consider the impact of what they are typing into a search box, the idea is the same. Teach people the appropriate behavior, provide clear guidelines, monitor compliance, and enforce the rules.

The Policies of Online Companies

The policies of online companies are at the heart of the debate surrounding web-based information disclosure. They can include usage and privacy policies, but also how your information is protected internally. For example, although detailed public information does not exist, anecdotal evidence suggests that Google enforces stringent internal data-access controls.

However, corporate privacy and usage policies are generally malleable. At the stroke of a pen, policies can, and do, change based on corporate needs. Largely written by lawyers for lawyers, many policies are difficult to understand, and they are written to protect the company, not you. Given the spotlight that this book places on Google, it is important to note that Google's public facing privacy policies are generally clearly written. In some places, the policies are vague or enigmatic, but when compared to others across the industry, the intelligibility of Google policies is a cut above the rest. As the industry leader, Google was the first to face many challenges that its competitors will face at some point in the future. Google's competitors should emulate their emphasis on well-written policies.

Because online companies write their own policies, they control the changes we desire. The best we can do is pressure them to change. These potential strategies should be part of any online company's policy:

- Protect our data as if it is Fort Knox, including physical security, network security, internal controls to govern access, employee background checks, and verified destruction of data. Don't share our data unless absolutely necessary, including with governments, business partners, and advertisers. In fact, you should fight to protect it. The more sensitive the data, the better you should protect it. Companies such as Google are sitting on the treasure trove of the century (perhaps in the history of mankind)—protect it accordingly.

- Make usage and privacy policies easy to read and understand by normal users, not just legal professionals. Seek transparency and full disclosure about how you collect and use information. Don't hide important details in the fine print or behind legal- and marketing-speak. Don't forbid employees from mentioning or implying the name of your company in public.[44] Remember, the vast majority of your consumers aren't pedophiles or terrorists; don't treat us as such.

- Give us a better choice than all or nothing. Don't make the only choice abstinence. When it comes to using your services, provide us with options, such as opting out of data collection, even if we have to pay for the increased protection. Even better, enable us to opt in to such collection if we want improved customization.

- Minimize data collection and retention to what is strictly required to perform your business function, enable customization, and facilitate innovation. Do not implement a policy of indefinite data retention. Instead, delete logged user data quickly and limit the lifespan of cookies and other identifying technologies.

Even the most well-intentioned privacy-protecting policies don't guarantee a solution. Despite what is on paper, employees must follow the policies, some will and some won't. One hundred percent compliance is virtually impossible. Even the most rigorous background checks and stringent punishments for noncompliance won't eliminate an inside threat in which playful or malicious employees access data they shouldn't, nor will they protect you from eavesdroppers on the network.

Corporate policies vary widely, and we are in desperate need of industry standards. It feels as if online companies are similar to kids in a candy store, acquiring as much user data as possible before they are forced to stop. However, despite the hard decisions these companies face, it is up to them to seize the initiative and craft policies that protect our privacy.[45] Promising advances have developed. Ask.com recently announced that it would "allow search users to control how and whether their searches are recorded, marking the first time a major search engine modified their data retention policy to make it user controllable."[46] The metasearch engine Ixquick (www.ixquick.com/) promises to retain user data for only 48 hours and makes user privacy a core component of its business model (see Figure 9-16).

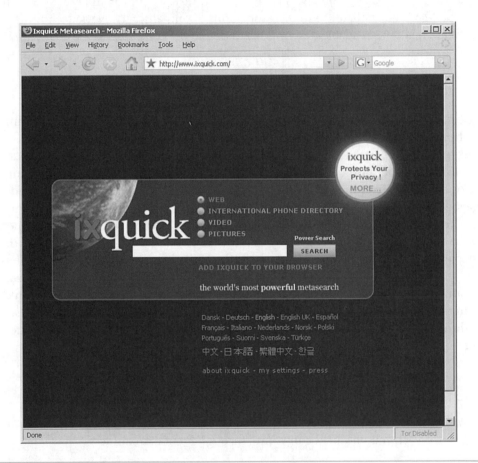

Figure 9-16 The Ixquick metasearch engine takes a strong pro-privacy stand. Note the prominently placed link to its privacy policy.

Although these are very positive steps, they are only a start. Ultimately, it is incumbent on Google, as the company with the greatest stature, to set the tone and direction. Others will follow its lead.[47]

> **NOTE**
>
> An interesting initiative coming out of the World Wide Web Consortium is the Platform for Privacy Preferences (P3P) project. Instead of providing only human-readable privacy policies to web visitors, online companies using the technique can provide machine-readable descriptions to define the collection and use of data.[48]

PETITION LAW AND POLICY MAKERS

I once called a hacker friend of mine to get together for a meal. When I reached him via cell phone, he said he wouldn't be able to make it. *He was in the Governor's Office.* Concerned that a particularly worrisome bill was about to be enacted into law, he took it upon himself to petition the governor directly. I was profoundly impressed with this type of activism. He didn't sit idly by and let things turn for the worse; he went and engaged senior decision makers directly. At the end of the day, online companies must obey the law of the land. If you are dissatisfied with the current state of affairs, appeal to your law and policy makers. If you feel that the government itself is making a bad decision, contact your elected representatives. In the United States, the government intervenes when business sectors can't police themselves. You might find a supportive ear. As an example, the United States Federal Trade Commission has taken a forward-thinking role in addressing the problem of web-based information disclosure and its abuses.[49] If you think your lone voice will not be heard, join a group that has a collectively louder voice.

> **NOTE**
>
> Lawmakers are not the only external parties who can shape corporate policies. You can also reach publicly held companies through their shareholders.[50]

SUPPORT PRIVACY ORGANIZATIONS

No single individual has the time to keep track of all the technical and policy issues surrounding online privacy. However, several notable groups make it their policy to monitor the privacy landscape and take an active role in protecting our freedoms. If this book has struck a chord, I suggest that you consider supporting the Electronic Frontier Foundation (www.eff.org) and the Electronic Privacy Information Center (www.epic.org).

DATA GENERATION, RETENTION, AND ANONYMIZATION

The problem of web-based information disclosure centers on data retention by online companies. Recall that a dearth of legal protections and consumer-centric best practices exist to inform (or compel) online companies to behave appropriately; therefore, a wide range of differing corporate policies exists. As I've mentioned earlier, you should assume that the information you disclose is scrupulously logged and retained indefinitely, with few exceptions. This data is valuable to online companies to support business models of targeted advertising and their research programs. However, absolute data retention isn't always necessary. Let's look at three potential solutions.

Reduce or Eliminate Data Generation

The most effective way to eliminate the problem of web-based information disclosure is to never generate the data in the first place. Unfortunately, the extreme example, abstinence, isn't practical. By simply not using the powerful tools society has at its disposal, you avoid key benefits of being part of the modern world. However, we can reduce data generation by employing some of the technical solutions I presented earlier in the chapter, along with a good helping of common sense. By pausing and reflecting before you search for something sensitive and using techniques such as Kulsoom Abdullah's self-monitoring tool, you will make far better decisions and reduce the risk of personal information being transmitted across the Internet and stored on someone else's servers.

Reduce or Eliminate Data Retention

From a privacy standpoint, it's best for user data to not be logged in the first place, but this solution isn't practical from the perspective of most online companies. Your data gives these companies a competitive advantage and maximizes profits—the more data, the better. However, I believe a middle ground could exist between indefinite retention and no retention. For example, user data could be sampled—only a portion of the overall data could be collected.[51] Far from a complete solution, sampling has the potential to greatly reduce the amount of information collected.[52] Data could also be destroyed after a given period of time, as Google promised to do after 18 to 24 months with IP address information in its search query logs. Of course, a comprehensive policy will cover all facets of disclosure, not just search queries.[53] Individual users could be given the chance to opt in for longer periods of data retention if they believe such retention will truly improve their online experience or would otherwise be in their own best interest.

> **NOTE**
>
> Viktor Mayer-Schönberger, a professor in Harvard's JFK School of Government, approaches this solution in a very insightful way. He proposes that computers should learn to "forget."[54, 55]

Pay for Privacy

Usable security researchers at Carnegie Mellon University have proposed an interesting alternative solution to providing user privacy. We currently enjoy a "free lunch" when it comes to most online tools. Companies such as Google give away these tools for free, and we quietly pay for them with our privacy. But what if companies offered a different business model in which you could pay a small amount of money in return for not being tracked? Researchers Janice Tsai, Serge Egelman, Lorrie Cranor, and Alessandro Acquisti conducted an experiment in which they discovered that participants were willing to pay more for items from sites that had better privacy policies.[56, 57] The group used a modified shopping search site (www.privacyfinder.org) that rated sites based on their privacy policies and provided a summarized privacy report that made it easy to compare policies among different online retailers. If their results could be generalized to companies such as Google, perhaps a viable alternate business model does exist in which users might pay for privacy.

Data Anonymization

Data anonymization seeks to remove identifying information from logs in a way that safeguards anonymity but still provides useful insights. Anonymization might appear easy at first glance, but it is quite difficult. Data anonymization represents a trade-off between removing information and retaining value to the online companies. Remove too much information, and little value is left. A common approach is to remove specific data and combine the remainder into categories. A bad anonymization decision today might erase a great deal of future value, thanks to advances in data mining. Remove too little information, and users are not protected. We saw a failed attempt at anonymization in the AOL data spill when AOL researchers replaced usernames with a unique numeric identifier. Although it's a good start, Google's March 2007 pledge to anonymize IP addresses after 18 to 24 months doesn't go far enough, apparently removing only portions of IP addresses from search query logs. As you saw earlier in the book, many other services that aren't addressed by the policy and search queries themselves can contain sensitive information even if not attributable to a precise IP address. Unless mandated by law or driven by the marketplace, online companies that depend upon high-quality information to target advertising find little reason to anonymize data.

Although a trade-off currently exists between the anonymization of logs and their value to online companies, this doesn't have to be the case. Academic researchers are working on solutions.[58] Academics have a vested interest in seeking solutions; they need high-quality logs to research new innovations. Currently, only researchers internal to online companies, and a select few trusted partners,[59] have access to high-quality logs. This makes it very difficult for the scientific community to validate, extend, and peer-review research contributions of those with access to proprietary data. Because of the dearth of publicly available query logs, only a few published studies exist.[60] By involving the broader research community, better solutions will be possible more quickly. Research is ongoing, and solutions might ultimately require different levels of anonymization—when data is stored and used internally, and when it is shared externally.[61]

SUMMARY

Attempting to completely anonymize your online activities is a difficult, if not impossible, proposition because of the semantic information you disclose when you use online tools. Unfortunately, a bulletproof, anonymous web-browsing experience doesn't exist. In the future, it might, but we must work together to ensure that solutions are not just for the technological elite and, instead, are usable by all web surfers. Online companies are a key component to make this happen. However, a unilateral solution surrounded by marketing spin is unacceptable. The companies must work together with all parties—most importantly, end users—to ensure that the result is satisfactory, robust, and usable.

In this chapter, I've given you a survey of user-based, technological, and policy countermeasures you can use to limit the disclosure of this semantic information and sensitive network level information. A full discussion would take an entire book, but applying some of these techniques will limit the magnitude of your disclosures, reduce your exposure, and minimize the probability that you will be personally identified. The key is finding the right balance between solutions that are effective and usable. With that in mind, I encourage you to go out and explore solutions now and into the future. By doing so, you will help accelerate and shape a future in which your activities won't be silently logged, data mined, and used to erode your privacy. Scott McNealy, former CEO of Sun Microsystems, famously said, "You have zero privacy. Get over it."[62] I respectfully disagree and hope you do, too.

ENDNOTES

1. Information disclosure isn't constrained to the web. Consider grocery store loyalty cards that give you a small price discount, but you have to give them personal information and buying habit data in return. Such perks aren't "free."

2. Such a configuration also lets the company know when you've upgraded your browser because the browser's header information changes.

3. One alternative is to set the default home page to "about:blank," which starts the browser on a blank page.

4. Note that these screenshots were taken of the Firefox 2.0 browser, but cryptic error messages are endemic across many popular browsers.

5. "Call for Papers," Symposium on Usable Privacy and Security (SOUPS). http://cups.cs.cmu.edu/soups/2008/, last accessed 9 November 2007.

6. See the University of Pennsylvania Positive Psychology Center's web site for more information on learned helplessness: www.ppc.sas.upenn.edu/lh.htm.

7. One way to make cookie management easier is to use the Cookie Culler add-on for Firefox, https://addons.mozilla.org/en-US/firefox/addon/82.

8. "Five Data Leak Prevention Companies to Watch," *Network World,* 7 January 2008. www.networkworld.com/research/2008/010708-data-leak-prevention-watch.html, last accessed 4 July 2008.

9. You can find the Greasemonkey Firefox plug-in at https://addons.mozilla.org/en-US/firefox/addon/748.

10. Kulsoom Abdullah, Gregory Conti, and Edward Sobiesk, "Self-Monitoring of Web-Based Information Disclosure," Workshop on Privacy in the Electronic Society, October 2007.

11. "Web History Privacy Notice," Google, 22 February 2007. www.google.com/history/privacy.html, last accessed 3 July 2008.

12. Some work has been done on corporate self-monitoring. For an offerings comparison of managed web-filtering services, see www.isp-planet.com/technology/mssp/2006/mssp_web.html.

13. Daniel Howe and Helen Nissenbaum, "TrackMeNot" project web page. http://mrl. nyu.edu/~dhowe/trackmenot/, last accessed 3 November 2003.

14. See http://en.wikipedia.org/wiki/Cryptography and http://en.wikipedia.org/wiki/ Encryption for quick overviews.

15. Jon Callas, "View from the Top—Why You Need Enterprise Data Protection." *PGP Newsletter: Encryption Matters* 2, Issue 4 (June 2007). www.pgp.com/newsroom/ newsletter/volume2_issue4.html, last accessed 7 November 2007.

16. You have to make your own assessment of how "well resourced" you believe ISPs are.

17. SSL can also be vulnerable to man-in-the-middle attacks. See www.monkey.org/ ~dugsong/dsniff/ for an example. Commercial appliances are also available that provide SSL visibility and control. See the offerings by BlueCoat for one example, www.bluecoat.com/solutions/businessneeds/secureweb/sslvisibility.

18. See www.networkworld.com/news/2007/030807-ssl-optimization.html for an interesting article on SSL optimization over wide area network (WAN) issues.

19. See http://en.wikipedia.org/wiki/Traffic_analysis for an overview of traffic analysis.

20. "Merely Cloaking Data May Be Incriminating?" Slashdot.org, 27 July 2007. http:// yro.slashdot.org/yro/07/07/27/2310247.shtml, last accessed 20 November 2007.

21. "Shredded East German Secret Police Files Being Reassembled by Computer," *Associated Press*, 9 May 2007. www.komotv.com/news/national/7423656.html, last accessed 7 November 2007.

22. "EFF DES Cracker," Wikipedia.org. http://en.wikipedia.org/wiki/Deep_Crack, last accessed 7 November 2007.

23. To see the latest high-level allocations, visit www.iana.org/assignments/ ipv4-address-space.

24. Although DHCP can update IP addresses frequently, it is constrained in the range of addresses it can issue.

25. You can give this a try by visiting www.arin.net/whois/ and typing in your IP address.

26. It is an open-research question whether adding more than three nodes increases anonymity.

27. You can find SwitchProxy at https://addons.mozilla.org/en-US/firefox/addon/125 and FoxyProxy at https://addons.mozilla.org/en-US/firefox/addon/2464.

28. "Tor: Anonymity Online," Tor Project home page. www.torproject.org/, last accessed 21 November 2007.

29. You might also want to explore FoxTor, http://cups.cs.cmu.edu/foxtor/, which is a similar deployment bundle.

30. "Torbutton," Firefox Add-Ons. https://addons.mozilla.org/en-US/firefox/addon/2275, last accessed 22 November 2007.

31. You can find listings of much of this work at http://torbutton.torproject.org/dev/, http://freehaven.net/anonbib/topic.html#Anonymous_20communication, http://en.wikipedia.org/wiki/Tor_(anonymity_network), and www.onion-router.net/.

32. Steven Murdoch and George Danezis, "Low-Cost Traffic Analysis of Tor," *Proceedings of the 2005 IEEE Symposium on Security and Privacy,* 2005: 183–195.

33. To read the story of a security researcher who did just this, see www.theregister.co.uk/2007/11/15/tor_hacker_arrest/.

34. "Tor Anonymization Network Phished, Part 2," *Heise Security,* 21 November 2007. www.heise-security.co.uk/news/99333, last accessed 22 November 2007.

35. "De-Anonymizing Tor and Detecting Proxies," ha.ckers blog, 26 September 2007. http://ha.ckers.org/blog/20070926/de-anonymizing-tor-and-detecting-proxies/, last accessed 24 November 2007.

36. "Warning: Want Tor to Really Work?" TorProject web site, 17 November 2007. www.torproject.org/download.html.en#Warning, last accessed 23 November 2007.

37. See the media archives of the 2006 Hackers of Planet Earth conference, www.the-fifth-hope.org/hoop/5hope_speakers.khtml, for a number of high-quality talks on this subject.

38. Others choose to surf from unsecured access points of homes and businesses. However, this practice is illegal in many jurisdictions, and I don't recommend it.

39. Bruce Potter, "Wireless Hotspots: Petri Dish of Wireless Security," *Communications of the ACM* 49, no. 6 (June 2006): 50–56.

40. You can find a copy of "Privacy-Enhancing Personalized Web Search" at www2007.org/paper247.php.

41. Corey Benninger, "Finding Gold in the Browser Cache," Blackhat USA, 2006.

42. A reasonable starting point is *PC Magazine's* "Trace Removers" article, by Neil J. Rubenking, http://www.pcmag.com/article2/0,2817,1922882,00.asp, 4 May 2005.

43. Christopher Rugaber, "Privacy Groups Seek 'Do-Not-Track List,'" MSNBC, 31 October 2007. www.msnbc.msn.com/id/21563914/, last accessed 20 November 2007.

44. "Google's Evil NDA," Slashdot.org, 3 May 2007. http://slashdot.org/articles/07/05/03/1352224.shtml, last accessed 25 November 2007.

45. For one interesting approach, see privacy advocate Lauren Weinstein's "An Open Letter to Google: Concepts for a Google Privacy Initiative," at www.vortex.com/google-privacy-initiative.

46. Ryan Singel, "Ask to Allow Users to Control Data Retention," Wired Blog Network, 20 July 2007. http://blog.wired.com/27bstroke6/2007/07/ask-to-allow-us.html, last accessed 25 November 2007.

47. An excellent example is Google's pledge to anonymize portions of IP addresses after 18 months. Other large search firms soon made similar announcements. See http://news.bbc.co.uk/2/hi/technology/6911527.stm.

48. Platform for Privacy Preferences (P3P) Project, World Wide Web Consortium, 10 December 2006. www.w3.org/P3P/, last accessed 4 November 2006.

49. In November 2007, the Federal Trade Commission hosted a workshop entitled "eHavioral Advertising: Tracking, Targeting, and Technology" that directly addressed the problem of web-based information disclosure. Video and transcripts from this event are available at http://htc-01.media.globix.net/COMP008760MOD1/ftc_web/FTCindex.html#Nov1_07.

50. Erik Larkin, "Google Shareholders Vote Against Anti-Censorship Proposal," *PC World*, 10 May 2007. www.pcworld.com/article/id,131745-pg,1/article.html, last accessed 25 November 2007.

51. You can find a quick overview of sampling at http://en.wikipedia.org/wiki/Sampling_(statistics).

52. An eavesdropper between you and the online company might not decide to sample.

53. Such a policy should also include all backup tapes created by online companies.

54. Nate Anderson, "Escaping the Data Panopticon: Prof Says Computers Must Learn to 'Forget,'" Ars Technica, 9 May 2007. http://arstechnica.com/news.ars/post/20070509-escaping-the-data-panopticon-teaching-computers-to-forget.html, last accessed 17 November 2007.

55. "Useful Void: The Art of Forgetting in the Age of Ubiquitous Computing," Faculty Research Working Paper, Harvard University, John F. Kennedy School of Government, April 2007. Available online at http://ksgnotes1.harvard.edu/Research/wpaper.nsf/rwp/RWP07-022/$File/rwp_07_022_mayer-schoenberger.pdf.

56. Janice Tsai, Serge Egelman, Lorrie Cranor, and Alessandro Acquisti, "The Effect of Online Privacy Information on Purchasing Behavior: An Experimental Study," 2007 Workshop on the Economics of Information Security. http://weis2007.econinfosec.org/papers/57.pdf, last accessed 23 November 2007.

57. A quick overview of their study is available at www.news.com/Study-Shoppers-will-pay-for-privacy/2100-1029_3-6189380.html.

58. See the proceedings from the 2007 World Wide Web Conference's Query Log Analysis Workshop for promising solutions at www2007.org/workshop-W6.php.

59. For one example, see http://research.microsoft.com/ur/us/fundingopps/RFPs/Search_2006_RFP_Awards.aspx.

60. The 2006 AOL dataset will generate interesting academic research, but it will not retain its research value indefinitely.

61. Judit Bar-Ilan, "Position Paper: Access to Query Logs—An Academic Researcher's Point of View," *Proceedings of the 2007 World Wide Web Conference's Query Log Analysis Workshop*, 8–12 May 2007. Available online at www2007.org/workshops/paper_39.pdf

62. Polly Sprenger, "Sun on Privacy: 'Get Over It,'" Wired.com, 25 January 1999. www.wired.com/politics/law/news/1999/01/17538, last accessed 23 November 2007.

Conclusions and a Look to the Future

What will Google be in five years?

Bigger and more powerful than Microsoft	*23%*
Brought down a notch by competitors, lawsuits	*32%*
Giant eye that knows more about me than I do	*45%*

—San Francisco Chronicle Online Survey Results[1]

The study of web-based information disclosure, including the tools of Google and its competitors, is a fast-moving target. One of my primary aims with this book has been to provide you with long-lasting fundamentals that will stand the test of time, because change is inevitable. The future is notoriously hard to predict, but a number of trends and warning signs yield useful insight. Most of these signposts indicate that we will continue to wrestle with the problem of web-based information disclosure, as well as the risky reliance upon a few major online companies for critical infrastructure information-processing needs. These key issues boil down to a few basic ideas about data: what is disclosed and how the data is communicated, stored, shared, processed, protected, and destroyed. Looking to the future requires looking at these facets and extrapolating the direction they are heading.

The future promises many technologic advances, capable of enriching our lives, but, at the same time, capable of creating the dystopia envisioned in George Orwell's *1984*. Advances in processing power, storage, and networking technologies will surely occur, as will advances in artificial intelligence, machine learning, data mining, and sensor technologies. Online companies will employ these technologies to create amazing new online tools that will entice us to seek a short-term benefit instead of long-term security and privacy. Users and organizations worldwide will have to understand the threat and consider how to employ current and future tools—even whether to use the tools at all. Every time developers create a web-enabled application that relies on Google or any other third party's web service, people must consider what information is being disclosed and evaluate the risk accordingly. The threat of information disclosure doesn't exist in a vacuum; each new end-user tool and compelling web service will occur against the backdrop of changing political and corporate climates and globalization. In short, changes in the larger environment must also be considered to fully evaluate the threat of information disclosure.

Are Google and most online companies evil? No. Are they entirely altruistic, providing free services out of the kindness of their hearts? No. Ultimately, businesses require profit to survive. Currently, advertising is the profit-generating engine that allows most online service providers to exist and pays the bills for the myriad "free" online tools. This business model is unlikely to change in the near future. Advertising will continue to be an arena where the most effective—and, hence, most valuable—advertisements will yield the greatest competitive advantage. Precisely targeted advertisements will be the most valuable of all but will raise the specters of data disclosure, data retention, data mining, and user profiling. Don't expect information disclosure issues to dissipate in the future; if anything, the issues will increase in magnitude as users become desensitized to the act of disclosing information and as more and better services become available.

The following sections describe areas to watch closely as we move into the future. The Internet itself is no longer simply a utility that reliably delivers data, unaltered, from point A to point B. Instead, ISPs are awakening the power they possess to control flows of information. Online companies will continue to develop new services that will accelerate the information we disclose. Along with these disclosures come continued risks of information spills and information leakage, some intended and some not. Finally, advances in artificial intelligence will allow online companies to more deeply mine the troves of information that grow significantly larger on a daily basis.

Despite all of these concerns, I do believe the world is a better place with the free tools and services offered by companies like Google. As I made clear earlier in the book, there are hundreds of millions of avid Google users, who by no means want to see the company wink out of existence. However, users must use the tools wisely, and online companies must work together with their constituents to jointly seek an equitable balance between productivity, privacy, and security, particularly as the world moves off the desktop toward web-based applications, cloud computing, and Internet-enabled refrigerators.

FOUNDATION AND GOOGLE

Any dogma, primarily based on faith and emotionalism, is a dangerous weapon to use on others, since it is almost impossible to guarantee that the weapon will never be turned on the user.
—Isaac Asimov, Foundation

The Foundation series are masterworks of science fiction, depicting a time when history, sociology, and statistics (*psychohistory*) were used to scientifically predict future events and assist the continued existence of a galactic empire. Although I'm not really suggesting that such technology exists today, there is a striking similarity between Google and the Foundation series.[2] This comparison raises an interesting question: Given the information and resources at Google's disposal, is it possible to subtly alter the information Google provides to users in a way that influences the behavior of individuals, groups, and perhaps even nations?[3] You might believe this is far-fetched, but I argue this is a happening now in the form of advertising. Advertising is the driving force behind Google's success, and influencing people to buy things is at its core.[4] To improve the effectiveness of advertising is to increase profit, a key goal of any company. The web is an excellent forum for testing and evaluating the effectiveness of candidate advertising techniques. Because many users visit their corporate websites, companies can present a test population—say, 10,000 users—with a new form of advertising.[5] If successful, the technique can be adopted; if not, it can be changed and a new technique tested. The process can even be automated, such as by using genetic algorithms to modify and mutate advertisements, and using click-throughs or purchases as a *fitness function*, a metric of the algorithm's success.

Genetic algorithms are only one small weapon in the arsenal of techniques that Google and other online companies will employ as they attempt to gain strategic advantage. Artificial intelligence techniques are also extremely promising. Google's cofounder Larry Page sees one potential future: "[T]he ultimate search engine would understand everything in the world. It would understand everything you asked it and give you back the exact right thing instantly." He continued to state that artificial intelligence could be a reality within a few years.[6] Contrast these statements with the proceeding paragraph, in which I argued that influencing people to buy things is the core of Google's success. Perhaps this suggests that the ultimate search engine does not give you back the exact right thing, but instead directs your attention to the things that advertisers want you to see. Consider Overture, which was a paid-placement search engine. It was somewhat successful, but not nearly as successful as Google, perhaps because its users knew they were being manipulated. Artificial intelligence is one means of accomplishing Google's goals, both stated ("organize the world's information") and unstated ("increase advertising revenue").

Artificial intelligence was an extremely active research area in the late 1960s and early 1970s, but it stalled, leading to a period sometimes called an AI winter. My belief, however, is that AI suffers from a perception problem; any success in AI isn't called AI anymore. A wide range of successes have emanated from AI research, including data mining, machine translation, speech recognition, and—the Google search engine. Google has long been employing advances from the AI community to better help humans locate information.[7, 8, 9] AI, particularly data mining, is also an extremely powerful tool to provide more effective, better targeted advertising and increased profitability. Advances in artificial intelligence will lead to innovative new products and services. More concerning, however, is that future AI, combined with the unprecedented stockpile of information under Google's control, will lead to security and privacy concerns that are difficult to imagine today. Current AI technologies pale in most ways to the capability of the human brain. Today scientists are attempting to simulate the neocortex of a two-week-old rat[10] and create a Second Life being with the intelligence of a four-year old.[11] Advances in processing power will fuel AI, and vice versa. Quantum computing is another important technology to watch. If successful, quantum computing promises a discontinuity in Moore's law. In the middle of this century, experts believe machines will begin to approach the computational capacity of the adult human brain, and at this point, all bets are off. Unanticipated capabilities will surely create new privacy and security threats to online users. Two areas, in particular, to watch for advances are user profiling and user fingerprinting. More accurate profiles and precise user identification allows better services *and* more profitable, targeted advertising.

THE GLOBAL BATTLE FOR THE NETWORK CONTINUES

Another major battleground is control of the network. Networks are critically important because each of the information disclosures outlined in this book occurs on a network. To control the network is to control the information. In an ideal network, messages sent are received by the correct party, unaltered and in a timely fashion. This is usually the case now, but the future is another story. As with the supply of oil to the world, there are only a limited number of suppliers of high-bandwidth network connectivity. Historically, network service providers simply provided unbiased connectivity, akin to a utility such as a water or electric company, but such unbiased connectivity provided only borderline profitability. Major telecommunications firms are awakening to the fact that they can alter the speed of communications, providing some customers with better service and others with slower, or no access as a business model to increase profit. Initial forays into this area have largely met resistance and have given rise to the network neutrality countermovement, which calls for unbiased utility-like access. The battle is waging now.

Network service providers wield a great deal of power. They have the capability to eavesdrop on traffic that crosses their networks, including the ability to identify the amount and type of traffic and the owners of some IP addresses. Unless this is encrypted, network providers have access to each of the information disclosures discussed in this book, including most forms of web surfing and e-mail. For example, airlines are planning to filter and censor in-flight Internet access.[12] Even if encrypted, large network companies could have the resources to perform some cryptanalysis, although this is an unlikely scenario. A more plausible scenario involves ISPs distributing trusted root certificates to their customers, perhaps as part of an install disk or a browser toolbar. With a trusted root certificate in the user's browser, ISPs could then conduct man-in-the-middle observations of their SSL communications with secure websites. Products such as BlueCoat (www.bluecoat.com/) provide this capability for enterprises that want to monitor their employees' encrypted web accesses. If an ISP did this surreptitiously today and it was later discovered, it would cause a public relations uproar, but I can see certain future scenarios in which people consensually agree to this observation, perhaps in exchange for better protection from malware, or where certain-nation states would require this of their citizens. The technology is productized today; using it is only a policy decision.

However, if cryptanalysis and certificate distribution schemes do not occur, traffic analysis is another plausible threat. The power to observe traffic crossing their networks provides network service providers the data they need to identify popular—and potentially highly profitable—classes of traffic to slow or deny, effectively holding the users hostage in return for greater access fees. For example, millions of users worldwide have used the Internet for free or at very low cost. Because of this, services such as Internet telephony are becoming extremely popular. After apparently catching network service providers off-guard, Internet telephony is now causing these providers to leverage their power by blocking VoIP calls.[13] Similarly, some network service companies have begun charging users more for Virtual Private Networks (VPNs), often used by telecommuters, to communicate with their employer's internal network assets.

Both blocking and charging higher service fees for VoIP and VPN services are important, but some ISPs are taking a more aggressive step by altering the content of the communications themselves. Some ISPs are inserting on-the-fly advertisements into web pages requested by end users.[14, 15] Current and future technologies would allow even more drastic alterations, such as using AI to alter information flows and deeply inspecting packet contents. [16, 17, 18] Even a change such as charging users per gigabyte of download could drastically alter the network landscape, by forcing users away from bandwidth-heavy services, such as video, to lighter-weight textual services.[19] Third parties who do not directly control the networks themselves also attempt to influence network providers; these include the Recording Industry Association of American (RIAA) and the Motion Picture Association of America (MPAA) which have been pressuring colleges and universities, both de facto ISPs, to crack down on illegal file sharing.[20, 21] More powerful entities, such as national governments, are also leveraging their control of networks within their territory for a variety of aims. Consider the following examples.

- In Japan, the nation's four major providers of Internet access, representing about 1,000 smaller ISPs, agreed to forcibly cut the Internet connections of users of file-sharing programs.[22]
- The Chinese government denied Internet users access to YouTube because of politically sensitive Tibeten protest videos. This is part of an overall movement by the Chinese government to use online filters to block access deemed subversive.[23]
- The Australian government mandated that all ISPs provide "clean feeds" to schools and homes that are "free of pornography and inappropriate material."[24]
- In the United States, a bipartisan group of U.S. senators called for universal Internet filtering.[25]
- The Malaysian government warned that it would use tough antiterrorism laws against bloggers who insult the country's king.[26]

Although the reasons to perform these actions might appear legitimate to some readers, the key point to take away is that control of network connectivity provides tremendous power, particularly as we increase dependence in the future. Today the reason might be to protect the children[27] or to stop illegal file sharing, but tomorrow it could be used to shut down the free press. In short, we see the warning signs now that network services as we know them could change drastically for the worse.

> **NOTE**
>
> Tremendous power lies in the hands of ISPs. The content they carry, such as peer-to-peer file-sharing services, VoIP, or VPNs, can be ignored, throttled, or blocked, at their whim.[28]

The importance of network control is not lost on Google, who, after months of conjecture, was unable to secure a portion of wireless spectrum during a recent Federal Communications Commission auction.[29, 30] Some analysts believe the outcome was still favorable to Google because, as a result of the auction, users can use any wireless device, as well as download any application and content they want.[31, 32] Speculation surrounding Google and the acquisition of network access and networking technologies is rampant, including some unconfirmed wireless balloons[33] and others well known, such as free wireless access in San Francisco and participation in the Unity transcontinental fiber-optic cable project.[34, 35] For now, the power of the ISPs and Google is split. If somehow Google emerges as a full-blown ISP at some point in the future, perhaps funded by advertisements,[36] the information-disclosure risks of Google will be combined with those of an ISP, essentially putting all information into the hands of a single company.

GOOGLE IS DEAD, LONG LIVE GOOGLE

"The King is dead, long live the King!" is a traditional proclamation used to announce the ascension of a new monarch.[37] The phrase is meant to convey the continuity of leadership. Google is currently king, but there is a growing pack of would-be monarchs hot on Google's heels seeking the throne. Whether it be a large company such as Microsoft pondering the acquisition of Yahoo!, the Japanese government creating an Internet search engine to rival Google,[38] or any number of smaller companies, Google is under constant pressure to retain its dominance. This pressure will certainly fuel Google's innovation, but it may also cause the company to reconsider its motto of "Don't be evil."

GUNNING FOR GOOGLE

Google might be the big kid on the block today, but many companies, and even governments, are waiting to capture its turf. Search is Google's core area of competency, and it is a sure bet that Google will work to advance the state-of-the-art. As an example, Google is testing a health-related service in which Google will store and provide search services for several thousand health records of (volunteer) patients at the Cleveland Clinic. If successful, it is reasonable to believe that Google will expand the service. Innovations such as this are necessary to maintain Google's competitive edge. Such innovation is necessary because, hot on Google's heels, are innovative contenders such as Swicki (www.eurekster.com/) and Rollyo (www.rollyo.com/), both providing community-driven search; Clusty (http://clusty.com/), which group similar items and groups search results into folders; Wink (http://wink.com/), which enables users to tag their favorite results; and Lexxe (www.lexxe.com/), which uses linguistic techniques to help provide answers to short questions.[39, 40] These search competitors and the thousands of other companies fielding new online services provide intense competition, pushing Google to offer new services of its own and leverage its substantial assets. Rumors abound about Google PCs, Google browsers, and Google operating systems. While none of these has publicly emerged, it is safe to say that Google will quietly continue to innovate, and these new innovations carry information disclosure risks that must be carefully evaluated.

A continued stream of compelling new services isn't enough, however, to provide the profits needed for Google to survive and thrive. Google will continue to innovate in advertising techniques. Expect Google to leverage its technical expertise, information-processing resources, and information stockpile to both develop new services and innovative advertising techniques to provide its income stream.

POWER STRUGGLES CONTINUE

Research, development, and innovation are key to maintaining and extending Google's user base, despite intense competition. But fascinating new services aren't enough. As mentioned earlier in the chapter, Google is beholden to network providers to bring them their millions of users. Google and other online companies are also subject to the whims of the governments where they operate. On one hand, many governments covet the financial gains Google's business provides and the information Google possess. On the other hand, too much collaboration with governmental entities raises the specter of privacy concerns, which is bad for Google's business.[41] I expect that Google will continue to engage governments worldwide to help balance these two extremes. For example, Google recently opened a new permanent office in Washington, D.C., where Google "welcomed a veritable who's who of Washington."[42]

MERGERS, ACQUISITIONS, AND THE DEATH OF GOOGLE

Each company has a lifespan, and none exists forever. The business world is an ecosystem, where companies evolve and thrive, and others fall prey to competitors. Given today's environment, I know it is hard to conceive, but sooner or later Google will die.[43] Whether Google passes on quietly because of some unanticipated competing technology or is acquired in a public spectacle, the question to ask is, who will gain control of Google's immense information stockpiles? What happens to those who rely on Google for critical components of their infrastructure or business processes? These questions aren't relevant just regarding Google, but for every online company. One day users may trust a company's sock puppet mascot,[44] the next the company may disappear, its information assets shared with parties unknown and its relied-upon services a thing of the past. Currently, Google is in the position to acquire smaller companies, but one day the tables will be turned.

Corporate death might be the ultimate outcome for any business, but plenty of less severe events also occur in the business ecosystem, each with its own impact on web-based information disclosure. Corporate leadership will change, ushering in a new set of corporate ideals. A company might switch from being privately held to publicly held, and become legally bound to operate in the best interest of shareholders, not necessarily that of their end users. Competition might intensify, pressuring companies to move a little farther from their "don't be evil" ideals. Expansion of business markets might require adopting the policies of foreign governments as a cost of doing business in the region, as seen in Google's censorship of its search services in China. This list isn't intended to be comprehensive, but instead to illustrate that, although a company's business models and ideals might appear fixed today, they certainly are not over time. The end result is uncertainty about how databases of information disclosures will be used and misused in the future.

NEW VECTORS AND NEW USERS

If you've ever been to a hacker convention, you know you're surrounded there by the most security-aware people on the planet. Over the past decade, I have had the opportunity to attend about 20 hacker conferences, and I was surprised to find that many of the speakers directed their audiences to google this or that subject to find more information. Although this philosophy stays true to the RTFM (Read the Manual) philosophy permeating computing culture, it did get me thinking. Search has become an integral part of the wired world, and even the most security aware are desensitized to the risks associated with disclosing information to online companies. Advances in technology will provide additional high-value tools to end users, each service bringing with it new ways to disclose sensitive information. The adoption of these improved services will be magnified by the global ubiquitous use of mobile devices. The end result is that information will continue to be disclosed via traditional mechanisms such as search and e-mail, but also via new services.

> **NOTE**
>
> The more valuable the information collected by a given service is, the more likely it will be sought after by attackers, competitors, lawyers, and governments.

Disclosure vectors will ebb and flow over time. Some will fall out of favor, as e-mail is apparently doing with younger users in lieu of social-networking sites such as MySpace and Facebook,[45] but it could regain favor at some future point. Regardless, it is safe to say that demand for relevant information will continue to grow, while the mechanisms for sharing and acquiring the information will change.

WEB APPLICATIONS

Another technology to watch is web-based office applications. Web-based office services, along with remote file storage offerings, provide many compelling reasons to switch from desktop applications, including the capability to access and share word processing documents, spreadsheets, and other data files from anywhere with Internet access. Software upgrades need occur only on the server, not on every individual workstation. However, the security risks are many. If such services become popular, they will become a prime target for attackers. If a vulnerability is found, attackers could have access to millions of sensitive documents. From the perspective of web-based information disclosure, these documents will exist on someone else's servers, a very bad idea. One need only look to the news to see that new vulnerabilities are discovered every day across virtually all types of web-based applications. The future doesn't offer much hope for improvement.

Web-based office applications also raise concerns about dependency on third-party services, which could become cost-prohibitive or disappear without warning. Back-up procedures and regulatory compliance are impossible to monitor. End users cannot control access to the corporate back-up media. Web-based office applications also have the potential to lock in users. User lock-in means users might have difficulty moving to another service, a popular tactic businesses use. Perhaps the best example is Apple's iTunes, which restricts users from moving their song purchases to non-Apple media players. When Apple's popularity inevitably fades, users may find themselves collectively with billions of worthless songs. By ceding control of their documents to a third party, users could find themselves in similar circumstances.

> **NOTE**
>
> Web-based information disclosure isn't isolated to just end users. Web services and machine-to-machine interactions also disclose tremendous amounts of information. Such services are very popular and will grow dramatically in the future.

Finally, it is important to note that U.S. law provides weaker protections to documents stored on third-party servers than for documents stored on home computers. This increases the privacy risks associated with using web applications to store documents because your documents could be more vulnerable to disclosure under legal compulsion.[46]

SENSORS AND RFID

Cheap, ubiquitous sensors and RFID tags are yet other sources of information disclosure. Everything from toasters and refrigerators to stoplights, to the clothes we wear are starting to contain such devices. When the information these devices provide is publicly or privately shared (and this sharing is starting to occur now), we will face an order of magnitude or greater increase in information disclosure. Science fiction writer Bruce Sterling even posits that we will be able to search for lost car keys one day.[47] In another example, cable provider Comcast is allegedly experimenting with camera technologies to embed in set-top boxes to determine whether viewers are in the room.[48] How the data from networked sensors will be used and shared is difficult to predict, but assuredly the outcome will not be entirely positive.

WEB 2.0

It is impossible to predict all the new services that will be offered in the future. Web 2.0 and technologies such as AJAX promise much. This section provided a few examples, but it is clear that is well worth the time to consider the implications of each new service as it becomes available, whether it is a mainstream evolutionary development such as a new form of search or radically disruptive changes such as virtual worlds. New information-disclosure vectors generate additional user information that will be used to profile and more easily identify users. One surety is that information will continue to spill or otherwise be used in ways unintended by the end user.

PARTING THOUGHTS

As the world enters the second decade of web-based information disclosure, the importance of this threat has never been more significant. Despite the extreme popularity of online tools and their casual use by many, beware blindly following the crowd. The information-disclosure risks and misuses outlined in this book are real. A healthy measure of skepticism is required to gauge the true cost of free online tools, now and into the future. There's no such thing as a free lunch. Current countermeasures are insufficient protection against data loss, theft, misuse, legal compulsion, and the long reach of governments worldwide.

My intent with the book was to change the way people view online disclosures, networked communications, and trust of online companies. Once attuned, you will see sensitive disclosures occurring every day, at both the personal and organizational levels. Some signs will be small, such as a slight change in a privacy policy or an innovative new tool; others will sound claxons of warning, as with Google's acquisition of DoubleClick. Regardless, it is critical to continually reevaluate the threat to you, your company, your country, and your family and friends as each shiny new tool and service is proudly publicized. Small disclosures aren't small when aggregated over years. If anything, advances in data mining and artificial intelligence will magnify the importance of the threat, under the guise of improving your experience. Weigh the short-term gain versus the long-term loss.

Apathy is the enemy. As you become aware of the magnitude of the threat, you will see it grow day by day. The next step is to take action, whether it be to take your business elsewhere, petition lawmakers, or help develop technological countermeasures. Failure to do so is the biggest risk of all. Privacy could be a thing of the past otherwise. One day soon, you might find that every facet of your existence is instrumented to collect data and help increase advertising revenues, data that will be cherry-picked or taken en masse by others. Ask yourself, are corporations becoming offline storage sources of personal information for law enforcement and government? Think of China as an early adopter— trends and abuses you see there are slowly working their way around the globe. For now, in the West, the stated goal of similar encroachment is to prevent piracy, protect children, and fight terrorism. Just as a dog that has tasted human blood can no longer be trusted, I'm concerned that when online companies, and governments, feel the surge of power that online stockpiles of information provide, there will be no turning back. When we cede control of lives, we may have no other option than to live with the status quo of a steady decline.

Not many years ago, I found the topics of privacy, ethics, and anonymity uninteresting. Now I consider these subjects critically important. My personal indifference began changing when I observed the direction of civil liberties in a post–9/11 world, and the happy smiling face of the Google search box turned into something nefarious, a seductive gateway to undermining my civil liberties—and yours.

Grass-roots efforts might not be enough to stem the tide, but perhaps the greatest champion is Google itself. Google, the nation-state, could stake out the higher ground by moving beyond "improve your online experience" propaganda and is best positioned to develop the new technologies, policy, and other solutions we need to allow our security and privacy to coexist with successful business profitability and innovation. With the tremendous power at Google's disposal comes great responsibility. I hope they use it wisely.

ENDNOTES

1. Verne Kopytoff, "Who's Afraid of Google?" SFGate, *San Francisco Chronicle*, 11 May 2007. www.sfgate.com/cgi-bin/article.cgi?file=/c/a/2007/05/11/ MNGRIPPB2N1.DTL, last accessed 24 March 2008.

2. There is also a striking similarity between a future Google and Skynet of the *Terminator* movies, in which an AI became self-aware and turned on its human creators, but I leave this thought experiment as an exercise to the reader.

3. While we are talking science fiction, an interesting book on the subject of controlling information flows to influence the population is *Echelon,* by Josh Conviser.

4. Advertising aside, this statement doesn't mean that influencing people to do other things by controlling the information they are provided isn't beyond the realm of technical possibility. As an example, ask yourself whether a search engine could convince citizens to vote for a given candidate in an election by providing only certain types of search results.

5. This Google Blog entry provides some insights into Google's online experiments; see http://googleblog.blogspot.com/2006/04/this-is-test-this-is-only-test.html.

6. Richard Wray, "Google Users Promised Artificial Intelligence," *The Guardian,* 23 May 2006. www.guardian.co.uk/technology/2006/may/23/searchengines.news, last accessed 30 March 2008.

7. Stefanie Olsen, "Newsmaker: Google's Man Behind the Curtain," CNET News.com, 10 May 2004. www.news.com/Googles-man-behind-the-curtain/2008-1024_ 3-5208228.html, last accessed 29 March 2008.

8. Caroline McCarthy, "Google Backs Character-Recognition Research." CNET News, 11 April 2007. www.news.com/Google-backs-character-recognition-research/ 2100-1032_3-6175136.html, last accessed 30 March 2008.

9. Stefanie Olsen, "Spying an Intelligent Search Engine," CNET News, 18 August 2006. www.news.com/Spying-an-intelligent-search-engine/2100-1032_3-6107048.html, last accessed 30 March 2008.

10. Clint Witchalls, "Lab Comes One Step Closer to Building Artificial Human Brain," *The Guardian,* 20 December 2007. www.guardian.co.uk/technology/2007/dec/20/research.it, last accessed 30 March 2008.

11. Liz Tay, "Child-Like Intelligence Created in Second Life," iTnews, 14 March 2008. http://itnews.com.au/News/72057,childlike-intelligence-created-in-second-life.aspx, last accessed 30 March 2008.

12. Jacqui Cheng, "Airlines Planning to Filter, Censor in-Flight 'Net Access.'" ArsTechnica, 24 December 2007. http://arstechnica.com/news.ars/post/20071224-airlines-planning-to-filter-censor-in-flight-net-access.html, last accessed 24 December 2007.

13. John C. Dvorak, "Inside Track v25n3," PC Magazine Online, 1 February 2006. www.pcmag.com/article2/0,1895,1916760,00.asp, last accessed 26 March 2008.

14. "ISPs Inserting Ads into Your Pages," Slashdot, 23 June 2007. http://yro.slashdot.org/article.pl?sid=07/06/23/1233212&tid=17, last accessed 23 March 2008.

15. For an interesting countermeasure for "in-flight" web page alterations, see http://yro.slashdot.org/article.pl?no_d2=1&sid=07/07/25/155200.

16. Mark Evans, "A New, Better Approach to RSS," MapleLeaf 2.0, 19 July 2007. www.mapleleaftwo.com/a-new-better-approach-to-rss/, last accessed 31 March 2008.

17. Nate Anderson, "Deep Packet Inspection Meets 'Net Neutrality, CALEA," ArsTechnica, 25 March 2007. http://arstechnica.com/articles/culture/Deep-packet-inspection-meets-net-neutrality.ars, last accessed 31 March 2008.

18. I once worked in an organization that used antivirus software to censor information flows. By adding the filename of a banned document to the AV software's signature database, the software would delete the attachment and alert organizational leaders of the transgression.

19. Steven Levy, "Pay Per Gig," Washington Post Online, 30 January 2008. www.washingtonpost.com/wp-dyn/content/article/2008/01/29/AR2008012903205.html, last accessed 31 March 2008.

20. Therese Poletti, "RIAA Tactics to Combat Piracy Again in Question," MarketWatch, 20 March 2008, www.marketwatch.com/news/story/does-riaa-engage-mob-tactics/story.aspx?guid=%7B66666B25-1C23-4377-8C99-0BA530FD7577%7D&siteid=yhoof, last accessed 30 March 2008.

21. Brian Krebs, "MPAA University 'Tookit' Raises Privacy Concerns," Security Fix, Washington Post Online, 23 November 2007. http://blog.washingtonpost.com/securityfix/2007/11/mpaa_university_toolkit_opens_1.html, last accessed 31 March 2008.

22. Yomiuri Shimbun, "Winny Copiers to Be Cut Off the Internet," Daily Yomiuri Online, 15 March 2008. www.yomiuri.co.jp/dy/national/20080315TDY01305.htm, last accessed 23 March 2008.

23. "China Blocks YouTube over Tibet Videos," *Wired News,* 17 March 2008, http://news.wired.com/dynamic/stories/C/CHINA_YOUTUBE_BLOCKED?SITE=WIRE&SECTION=HOME&TEMPLATE=DEFAULT&CTIME=2008-03-16-10-08-59, last accessed 23 March 2008.

24. "Conroy Announces Mandatory Internet Filters to Protect Children," ABC News Australia, 31 December 2007. www.abc.net.au/news/stories/2007/12/31/2129471.htm, last accessed 23 March 2008.

25. Adam Thomas, "U.S. Senators Call for Universal Internet Filtering," Press Esc, 25 July 2007. http://pressesc.com/news/78225072007/us-senators-call-universal-internet-filtering, last accessed 23 March 2008.

26. "Malaysia Cracks Down on Bloggers," BBC News, 25 July 2007. http://news.bbc.co.uk/2/hi/asia-pacific/6915002.stm, last accessed 23 March 2008.

27. For a look at the "think of the children" trend, see http://yro.slashdot.org/tags/thinkofthechildren.

28. Andrew Colley, "Big Three ISPs Say Peer-to-Peer OK," *Australian IT,* 21 February 2006. www.australianit.news.com.au/story/0,24897,18213133-15306,00.html, last accessed 31 March 2008.

29. John Letzing, "Verizon Wireless Wins Bids on 'Open' Spectrum," *MarketWatch,* 20 March 2008. www.marketwatch.com/news/story/verizon-wins-bids-open-spectrum/story.aspx?guid=%7BDE7234BA-A8EC-4108-BDD7-DF54F9355AC8%7D, last accessed 26 March 2008.

30. Brad Stone, "Google to Join Spectrum Auction," The New York Times Online, 1 December 2007. www.nytimes.com/2007/12/01/technology/01google.html?_r=3&em&ex=1196744400&en=6c9bd6fe4276d660&ei=5087%0A&oref=slogin&oref=slogin&oref=slogin, last accessed 26 March 2008.

31. Dan Frommer, "Spectrum Auction: Verizon Big Winner, Google 'Happy Loser,'" *Silicon Alley Insider,* 20 March 2008. www.alleyinsider.com/2008/3/spectrum_auction_verizon_big_winner_google_happy_loser_, last accessed 26 March 2008.

32. Richard Whitt, "The End of the FCC 700 MHz Auction," Google Blog, 20 March 2008. http://googleblog.blogspot.com/2008/03/end-of-fcc-700-mhz-auction.html, last accessed 26 March 2008.

33. "Google Floating Wireless Balloon Idea?" *Telecoms,* 21 February 2008. www. telecoms.com/itmgcontent/tcoms/news/articles/20017507674.html, last accessed 26 March 2008.

34. "Peek-a-Boo, Google Sees You," *CNNMoney,* 7 April 2006. http://money.cnn.com/ 2006/04/06/technology/googsf_reut/index.htm, last accessed 26 March 2008.

35. Barry Schwartz, "Google Unity Project to Build Submarine Cables Across Pacific Ocean," Search Engine Land, 21 September 2007. http://searchengineland.com/ 070921-143819.php, last accessed 31 March 2008.

36. Dawn Kawamoto, "Google Employees' Wireless Patents Published," *ZDNetAsia,* 28 March 2008. www.zdnetasia.com/news/communications/ 0,39044192,39346317,00.htm, last accessed 31 March 2008.

37. This phrase is based on the traditional proclamation used to announce the ascension of a new monarch. See http://en.wikipedia.org/wiki/The_King_is_dead._Long_live_ the_King! for more information.

38. "Japan Aims to Give Google Some Competition," *Newindpress,* 19 December 2005. www.newindpress.com/NewsItems.asp?ID=IEN20051219042803&Page=N&Title=In fotech&Topic=0&, last accessed 30 March 2008.

39. Ebrahim Ezzy, "Search 2.0 vs. Traditional Search," ReadWriteWeb, 20 July 2006. www.readwriteweb.com/archives/search_20_vs_tr.php, last accessed 28 March 2008.

40. Other challengers to watch are Blekko (www.blekko.com/) and Wikia (http://alpha. search.wikia.com/); see www.techcrunch.com/2008/01/02/the-next-google-search- challenger-blekko/.

41. Verne Kopytoff, "Google Has Lots to Do with Intelligence," SFGate, 30 March 2008. www.sfgate.com/cgi-bin/article.cgi?f=/c/a/2008/03/30/BUQLUAP8L.DTL, last accessed 31 March 2008.

42. Adam Kovacevich, "Our New D.C. Digs," Google Public Policy Blog, 18 January 2008. http://googlepublicpolicy.blogspot.com/2008/01/our-new-dc- digs.html, last accessed 31 March 2008.

43. Robert X. Cringely, "The Final Days of Google: It Is Going to Be an Inside Job," I, Cringely Blog, 24 May 2007. www.pbs.org/cringely/pulpit/2007/pulpit_20070524_ 002134.html, last accessed 4 April 2008.

44. This is a reference to Pets.com; see http://en.wikipedia.org/wiki/Pets.com for more on the sock puppet and the demise of Pets.com.

45. Stefanie Olsen, "Kids Say E-mail Is, Like, Soooo Dead," CNET News, 18 July 2008, www.news.com/Kids-say-e-mail-is,-like,-soooo-dead/2009-1032_3-6197242.html? tag=nefd.lede, last accessed 6 April 2008.

46. Orin Kerr, "The Case for the Third-Party Doctrine," *Michigan Law Review* 107, May 2008. Available online at http://papers.ssrn.com/sol3/papers.cfm?abstract_id= 1138128, last accessed 19 June 2008.

47. "The Internet of Things—What Is a Spime?" Slashdot.org, 3 May 2007. http://it. slashdot.org/article.pl?no_d2=1&sid=07/05/03/2031218, last accessed 6 April 2008.

48. Chris Albrecht, "Comcast Cameras to Start Watching You?" *NewTeeVee,* 18 March 2008. http://newteevee.com/2008/03/18/comcast-cameras-to-start-watching-you/, last accessed 5 April 2008.

Index

G

X-Y-Z

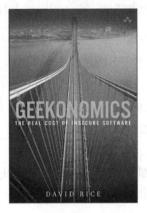

The Electronic Frontier Foundation (EFF) is the leading organization defending civil liberties in the digital world. We defend free speech on the Internet, fight illegal surveillance, promote the rights of innovators to develop new digital technologies, and work to ensure that the rights and freedoms we enjoy are enhanced — rather than eroded — as our use of technology grows.

PRIVACY   EFF has sued telecom giant AT&T for giving the NSA unfettered access to the private communications of millions of their customers. eff.org/nsa

FREE SPEECH   EFF's Coders' Rights Project is defending the rights of programmers and security researchers to publish their findings without fear of legal challenges. eff.org/freespeech

INNOVATION   EFF's Patent Busting Project challenges overbroad patents that threaten technological innovation. eff.org/patent

FAIR USE   EFF is fighting prohibitive standards that would take away your right to receive and use over-the-air television broadcasts any way you choose. eff.org/IP/fairuse

TRANSPARENCY   EFF has developed the Switzerland Network Testing Tool to give individuals the tools to test for covert traffic filtering. eff.org/transparency

INTERNATIONAL   EFF is working to ensure that international treaties do not restrict our free speech, privacy or digital consumer rights. eff.org/global

EFF.ORG

ELECTRONIC FRONTIER FOUNDATION

Protecting Rights and Promoting Freedom on the Electronic Frontier

EFF is a member-supported organization. Join Now! www.eff.org/support

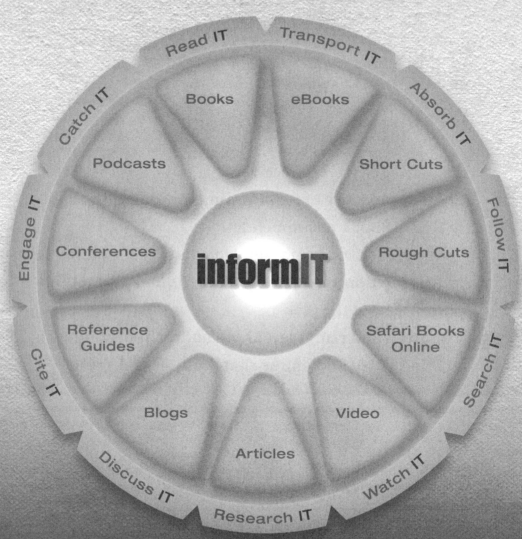

LearnIT at InformIT

Go Beyond the Book

11 WAYS TO LEARN IT at **www.informIT.com/learn**

The online portal of the information technology
publishing imprints of Pearson Education

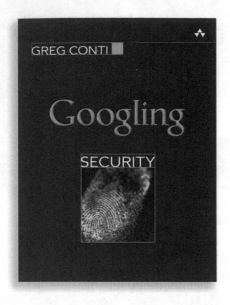

FREE Online Edition

Your purchase of *Googling Security* includes access to a free online edition for 45 days through the Safari Books Online subscription service. Nearly every Addison-Wesley Professional book is available online through Safari Books Online, along with over 5,000 other technical books and videos from publishers such as Cisco Press, Exam Cram, IBM Press, O'Reilly, Prentice Hall, Que, and Sams.

SAFARI BOOKS ONLINE allows you to search for a specific answer, cut and paste code, download chapters, and stay current with emerging technologies.

Activate your FREE Online Edition at www.informit.com/safarifree

> **STEP 1:** Enter the coupon code: CAMAQWA.

> **STEP 2:** New Safari users, complete the brief registration form.
> Safari subscribers, just login.

If you have difficulty registering on Safari or accessing the online edition, please e-mail customer-service@safaribooksonline.com